THINKING ABOUT TOMORROW

Excerpts from the Life of Keith West

IAN L. CLAY

HAWKSMOOR
PUBLISHING

First published 2020 by Hawksmoor Publishing

Kemp House, 152-160 City Rd, London, EC1V 2NX

www.hawksmoorpublishing.com

ISBNS: 978-1-8380990-1-5 [Hardback]
978-1-8380990-8-4 [Softback]

A CIP catalogue record for this book is available from the British Library.

KEITH'S ACKNOWLEDGEMENTS

I'm dedicating this book to my wife Pat, and my three daughters, Shelley, Jodie, and Carrie. My family has always come first, and although music took me to places I never thought I'd see, they will always be my proudest achievement, without a doubt!

I would also like to thank the following, in no particular order:

Ken Burgess, my writing partner, who now lives in Israel.

Roy Pitt who was a shining light and great company.

Malcom Forrester, my first publisher and still a good mate.

Martin Costello, a real music fan and a friend for life.

Antony Rufus Isaacs, a true gentleman. We were from two entirely different backgrounds and he showed me another side of life, I can't thank him enough.

Steve Howe, guitarist extraordinaire, my oldest friend, and sidekick.

John (Twink) Alder - Richard Morton Jack - Dana Gillespie - Ken Lawrence who supplied many unseen photos and anecdotes - Joe Boyd - Gita Renik - John Jessup - all the guys at Cherry Red Records - Mark Stratford - Sony ATV.

R.I.P. John (Junior) Wood.

ABOUT IAN L. CLAY

Thinking About Tomorrow is Ian Leslie Clay's first book after a lifetime of writing as a journalist and PR agent. Starting as the sports, music, and film correspondent at Reading University's *Spark* newspaper he then gained experience on the local newspaper scene in Kent before entering trade publishing in 1995. As part of Nexus Media's Music Division, he worked on the brilliantly titled *Disco International* (where he got to interview everyone from Peter Stringfellow to Michael Grade) before settling down and getting a 'proper' job with Western Business Publishing in 1998.

After more than a decade as a tech journalist, he 'went to the dark side' and became a partner in a small PR agency – Technical Publicity – which, along with his business partner Sylvia Laws, they grew before selling to Publitek through their PLC holding company Next 15 Communications in 2018. He is currently working on a screenplay, has a second book project in development, and returns to Publitek in late 2020.

Ian L. Clay was born in 1971 and went to school at RHS near Ipswich. He graduated from The University of Reading in 1993 where he read English, Film, and Drama.

IAN'S ACKNOWLEDGEMENTS

Firstly, the author would like to thank Keith West for giving so generously of his time and believing that this project would capture his story in the way it deserved. I hope you are pleased with the outcome!

Secondly, I'd like to thank all the interviewees who not only provided excellent stories but who also, on many occasions, sent photographs and documents to help piece together the story. These were: Steve Howe, Ken Lawrence, Joe Boyd, Dana Gillespie, Malcolm Forrester, Martin Costello, Bruce Thomas, Mike Reid, John Jessup, Antony Rufus Isaacs, Gita Rennick, Barry Gibson and John Alder (Twink).

Thirdly, a debt of thanks to James Lumsden-Cook and his team at Hawksmoor for their initial enthusiasm for the project and wise counsel and editing along the way. Also, thanks to Richard Morton Jack and Nick Warburton whose research and knowledge for the 2012 article in *Flashback* magazine about Tomorrow they freely shared.

Fourthly, I would like to thank my wife, Lynn, and daughter, Amber, for their unfailing belief that I could write this book. Also, to my parents Stuart and Carol, and in-laws Denis and Mary, for their support and enthusiasm. I promise I might be able to talk about a different subject in 2021!

Inevitably, when documenting events from over 50 years ago, some of the main actors are no longer with us or are too ill to contribute. It was a great sadness to me that I was not able to speak with Ken Burgess who is currently undergoing intense treatment nor to Mark Wirtz who died shortly before the first draft of the book was completed. Plus, to not be able to meet or speak to John 'Junior' Wood will remain a regret, as he was the catalyst for all of these adventures.

Lastly, I'd like to thank Bob Good and Maggie for their teaching and support during my time at RHS. Their love and enthusiasm for literature and the creative arts stoked a fire which has burnt for a lifetime.

CONTENTS

Prologue: lost in music

Romford Hospital, in the run-up to Christmas 1955, was not the place Keith Hopkins expected or wanted to be. During the summer, after a visit from his eldest sister Anne and her husband Barry, he started to have difficulty breathing and was sometimes out of breath after just walking up the road.

After a visit to the family doctor, young Keith was bemused to be diagnosed with a shadow on the lung, or to give it its medical name pleurisy, caused by a form of tuberculosis or 'the dreaded TB' as it was known. His other sister, Mavis, had also tested positive for TB, and both were transferred to Romford hospital as in-patients.

Hospitals in Britain, in 1955, were pretty much akin to army barracks with austere matrons playing the role of drill sergeants, and nurses and porters acting as foot soldiers. Unlike today, where hospitals operate a patient-first approach, and the needs of the individual and family are given priority, post-war military efficiency was the order of the day and visiting time was limited to one hour – Monday to Saturday – with two hours being allowed on Sunday afternoons. As such, when Mavis was given the all-clear and discharged, Keith was left – if not to fend for himself exactly – then certainly to his own devices for a great majority of the week.

Sitting on his hospital bed, with its tubular iron frame and pale blue curtain, that could be quickly whipped around the curtain rail if required, he was able to watch the coming and going of the staff and store some comics and books in his small wooden locker. The rhythm of the day was only punctuated by the ritual of a nurse spoon-feeding him some foul-tasting medicine.

Every so often, a tall, commanding man who the nurses called 'doctor' – and to whom the matrons practically genuflected in front of – would appear. He would pull the curtain around and listen to Keith's chest giving, on occasion, a firm 'hmmm', or a less positive 'tsk'. Either way, Keith was pretty much in the dark about his progress and would eventually stay in Romford Hospital for ten months. When you are 10-years-old, that seems like a lifetime.

Over time, visits from the family dwindled a little. His father's job as a lorry driver and his mum's job as a seamstress (plus looking after two other children) kept them away. Fortunately, salvation was at hand as, unexpectedly, about half-way into his stay at the hospital, a boy called Billy arrived as an in-patient on the ward. Being about the same age as Keith, they started chatting. They weren't the most natural of allies as Billy was well-spoken and his parents seemingly well-heeled; they always brought Billy the latest comics and some sweets, which he generously shared with Keith.

Most importantly of all, Billy's father brought him a Bakelite radio and, once Billy had listened to some of the light entertainment programmes of the day – detective shows mainly, like *Dick Barton Special Agent* – he would pass the radio and the headphones over to Keith. This was mainly done close to lights-out time, and Keith would make a little tent out of the heavy brown blankets and boiled-to-a-crisp white sheets. To the nurses passing on patrol, Keith was just a ball, curled up on his bed. But in his dark cave, he could pick up the pirate radio station Radio Luxembourg which, unbeknownst to him, was broadcasting commercial radio illegally into the UK. In the eyes of some, it was corrupting the nation's youth; naturally, the nation's youth loved it, and could not get enough.

The programmes on Radio Luxembourg were great, Keith thought, with *Boys Own* programmes like *The Adventures of Dan Dare,* as well as *Movie Magazine* with Wilfred Thomas (which talked about all the latest new films). Indeed, the movies all sounded terrific, even if he was too young to get in to see many of them. But then came new discoveries, a batch of music programmes such as *The Capitol Show* which talked about and played all the new releases by Capitol Records; *Rockin' to Dreamland* that played all the latest hits from both the UK and the USA; *Record Hop* which was on Friday evenings; and *Jamboree,* on Saturdays, where Alan Freed – the American Disc Jockey – played all the new rock and roll records. Here, young Keith was drawn inexorably to the sound of the electric guitar and rock and roll, from the harmony singing and flashy guitar runs of Les Paul and Mary Ford to the teenage rebellion that Bill Haley's timeless *Rock Around the Clock* would signify. These nightly forays into the distant, wildly exciting world of the newly burgeoning rock and roll scene helped Keith to escape from the daily nightmare of the hospital routine with its early mornings, unpalatable food, and long passages of nothing to do. Then, just after Christmas, in January 1956, he heard something on Radio Luxembourg which would change the course of his life forever.

Keith heard Elvis.

'*Heartbreak Hotel* was the first record I ever bought,' says Keith. 'I must have made my sister run out and get it for me, but it totally blew me away. From the first lyric 'Well since my baby left me' and the title – what a great title for a song – it's kind of jazzy and bluesy at the same time with that descending bassline and twinkling piano. I was totally mesmerised. I couldn't get enough of it, and when Scotty Moore's guitar solo kicked in, my little world just splintered apart. I knew what I wanted to do with my life. I wanted to be a rock and roll singer, and I wanted to play the guitar. I was totally lost in music.'

1. See me walking around, I'm the boy about town

At the unfeasibly young age of 15, in December 1959, Keith Hopkins left school armed with no qualifications save a school leaving certificate. Viewed through today's lens, such a short education would be seen as a modern tragedy and a failure of the system, but at the beginning of 1960 the world – and more importantly Keith – saw things entirely differently. He was eager to get out into the adult world – with all its possibilities – and escape the clutches of schoolmasters who were either traumatised by, or had their ideas shaped by, wartime thinking.

Keith aspired to be a musician or, as he excelled in English, to be a journalist. However, his careers master poured cold water on his dreams and attempted to steer him towards something more fitting to the station of a working-class young man, with basic education, in Dagenham. This meant either the docks, or the fast-growing automotive industry in the area, which was powered by Ford Motors and the supply chain that had grown up around it.

Keith, like many others of his age, wanted more; and you have to admire the chutzpah here of the boy that Keith still was. He was at the forefront of a new generation who would not be contained by the dutiful thinking of his parents' generation, and the make do and mend attitude that came with it.

Richard Weight, in his excellent book *MOD: From Bebop to Britpop, Britain's Biggest Youth Movement,* identifies a new way of thinking – originally exhibited among the Bebop followers and jazz aficionados of Soho. The Mod culture started to spread outside of London and would continue to be influential, he argues, through all the youth movements from the 1950s onwards. An early example of a mod is to be found in Colin MacInnes' classic 1958 novel *Absolute Beginners* where the central character is only 18 but forging a new life for himself in a hip community of artists who cherish style, fashion, music, and entrepreneurial endeavour, and who reject just about every aspect of their parent's lives.

Pete Meaden, an influential mod (short for modernist) defined this new thinking, and the way in which it translated into the world of the young British working class, as 'clean living under difficult circumstances' and Keith – whether he knew it or not – was one of the original mods. He would continue to be one throughout his extraordinary life.

Looking the part was made easier as Keith's Mum was a seamstress and worked for Hector Powe, the gentlemen's outfitters which still exists today, and he exhibited an interest in clothes that she could help facilitate. Despite being only 15, pencil slim, and some way yet from reaching the six feet in height that he would eventually attain, Keith Hopkins, having rejected his path as factory fodder, managed to get himself a job at the *Daily Express* newspaper.

On his first day of working, he was well turned out with a made-to-measure three-piece suit replete with starched collar. He looked both cool and smart at the same time. Keith, always something of a peacock, fondly remembers these early adventures into the working world, where he would jump on the train at Dagenham Heathway Station and disembark at Fenchurch Street. 'The dressing up thing I didn't mind too much. A nice uniform to wear with handmade shirts and good shoes. I looked pretty dapper, even if I do say so myself.'

While Richard Weight identifies a collective movement, it still takes extraordinary individuals to form that movement. So, where did the 15-year-old Keith get that confidence from? In some ways, his confidence and sureness – that he could pursue the path *he wanted* – came from the fact that, following his eureka moment in Romford Hospital, he had thrown himself into music and had already achieved some success.

Indeed, he had already earnt some decent money as a gigging musician.

Before he left school, Keith was more interested in music than formal education and along with his lifetime school friend, Ken Burgess, he started to immerse himself in music. 'My dad played piano,' says Keith, 'and we did have a piano in the house. I even had some lessons at one point, but it was all about the guitar for me. Jet Harris from The Shadows was the inspiration for that. Everybody, all our family, all the kids that I knew, were into The Shadows as they were our best band at the time. They could actually compete with the Americans on some sort of level. Cliff was doing the Elvis thing, but the band were really good musically, and had a great career over the years.

'Jet looked like James Dean. He's a great looking character – very cool – and a good musician. You have to remember, there weren't a lot of electric bass players around in those days. It was a new instrument.'

Even at the young age of 12, Keith would demonstrate an aesthetic appreciation which would surface throughout his career. 'As well as the sound, the image was very important for me too. It definitely was. It's the look of it. I mean the Stratocaster. The first time I saw one – everybody, Mark Knofler, Eric Clapton, they'd all say the same thing – it's like wow! They never designed a better-looking guitar.

'The balance, the sound, the tuner's all on one side. It's contoured. It's got everything going for it. These elements, the sound and the style, went hand in hand for me and even much later – with the changing of my name – it shows a certain vanity there. That's good, I think, because we're all a bunch of show-offs, basically.

'We want to get up on the stage and say look at me. I can do this. You've got to be like that; you've got to have some confidence, especially if you're the singer. You need more confidence than anybody else in a band because you're vulnerable. The voice is a fragile thing… anything can happen. You can get a cold, or you can not be feeling good. You're going to be tired sometimes, and the voice will go. You need to have a lot of balls to get up and do that in the first place.'

In thrall to Jet Harris, and the look and feel of rock and roll generally, Keith went down the well-travelled route of the first wave of rock musicians; he badgered his parents into getting a bass guitar on Hire Purchase, referred to, in the vernacular of the day, as 'on tick'.

'My parents put down a deposit on a Tuxedo bass and signed the agreement to pay it off monthly. God knows what the APR was. It was probably outrageous, but I wasn't aware of that.

'Anyway, the Tuxedo had a neck that was like a cricket bat, so I traded that after about six months and bought a Framus because I saw Jet Harris had played one. It's called a star bass and is a red colour. I was playing that through a homemade valve amp with a 15-inch speaker while Ken, whose parents were middle class, played guitar through a Selmer Truvoice amp which was quite popular at the time.'

In the linear journey of rock and roll biographies, the acquisition of instruments by teenage friends would usually lead to anything between two and five years of obsessive practice, before they emerge into the world as fully-formed and ferociously gifted musicians. Keith's journey was a little different as – in the first example of what was to be a continuing theme throughout his life – he came into close proximity with someone who was to have a long and varied career in the music business.

The story starts with Keith and Ken Burgess hanging around their usual Saturday afternoon haunt in Dagenham – the record store. It was owned by the dad of a friend and one afternoon, Ken – who was already a member of a local band called Tony Colton and The Teenbeats – asked Keith how he was getting along with his bass playing. Keith picks up the story, 'I replied 'okay', and he then told me that the Teenbeats' bassist was leaving and would I be interested in trying out for the gig. Well, I was very excited but also nervous as my playing was limited, but I did get hired!'

It was 1958, and both boys were yet to turn 15. This development is important for two reasons. Firstly, for who Tony Colton was, and who he went on to be; and, secondly, because of the experience they gained at this early age.

So, who was Tony Colton?

In 1958, he was among the first wave of musicians to jump on the rock and roll bandwagon and capitalise on playing live rock and roll to young audiences. From here, he graduated through a number of bands until he became part of an elite group of musicians and songwriters that would hang around The Flamingo Club, in Wardour Street, where he would befriend and work with the likes of Jimi Hendrix and Eric Clapton. By 1965, Tony was writing hits such *as I Stand Accused* for himself (and also The Merseybeats who covered it), and *Big Time Operator* for Zoot Money's Big Roll Band. He also wrote songs for Cream and produced albums for the likes of Yes, as well as many hits for Shirley Bassey.

Tony's name might not be as familiar to us as Clapton or Page or Plant, but it might have been, had his 1970s supergroup – Heads, Hands and Feet (which featured guitar supremo Albert Lee and Chas Hodge, later of Chas 'n' Dave fame, on bass) – reached its potential. After a period out of the spotlight, yet still punctuated with acts such as Elvis Costello covering his songs, a late-career renaissance saw his song *Country Boy* win awards after Ricky Skaggs did a cover version. He then relocated to Nashville to work as a songwriter and producer for the likes of Johnny Cash, Jerry Lee Lewis, Tom Waits, Willie Nelson and even Ray Charles! An incredible career and a hell of a force for the young, impressionable Keith Hopkins to work with in 1958 and early 1959.

Keith and Ken's time with Tony and The Teenbeats seems an odd mixture of incredible experience and child labour with faint overtones of *Oliver Twist* (with Keith and Ken playing the part of the small, young orphan, while Tony was a mix of both the Artful Dodger and Fagin). Almost immediately, on passing the audition, they were put to work gigging up and down the South Coast from Southend in Essex to Portsmouth in Hampshire, and all points in between.

Keith remembers, 'We were based in Dagenham, but were having to go all the way down to Hastings and Brighton for gigs. Tony would organise that. We'd just get in the van and off we'd go, wherever. We'd get home at all times of the night, two or three in the morning and stuff like that. We found places that were open to eat after the gigs, which were mainly Indian restaurants. That's where the love of Indian food comes from with musicians; they were the only places that were open.

'Plus, it wasn't just the gigs. We were also practising and learning new material which – in those days – had to be done by ear from the records. We'd pretty much copy the keys from the records. You'd listen to the record, practise it at home, and from there you would have your arrangement. Fortunately, in those days, it was mostly only three or four chords for most of the songs, and it's quite simple, but some of it was more complicated.

'Also, we were so young and so excited that we would have been pushing all the speeds. The adrenalin was going, and we were probably doing the numbers an awful lot faster than the records.'

Being around Tony Colton wasn't just an intense musical apprenticeship though; his behaviour also shined a light into the murky world of show business. 'I can remember one scam that Tony used to come up with,' says Keith. 'Tony had a friend that looked like Jet Harris – he *really* looked like him – and to get the crowd going, he would sometimes get on the mic and say, 'We've got a special guest tonight… Jet Harris', and the girls would go crazy screaming. It was a complete con. Then we would have to rush back to the dressing room quick, before anybody twigged it. He would tell the promoters that Jet Harris was coming along. That's the sort of things he used to get up to. You can't get away with that these days; now you could quickly Google what Jet Harris looks like. In 1959, if you hadn't seen him on the TV, you wouldn't know. He pulled that stunt quite a few times. It was every man for himself; it really was.'

While drumming up a little hype is one thing, Tony was also not afraid of going beyond that, and crossing the line into the frankly criminal. Keith recalls, 'He was a real hustler; he had the gift of the gab and could talk you both into, and out of, anything. He was older than we were, and he was up to all sorts. For some reason, even though we were working regularly and getting well paid, he never seemed to have any money.

'I can remember one of his scams where he would pull up at a petrol station late at night and say, 'Fill her up. Is Jack around?' And the attendant would go, 'Jack? Oh, do you mean John?' Tony would say, 'Yeah, yeah, John. Is he around?' The attendant would say no and then, without skipping a beat, Tony would say, 'I'm his son, just put it on the account', and then he would just drive off. Of course, in those days, there was no CCTV, so he got away with it.'

Keith would meet with Tony Colton again further down the line in their respective musical careers, but after one year, The Teenbeats came to an end. Tony was moving inexorably onwards and upwards and would soon form Tony Colton and The Big Money Band, and then Tony Colton and The Crawdaddies (with whom he would have a hit in 1965).

The band's dissolution coincided with Keith leaving school and getting himself a job at the *Daily Express* on Fleet Street. However, despite the forces that were gathering both within Keith and across the country, miracles were still not a daily occurrence. While landing a job on the *Daily Express* was an excellent start, there was a certain reality to be faced. Despite being on a national newspaper, Keith's first job was not the one he had dreamed about as a music or sports correspondent, with all the attendant glamour; it was actually on the printing side as a less-than-glamourous-sounding 'block room boy'.

'The block room was full of printing blocks, that's all they had in those days, no digital stuff,' says Keith, remembering back to his first job some 60 years previously. 'Up to the ceiling, full up with blocks. The printers would give you a list of the blocks they wanted, they're all numbered, and you'd dig them out, put them in the tray and deliver them to the printer.

'After about three months, I became head block room boy, because people working in the block room didn't seem to last very long. There was no future in it, no future in it at all. But, one of the guys liked me at the *Daily Express*, and when I was in his office one day, he said, 'If you want to be a journalist I'll show you a few things.'

'Then somebody came in from another office and said, 'What's *he* doing in here?' Even though the guy tried to argue my case and said I was smart, the response was, 'No, get him back in the block room.' So, it became clear that to try and make the progression from the printing side to the editorial team was going to prove impossible. There was nothing more I could do to impress them in the block room, so I left after six months and started to look for another job.'

Another phenomenon of the time, and one which seems incredible in the modern era of CV checking, and LinkedIn and Facebook due diligence, is that leaving a job before finding a new one was a common occurrence. Employment, particularly in junior positions was plentiful and therefore Keith's action, while eschewing the mantra 'you have to have a job to get a job', was not as brazen as it might seem to the modern reader.

Keith found new employment with the importer Mory and Co., and they certainly helped fulfil his ambitions as being a boy about town. The company was based in Leadenhall Street in the City and came complete with a great number of young women employees, all looking to define themselves in this new mod era. Most were happy to stop and chat to the slim, handsome, charming boy with the stylish suit and the sharp haircut who knew loads about music and the latest scene. The attraction was mutual and Keith, having two older sisters, was happy chatting and laughing with any number of girls from within his own company or beyond. It was to prove to be a talent not entirely without consequences.

'While it was a long working day that meant walking up to the bus stop, getting on a bus, getting on a train and getting up to Bank, I loved it,' remembers Keith. Mory and Co. were a big coffee importer and the guy that ran it was a former army colonel: Colonel E.A. Depas. I used to clean his desk, run around him, make him coffee and answer his phone and stuff like that. That's the character I wrote the song *Colonel Brown* about, actually. I wanted to get back at him because he was a real arsehole, he really was.

'I was there for quite a while. They promoted me to look after the clients that were coming in, so I obviously had a bit of a talent for charming and getting on with people. I don't know where it came from.

'One of the biggest clients was a flower importer from Amsterdam, who used to come into Southend airport. I used to go down there, meet this guy, take him out for a drink. It's incredible when you think of it as I was only 16, but he liked me, so that's why they promoted me.

'I'd get the train up to Southend, meet him there, have a bit of lunch. I'd take up some cigarettes with our brand name – Mory and Co. – we had our own cigarettes in boxes of 50. A sweetener basically, keep him sweet. He'd make a fuss of me, always asking when he came into the office, 'Where's Keith?' And they'd all go, 'Fucking hell, what is it about this skinny kid that people like? Never mind, it's good for business. Let's ensure he's looked after.''

It was all for the good that Keith was progressing up the career ladder as his personal life had taken an unexpected turn.

Among the number of attractive young women that Keith would seek out and chat to, there was one that had made a real play for him. Norma Lucas was more mature than Keith and set her stall out to ensure he started dating her. But, within a few months, Keith's introduction to the harsh realities of life was complete when Norma announced she was pregnant, and Keith's parents insisted on the pair getting married.

Parenthood and responsibilities hadn't played any part in Keith's plans so far, and it was to clip his rock and roll wings until 1963. He and Norma were married in February 1962 and his son, Stewart, was born six months later. The immaturity of the bride and groom is revealed by the fact that there would be no matrimonial home and they would be forced to live at Norma's parents' house during the course of their marriage – not the best of circumstances for harmonious wedded bliss.

2. Jimmy Saville fixes it for Four + 1

As has been recounted in innumerable rock biographies, and also many slow-motion soft rock sequences in sports movies, there is always a training period where the hero of the story locks themselves away and spends countless hours refining their craft, or sculpting their physique, or chopping down logs and running through snow (if various *Rocky* movies are to be believed). Keith's musical training period came as he entered the working world and became a young father. Burdened with new responsibility, and needing to be home more, as he lived nearby but not with his new wife and son, he spent hours training his voice by listening to and emulating the blues performers of the day. He also learned to play the harmonica, like his idol Little Walter, and improved his guitar skills beyond the bass guitar to include rhythm and lead skills.

But the itch which had started with *Heartbreak Hotel* and Elvis Presley in Romford Hospital had still not been scratched. In fact, it had become more intense from his experience with the Teenbeats, and when Keith saw a 'Singer/Harmonica player wanted' advert in the *Melody Maker,* in the latter part of 1963, he answered it with the dual intention of re-starting his rock and roll dreams, and also to make some extra money for his new family.

Unlike his experience with Tony Colton, the advert placed by John 'Junior' Wood (which also advertised for a bass player) would require a formal audition. This was new territory for Keith. As he recalls, 'It was in a hall in Kennington, near the Oval. I turned up, and there was a load of people there; I couldn't believe it when I walked in. All these people just from one little ad.

'I didn't rate my chances highly as the guy in front of me played the harmonica too and was unbelievable. I figured he would get the gig, but he didn't look right. That's all. It was the image thing they were looking for as well, which I've always been into a little bit. I got the gig because of my image, I think, more than anything else.'

Also auditioning that day was a charismatic bass player who had changed his name from Robert Alcock to Simon Alcot. Keith remembers him from the audition as, 'A very handsome guy, who looked like James Dean, which meant he was going to get the job regardless of how he could play. But he was an okay player, too. There were a lot of bass players there, and he got the gig. I was pleased about that. I started talking to him about the audition, the songs we were going to do, and when I approached him and addressed him as Simon, he responded, 'No, man, it's Boots. It's just Boots. Everybody calls me Boots.' So, that was what we all called him from then on.'

Junior gave the results to Keith and Boots that afternoon, confirming that they had passed the audition and were in the band. As the originator of the band, Junior is an important but somewhat lightly-drawn figure in music history. Originally a sheet metal worker, Keith recalls him as, 'A bit of a rough boy at the time who dyed his hair blonde to get the Brian Jones look. The result was that he looked a bit hard. But he was a good guy and a good player, certainly the founding member and, at first, leader of the band.

'But, with hindsight, I could see a problem straight away with the drummer. He didn't look right at all. His image was completely wrong. He was a nice guy, but he was never going to be in a rock and roll band.'

Nonetheless, despite Keith's misgivings, the first incarnation of Four + 1 – a band that would later mutate into The In Crowd and then Tomorrow and spawn members of Yes, The Jeff Beck Group, and Keith West himself – was born into the dark, cold winter of 1963.

One immediate effect of landing the Four + 1 gig was that Keith changed his name from the simple, typically English, Keith Hopkins to the more American-sounding 'Keith West'. Although West was the name under which he would achieve popular acclaim, Hopkins would still be used on the songwriters' credits on his records. Changing names unofficially and not by deed poll, as Boots Alcot had also done, was increasingly common at the time, particularly among entertainment industry people. Keith would use both Hopkins and West throughout his career, signing record contracts as Keith West while being paid royalties as Keith Hopkins. His names were totally interchangeable depending on mood and season!

The band started working almost immediately, doing gigs at youth clubs, but it became clear that Keith's initial thoughts around the drummer were to prove correct. Not only was his image wrong, but musically he wasn't right either. From the off, Four + 1 were a dynamic R&B outfit influenced by The Yardbirds, The Stones, and Black American music in general. In terms of their presentation on stage, they kept away from the uniform image of the Liverpool bands, and instead modelled themselves on incredibly dynamic, wilder bands such as the Downliners Sect, who were popular in London.

'So, we auditioned for a new drummer,' says Keith taking up the story, 'and Ken Lawrence, a posh boy from Chiswick, turned up. He was from a middle-class family. Not like us. We were all counted as trash. But he was a lovely guy and was really good. Fortunately, he signed up, despite the fact that he was drumming in quite a successful outfit of the time, The Tridents.'

Told from Ken Lawrence's point of view, his decision to join the band was all about the music. While The Tridents were a popular live act, and gigging frequently, Four + 1 had a dynamic element that they couldn't match. When he stepped in for his audition, he remembers being exhilarated by the sound produced when Boots on bass, Junior on guitar, and Keith on harmonica were in full flow. It was, as Ken maintains, 'different gravy'.

The new line up of Four + 1 was instantly successful. 'We got a lot of work,' says Ken. 'A lot of screaming girls, that kind of thing. The Rolling Stones ruled at the time, but we were the next best thing. So, we cashed in on that quite a bit if we are being honest.'

No rock and roll story from that era is complete, though, without the accompanying tale of swindling managers and punitive contracts, and Four + 1 did not escape unscathed. They signed a contract with a youth club leader which would potentially keep them tethered to him for ten years, and entitled him to up to 50% of their earnings.

A typical tale of the time was that of the manager who saw bands at a gig, immediately imagined pound signs, and promised them the earth. As Keith says, 'He came backstage and said that we were fantastic, and that he would be able to get us a record deal, and all sorts of other promises. Then, he threw a contract at us. We were young and stupid, and we would have signed anything, basically.'

Unlike their peers, that both went before and after them in the music business, Four + 1 managed to extricate themselves from the clutches of this individual in a completely unique way. They went public through the medium of television and exposed the exploitation via a *World In Action* documentary that was aired in September 1964.

In reality, Four + 1's escape wasn't as well-orchestrated, smooth, or smart as it superficially appears, and owes almost everything to luck. Keith continues, 'Boots was having a conversation with some people in a bar one day. In the bar, at the same time, was a guy called Mike Hodges who overheard what Boots was saying about the awful contract and whose ears pricked up. He asked Boots if we would be interested in appearing in a documentary he was making about the music business called *The Flipside* [a pun on the dark underside of the business and the B-side of a record]. Of course, we jumped at the chance as not only might it help us get out of the contract, it was great publicity.'

Available to view on YouTube, the short, three-minute section of the documentary, that also featured Mick Jagger and legendary producer Joe Meek, is a sweet document of the early days of Four + 1 and identifies them as: 'one of 10,000 beat groups in the country trying to make it'. Ken Lawrence (who turned down a place at college to join the band, the documentary's voiceover maintains) talks about working seven nights a week, while Boots, all stylish cigarette and Harry H. Corbett (from *Steptoe and Son*) diction, bemoans the investment needed and ongoing financial commitment of being in a group. His complaints would have fallen on deaf ears, though, as he reveals that the group was earning up to £40 a week, which was more than most working men in the country at the time.

The most revealing part of the film is the live footage of Four + 1, shot on their home turf – Club Noreik – on Tottenham High Road. Playing to an audience of young dancers, it's easy to see how the band created so much excitement with their beat-filled, bass-heavy, throbbing and authentic R&B sound. The heavily stylised stage gyrations of Boots (who looks like a blueprint for AC/DC's Angus Young) and Junior also gives an insight into their popularity. At the centre of it all is the collected figure of Keith. He holds a plethora of maracas, and sings the blues in a style reminiscent of the early Mick Jagger.

The film, however, was ironically (and unbeknownst to the filmmakers) as much about the group conning their way out of the contract as revealing the underhand, exploitative nature of their manager. In the film, their contract's most punitive clauses are highlighted, but the voiceover credits them with 'having read every page, thrown it out, and signed with another agent'. This was, of course, untrue but it did the trick as, in Keith's words, 'The guy dropped us like a stone after the programme went out; it was not the best start for him and his fledgeling management career.'

Four + 1, despite their relatively short time together, were certainly in the right place at the right time to capitalise on the fierce interest in R&B which The Rolling Stones had essentially started to create.

Before the documentary, a friend of the band, Tony Brainsbury, turned up at a gig and said, 'I know Laurie Boost, the owner of Club Noreik on Tottenham High Road; he's got a fantastic blues club. We should go down there and talk to him about getting you on there.'

Keith takes up the story, 'I remember that we went down there, and we did an audition, and we were doing our new music, rhythm and blues, Chuck Berry stuff, the Rolling Stones, etc. and Laurie signed us up straight away. He got rid of the resident band, Bobby Rio and the Roots Roulette or something cheesy, who were doing straight covers and were quite old fashioned, and we were straight in there, basically.

'Laurie got us a road manager, a van, and paid us 25 quid a week each, which was quite decent money. So, we had a regular income which meant everyone could go full-time. I packed my job in when I was 19. The club would always be packed on a Friday or a Saturday night whenever we played there. Quite a few hundred. No problem. You can see that in *The Flipside* clip. It's quite a big club, and we made really good money.

'Club owners were cashing in on this new music; there was a small cover charge, and then obviously bar takings improved massively. Most evenings, wherever we were playing, we'd do two 45-minute spots or something like that, and finish around 11pm or 11.30. Then you'd have an all-nighter in some of these places which would go on until six in the morning. We were fortunate in that we had a road manager, so we would turn up for a gig, and he would have set all the stuff up, and got it working, which was quite handy. It was a nice thing to have as we could concentrate on just doing the show.

'There's a lot of hanging around when you're doing shows, sitting in dressing rooms – you're doing this, you're doing that – and you've got to go on and give it your all for an hour-and-a-half, or whatever.

'But one problem was that the top boys, a lot of them, were doing the same numbers, the same R&B and blues covers. That's where this thing about trying to find something different, something new, or trying to write original material came from. It's what we all ended up having to do. Nobody ever sat down beforehand and compared setlists. There was none of that going on. Whoever got to go on first, got dibs.'

'The kids [at Club Noreik] loved it straight away,' says Ken Lawrence. 'We played once during the week, and then the Saturday all-nighter, and the place was full of mods, high on pills, going berserk. We rammed the place pretty much every time we played there, and we supported a lot of the blues artists that came through, which was a big plus for us. We did the warm-up and then, afterwards, they'd do their set and then, hopefully, we'd get backstage and get an autograph and a chat or something.'

Keith adds, 'I did get quite friendly with Chuck Berry as we supported him a few times. He's a notoriously difficult character, but he was okay with us for some reason, perhaps because we weren't all over him, fan-type people. There were others, Little Walter, for example, who is a big favourite of mine; he gave me one of his harmonicas. Howlin' Wolf, whose real name was Chester, you couldn't call him Howlin', he was a huge great guy with a massive voice. So, yes, all these guys were down there. We'd be literally on the side of the stage watching them from the back. It was a great experience!

'Another one was Jerry Lee Lewis. I saw him down there once with Kingsize Taylor and the Dominoes. He was a particularly rude guy. He threw a bottle at somebody that tried to get an autograph in the dressing room. He wasn't the sort of guy that you wanted to fuck with, either. He was an asshole, he really was, but an amazing performer. Incredible. He stirred up the audience and, of course, we were learning from these people all the time about dealing with audiences, firing them up. We were taking it all in.'

The blues acts that were playing at Club Noreik (the owner's son's name, 'Kieron', spelt backwards) point to a curious time in musical history which began with American jazz players coming over to the UK. Here, they were better treated and respected than within their own country. From jazz musicians, things naturally moved through to blues guys and then rock and roll originators. Keith reflects on that time saying, 'I think, because of the birth of the Rolling Stones, attention got drawn to that style of music.

'All of these clubs started to bring musicians over from America, which meant they probably earned some decent money for a change. I wouldn't have thought they were on very good money at home. But the audiences loved them in the UK, and they really liked coming over as people made a fuss of them. They were revered, and there was a natural respect due to their age and backgrounds.

'The music is so real, and you can relate to it somehow, though it's from America. You could connect to those stories, which are real stories. The music has got some truth to it, which is the key for me; even us lot from Essex can relate to this music for some reason. I've never really worked out what it is, but I think it's because it talks to and reflects working-class people fighting to make a living, and having the same problems we had.'

One of the oddities about Four + 1 is that there were only four members in the band. Ken Lawrence remembers that his interpretation of this (having joined when they were already named) was that it was for marketing purposes; it added a little 'mystery' to their aura. He remembers the band and their supporters engaging in some guerrilla marketing activities by putting up stickers around London that read 'Four + 1 = ?'

Keith's interpretation was that the '+1' was in reference to the audience and acted almost like an invitation, or a way to impart some sense of community and inclusiveness.

Before the *World in Action* documentary had been aired, though, Four + 1 did indeed have five members when Les Jones joined from The Tridents on lead guitar. Ken Lawrence had played briefly with Les in The Tridents, who by this time must have been heartily fed up with losing band members to Four + 1 (although this would be forgotten as The Tridents' place in musical history is assured through Les's replacement, one Jeff Beck), but Les would quickly turn out to be a divisive character amongst Four + 1's seemingly happy band. Keith remembers, 'Les played in a similar style to Jeff Beck and he was a good player. He really was. But he didn't fit in with the band. We didn't get on with him. He was just a cool character. Hard to explain.'

Ken Lawrence remembers Ken as, 'Moody and loud. He wouldn't turn down, and his move from The Tridents to Four + 1, who were on the verge of a recording contract and a national TV appearance, went to his head and altered his personality for the worse.'

While Les's tenure with the band coincided with their first forays into the recording studio, it also signalled a crucial change in the power dynamics within the band that would have ramifications all the way through to the eventual break up of Tomorrow in 1968. Keith continues, 'Pretty quickly, after a few months, I could see how disorganised it all was. I'm that sort of person, basically, and I think I'm quite a diplomat. I'm not a person who likes confrontation, so if somebody is having it out, I'll get in the middle of it and sort it out and broker some sort of deal. I'm quite good at that, I think. I might be accused of sitting on the fence, sometimes, but I don't like confrontation or problems. There's always some way you can sort it out with somebody, somehow, to iron the differences out.

'Bands argue a lot and Les was a great player, but as a character, he didn't fit in with the band. It wasn't right – a bit like Pete Best and The Beatles. There's something that was missing there, and they didn't gel. I always thought of it as my band. I thought, someday I'm going to have to take it over.

'Someone's got to be a leader in a band. Whether you like it or not, someone has got to make decisions. John was not capable of doing that, so I took it over. I would hire and fire. I would sort the money out, and bits and bobs like that. I think I was quite good at it, actually.

'One good thing was that we all agreed on the songs; it was never a problem with what songs we were going to do. It was all covers at the time, and was all blues stuff. We weren't Beatles fans; we weren't into that Liverpool sound. We were all into the Yardbirds, Stones, black American music, basically.'

As mentioned above, one of the things that prompted Les Jones to abandon the good ship of The Tridents was the prospect of a recording contract, which Four + 1 were on the cusp of, but from what turned out to be quite an unsavoury source. As Keith remembers, 'Whenever we played, we got booked back pretty much and, as well as in London, we were quite popular up north which brought us into contact with Jimmy Saville. After seeing us play, he said he wanted to help us.'

Saville, at the time, was a very well-known music and influential entertainment industry figure in the North of England after stints as a DJ on Radio Luxembourg and regular spots on Tyne Tees television. He had already created the cigar-smoking, Rolls-Royce driving, 'larger than life' persona that would carry him for the next half a century, and was also seen as the top northern DJ who had access to the best music, and who owned Beat City, the best club in Leeds.

Keith explains, 'He was just king of the hill up there. He really was. He was the first star DJ, no question about it. He created the whole thing and did all those records. I don't know where he sourced them from, but he used to get records flown in from America. All the best stuff, all the new releases. His club was very successful, and he basically took us under his wing.

'He would take me out to lunch. He had a flat in Russell Square which I used to go to if he was in town. While that sounds quite flash, whenever I did go for lunch with him, it was inevitably somewhere cheap – typically a greasy spoon – and there was inevitably some sort of scam or back-hander going on for him to be there. He didn't like to spend his own money.

'I remember he did take us all out, once, for breakfast. I think we stayed in Leeds overnight, and then the next day he took us out to breakfast for a chat. We were sitting there having breakfast in this café. There was a garage opposite, and he had a Rolls-Royce at the time. It wasn't a particularly nice one, but he used to park it on the forecourt, and the guy would fill his car up for nothing because he'd get a load of business; people would come by and see Jimmy Saville's Rolls-Royce on his lot. That was a scam he did. So, he was a businessman first.

'I remember Saville as a clever and sharp guy. A lot of the bands that worked up there, he was behind them all. He was very supportive on that side of things. I know what happened later was disgraceful, but we never knew, never saw, any of that at all. He was a real music fan, and he helped us get our first record out.'

'He was very helpful,' remembers Keith, 'we would go up there [to Beat City], and it would be rammed, absolutely rammed. He liked us a lot and he, along with his PR guy, a man called Richard Reese-Edwards, who was thinking about managing us, managed to get us a one-record contract with Parlophone. He recommended we record the song *Time Is On My Side*, which was a Norman Meade song, and which was about at the time.'

As would become a trait more associated with him as the years went on, Saville embroidered the truth somewhat with what he would be able to do for Four + 1, and even how he had sourced *Time Is On My Side.* He told the band that he had made a trip to America to source it exclusively on their behalf. As it turns out, the Rolling Stones had already recorded a version of the song, and it was to appear on their *The Rolling Stones No.2* album, as well as being released as a US single in September 1964, and as a UK single in January 1965, just as Four + 1's version was released.

Inhibiting the fledgeling recording artists' chances even further was the fact that their version, while perfectly serviceable, was little more than a copy of The Stones' version. *Record Collector* magazine, in an article published in 1995, relates that, 'Reese-Edwards produced the disc, weighing in with the same sparse, cavernous sound which Andrew Oldham conjured up for the Rolling Stones' version of the song with Les Jones playing a Keith Richards-like loose scratchy guitar and West even adopting Jagger's affected Southern States drawl.'

'It does sound the same,' concurs Keith, 'even down to the organ and stuff. I reckon Saville was thinking of it as a bit of a Rolling Stones scam. Thinking ahead, he probably thought that they weren't going to release it as a single, but figured it was a potential hit. If we did a similar cover of it, and put it out as something of a Stones 'sound-a-like', then he might be able to pull a fast one, and create another string to his bow.'

More promising, for all involved though, was the single's B-side which was a cover of Chuck Berry's *Don't Lie to Me* which was a Four + 1 live favourite. 'It got airplay, and it got attention, and we got work out of it,' Keith says. 'I think, at that time, the live aspect was the most important thing. The record side of it, not so much. I didn't really enjoy going into recording studios in the early days, to be honest. It was very tedious. I would rather we recorded live, but you couldn't do it in those days. I didn't like the atmosphere in the studio. It was cold, clinical, and unfriendly.'

Ken Lawrence too has mixed feelings about that first recording session. 'I prided myself on being a good drummer,' says Ken, 'but for some reason, I could not get the beat required for *Time Is On My Side,* and they brought in a session guy, which is what you hear on the recording. It infuriated me, but in those days, studio time was deemed as being very expensive. I understood, but I was very upset about that.

'Keith later apologised to me and said he should have been more forceful at the time, but we were young and very inexperienced. I was on the B-side, though, but all I think about when I hear that song [*Don't Lie to Me*] is of Keith playing the tambourine, and when the song stops, Keith puts in another beat on the tambourine!'

In review, *Record Collector* says *Don't Lie to Me* is, 'fuelled by a pumping rhythm and recorded with a commendable minimum of fuss, the track is a tight, accomplished interpretation of the original.'

Sadly, however, the song failed to chart, and the relationship with Saville and Reese-Edwards faded with it. But there were benefits of having been through the process; it helped the band get more and higher profile gigs, and on their posters they could now mention a TV appearance, a record, and an association with a major record label.

But the relationship with Saville can probably best be filed in the category of a lucky escape, of which there would be a few more for Keith down the years.

3. Part of The In Crowd

Although the instant success craved by Richard Reese-Edwards and Jimmy Saville did not materialise, Four + 1 were still attracting a good deal of attention in the music industry, and retained plenty of influential supporters. Amongst them was Malcolm Forrester who, at the time (early 1965), was running Gunnell Music, the music publishing company owned by Rik Gunnell (one of the infamous Gunnell brothers who ran the Flamingo Club on Wardour Street where Christine Keeler famously played off her lovers). Malcolm would be a long-term supporter of Keith's, and on this occasion, he introduced the band to Roy Pitt, the husband of his secretary Barbara, who worked as a freelance record producer through his own production company Riot Productions.

The fact that Malcolm Forrester knew of Four + 1, and was willing (and able) to help, demonstrates how small the music business community was at the time, and particularly those on Denmark Street frequenting the legendary Gioconda café. Speaking to Malcolm in 2020, he recalls that he first met Keith via his association with Tony Colton (who was now well-known as a performer and songwriter) and their former Teenbeats bandmate Ken Burgess. A small world indeed.

Roy would go on to play a hugely influential role in the band's development during 1965, acting as both record producer and a manager-type figure. He was obviously popular with the boys in the band as Keith is quoted in one interview as saying, 'He was a great guy – the best manager in the world.' He must have been a powerful figure, too, as his first action was to change the band's name to The In Crowd (after the Dobie Gray single which was a hit both in the USA and in the UK in the latter months of 1964 and early 1965).

There was also a conscious decision to smarten up the band's image and give them a recognisable mod style to go with their mod-sounding name. As well as applauding Roy's ability to sniff the winds of change, there was also a more prosaic reason to change the band's name as the similarly titled Unit 4 + 2 had scored a worldwide smash with their single *Concrete and Clay* at the beginning of 1965 (reaching the number one position in the UK in April), and all involved thought it best to avoid any confusion.

As well as the change of name, the freshly-monikered band's influences and setlist were beginning to change also. 'That's right,' says Keith, 'the music business was changing all the time, and we changed too. We were doing more blues and soul then, artists like Otis Redding. We did *a lot* of Otis Redding material, but I didn't try to copy his voice, not in a million years. We just loved his music, so we covered the stuff. *I Can't Turn You Loose* – we used to do that – and *I've Been Loving You Too Long*.

'We did about five or six Otis Redding numbers in our set, and we were doing different gigs by then too, different clubs such as The Marquee, Blaises, The Ricky Tick in Windsor, The Cromwellian, The Speakeasy, Bag O' Nails, Annabel's for the posh people, as well as still playing the Noreik. We were starting to hang out with all the faces that were on the scene at the time as well; people like Keith Moon.

'I went drinking with Keith on a few occasions, and we would go to all the clubs I have mentioned; there were loads of them at the time. They were doing such good business, all these bars and clubs, and you could go on, and on and on. There was always a party happening on a Friday or Saturday after the clubs shut at two or three o'clock in the morning. So, Keith and I would take off to a party somewhere for a couple of hours.

'But, frankly, you couldn't keep up with his drinking. He was taking speed as well, so he would disappear for 10 minutes, pop something, and then come back and say 'Come on, let's get another round in!' and we would all be fucking floored. We would eventually end up staying at his house in Chertsey where his mother-in-law lived, and she would wake everybody up in the morning with a vodka and tonic. It was a crazy, crazy place and he was a lovely, fun, but dangerous character.

'The same can be said for Dave Davies from The Kinks; we got quite friendly. He was a really nice guy. Dave, Keith, and I used to hang around together. I remember the many times that I stuck him in a cab when he was drunk and sent him home.'

As well as drinking with some of the most celebrated figures in rock music, Keith was also hanging out with them as part of the musicians' network where artists supported each other by attending shows and giving moral support. Keith remembers seeing The Who in their Marquee pomp, 'I did go backstage once at the Marquee. Keith [Moon] invited me to go to their dressing room, but there was a fight; there was aggro going on there.

'There was an argument going on with Roger, Pete, and Keith – they were on speed and stuff like that, you could see it. John Entwistle was sitting there, letting it all go on, and he quietly suggested to me that it might be best to come back on a different occasion. I went back out again, but they were my favourite live band of all time, definitely. [Their performance at] The Marquee, I'd never seen anything like that before. Fucking smashing guitars up, flinging them through the air, putting them through the amp, sliding them along the mic stand which was so dangerous to do in those days. When they came out on stage, they were fired up.

'Our band didn't have that level of energy at all. You could see what their appeal was straight away. It was there. You could see why everybody was jumping all over them. They were sensational, they really were. But I always thought that for Roger [Daltrey], dealing with that lot must have been really difficult.

'We also met Bowie; he was called Davy Jones at the time. It was during our residency at The Marquee when Jack Barry was running the place – it was *the best* venue, the most credible venue at the time – and we had a residency there as The In Crowd. Davy Jones and the Lower Third also had a residency, and we went and saw them a couple of times. They were good, too, and you could tell he had a lot of charisma on stage. What they were doing was interesting but very much in the mod, blues, and soul genre, as he was digging The Yardbirds as well.'

The change in the music scene, and the band's direction, was reflected in their first single with Roy Pitt, recorded at De Lane Lea studios for Parlophone. The song, a cover of Otis Redding's *That's How Strong My Love Is* gave them their one and only 'hit'. But, as Keith now reveals, 50 years after the fact, that hit only happened due to some nefarious assistance from another giant (now discredited) entertainment industry figure, Max Clifford. Well-known now as the PR guru who would eventually be jailed as part of Operation Yewtree, he was known at the time as 'The Blue Max', due to his affiliation with the adult entertainment industry.

'There was some chart manipulation,' concedes Keith, 'and it helped us get on TV. You would be provided with a list of the chart shops [those record shops whose purchases were used to determine approximate record sales and chart positions nationally], and then you would pay people to go around and purchase records in those shops. Sales from these shops would show up on the chart information, and 'The Blue Max' organised this on our behalf.

'He wasn't the only one, though; quite a few people were doing it. Actually, to be honest, it was rife at the time and a recognised tactic just to kickstart a band and get them going. I'm sure some of the bigger, more popular bands have done it as well in the past, just to get something moving, to get them on TV and to kick it all off. It's well deserved, sometimes, because the public can need a bit of a push in the right direction, but it was highly illegal.'

Being in the Top 50 (the single appeared for one week at number 48) gave The In Crowd's career a boost which culminated in an appearance on *Thank Your Lucky Stars*, a music show aired at primetime (5.30 pm on a Saturday) to the nation's pop-obsessed youth. At the time, the show was the only serious rival to the BBC's *Ready Steady Go!*

But, if the well-known saying is 'a week is a long time in politics', then a month in the music business in the mid-60s can be viewed as a lifetime. Almost unbelievably, after the recording and release of their new single and its B-side, in April 1965 (of which a little more later on), Les Jones was sacked by the band and replaced with a new guitarist who would go on to mime his parts on their May 1st television appearance.

As Ken Lawrence recalls, 'Les was a difficult character to live with throughout his time in the band, and I was told by my three bandmates that as I had been responsible for bringing him in, I would have to be the one to get rid of him!

'It was one of the most difficult things I have ever had to do. He broke down in tears and begged me not to sack him. Although you can probably tell what a difficult man he was because, recently, The Tridents were getting back together and Les had contacted them and wanted to meet up, and they weren't going to do it! Even after 50 years, their memories of him being a bandmate were so unpleasant that they wouldn't even do that!'

Despite having a new bandmate in tow, *Thank Your Lucky Stars* would prove to be an exciting TV appearance for the band which saw them miming to *That's How Strong My Love Is*. The show, hosted by Brian Matthew, also featured Cilla Black, The Merseybeats, Sounds Incorporated, Julie Grant, Bobby Jameson, John Hammond and Val McKenna. Ken Lawrence remembers flying up to the studio in Birmingham with Keith for the show, and there was certainly momentum gained from their appearance; just two weeks later, they would also appear on *The Saturday Club*, a popular BBC radio music show whose other guests that week were Manfred Mann and The Everly Brothers.

Aside from losing a band member in the process, the experience of recording their single had been a mainly positive one for The In Crowd. While the A-side did chart, and was a decent cover of a strong song, the B-side, *Things She Says*, has a story all of its own. It marked Keith West's first song to make it onto vinyl. Thought by many at the time to be a more exciting song and certainly a more accurate record of how the band were as a live outfit, *Things She Says* is an early example of freakbeat with *Record Collector* noting, 'fat booming bass, some particularly vindictive fuzz guitar and 'blueswailing' (a made-up word, but we know what they mean) harmonica.' The fact that it only clocks in at just over 100 seconds gives an insight into how little time and effort record companies put into B-sides at the time.

Keith remembers what should have been an important moment for him as being something of an afterthought. 'They asked what we were going to put on the B-side, and I said that I had a song prepared. Well, sadly, the B-side was like a throwaway in those days. Nobody really cared about a good B-side. The attitude was to just do anything because it doesn't matter. They didn't really care, so the A-side got all the attention.'

Recording the B-side was remembered as a highpoint for the band's members though. Keith recalls, 'It was like a one- or two-take bang. Les Jones was on guitar because he plays a lovely solo in it, a really cracking solo, and they should have kept the tape rolling at the end because it would have gone on and been something amazing. I love that, that's my favourite record probably out of all the stuff we've [The In Crowd] done. One or two takes, that's the way I wanted to work. But it was more usual that we would have to do it over and over again, and they would add more overdubs. *Things She Says* had no overdubs, nothing; it was straight – bang.'

Ken Lawrence, too, looks upon this B-side as being, 'The best thing we ever did. If I close my eyes and think back, I can still remember playing that particular rhythm, in the studio, full of beans, perspiring like mad, and high as a kite on blues.'

Keith would, however, not receive his first professional credit as a songwriter for *Things She Says* due to more underhand goings-on in the music business. It transpires that for aspiring acts to win the much-coveted TV slot on *Thank Your Lucky Stars,* a hit record was not the only thing you needed to have; you also needed to assign the songwriting credit of the B-side to a company controlled by the producer of the show. If the song was a hit, he would benefit on the royalties side. Therefore, tragically, Keith's debut on vinyl is not credited to him.

What the song does reveal, though, is that Keith was starting to develop his own songwriting abilities. 'I had a basic knowledge of playing guitar in those days, and I was always writing words down and putting them away in books and things like that. I had loads of lyrics lying around; I'd just hum the tunes to the boys, or more likely to Ken Burgess as he could play guitar and we both liked the same music. I would say to him that I had a new idea and he would work the chords out.'

Keith's friendship and organic songwriting partnership with Ken Burgess has endured across the years, although for many years Ken was a hospital porter and not a part of the music industry, per se. His name, however, remains a regular presence in Keith's history and the songs which were soon to arrive.

4. Behind every great frontman is a genius guitarist

Despite only joining Four + 1 in the latter part of 1964, it was already clear to Keith, by the time The In Crowd entered the studio in April 1965, they needed a replacement for Les Jones, whose attitude was poisoning the atmosphere in the band. As it happened, fate would intervene as Keith and his new, well-to-do friend Antony Rufus Isaacs (actually 'Lord' Antony Rufus Isaacs), went to check out The Syndicats on Eel Pie Island in the early part of 1965. They were blown away by the band's young lead guitarist, one Steve Howe.

Keith recalls, 'I was looking for a guitar player, and there was a music shop on Charing Cross Road called Selmers, where all the guitarists used to hang out. I was friendly with a guy called Dave Lewison who used to work there, and I asked him if there were any good guitar players around who were available. He told me that I should check Steve Howe out; a guy who was always in the guitar shop and a really good player. He also told me that people called Steve 'The Face', which as it turns out was because he could pull a face like a gargoyle as his party-piece, rather than for any good looks or mod reasons.

'We had previously seen Steve when he was with The Syndicats; they had released a couple of records and were being produced by Joe Meek. But it turns out Steve wasn't happy there.

'We hit it off straight away, and it was all done at the Gioconda, the little Italian café on Denmark Street. We had a meeting in there and – bang – he was in.'

Keen to get started with their new recruit, the band pulled together a rehearsal session at Club Noreik, and Steve's impact was immediate. Keith remembers, 'Steve could really play; it sounded like there were two guitarists on stage the way he was playing. He completely changed the dynamic of the band. I mean Les was a decent guitarist, but when you get Steve Howe, and he starts playing, you just think 'fucking hell!'

'He could play anything. You didn't have to worry about what was going on behind you as a singer. You don't want to have to keep saying to band members, 'Oh no, you're doing that wrong.' Everything he did was right, everything he played. You couldn't criticise anything he ever did.

'Steve added so much more to the band, and he was very supportive of what I was doing, trying to write and stuff like that. I said to him, recently, that I probably wouldn't have been able to do some of it without his input in the early stages. You're writing something; you've got to put it forward; you don't know what people are going to think of it, etc., etc. He would have a go at anything, you know? What was going on behind me I couldn't believe; it sounded like there were about six people on stage.'

One negative aspect of that first rehearsal, though, is recounted in Steve Howe's book *All My Yesterdays* when he notes that Les Jones turned up at the Noreik. Which must have been an incredibly awkward moment for all concerned.

In the book, Steve gives an insight into the no-nonsense mindset and approach that would sustain him during a long, successful and varied professional career. When it came to his first engagement with the band, Steve would be miming along to a track on the *Thank Your Lucky Stars* performance. 'If you joined a band,' he wrote, 'there were certain things you had to do. You didn't whinge about them you just got on with them.'

Ken Lawrence also talks about the leap forward in the band's sound which was brought about with Steve's recruitment. 'He was a brilliant guitarist and he also seemed stoned out of his head 24/7! When Steve joined, we moved away from the wild sound which we had developed, and he brought some more finesse to proceedings; we became a bit more technical. I liked his playing a lot as we were more organised. We became more orchestrated in a way.'

As for Steve and Keith, theirs was an immediate friendship built on mutual admiration. Steve's first impressions of Keith were, 'He looked like a singer, the kind of guy who led a band', while Keith latched on to Steve's relaxed, permanently-stoned approach. The two started hanging out at Steve's parents' house in Holloway where they would delve deep into Steve's collection of blues and jazz records, as well as pre-release records from the USA that they were given through their contacts in the music industry. Over many hours, the two deconstructed the pop successes of the day such as *Love Is Strange* by The Everly Brothers and The Byrds song *Why,* picking apart their musical structure and production qualities.

These sessions were inevitably accompanied by the two friends smoking hash, and Keith remembers that they would often be overtaken by fits of the giggles. Steve's mother would invariably knock on the door to see what all the commotion was about, and sometimes remarked on the odd smell that Keith seemed to generate when he visited but, as everyone smoked cigarettes at the time, it wasn't quite so noticeable as if it had been an entirely non-smoking household.

With the new band formed and gigging regularly, August 1965 saw them once again enter the studio with Roy Pitt for another shot at recording success. Their second single was to be *Stop! Wait a Minute,* written by Harrell-Bailey, another song picked by Roy Pitt. Listening to the song now, you can easily discern the reasons behind Roy Pitt's thinking. The song is an upbeat, danceable number with a tight, clipped beat. Its purpose was to have mod boys and girls around the country hitting the dancefloor with their elbows tightly pinned to their sides, and their chins struck forward trying to look effortless, as their feet worked in time to the beat. But, while you can see where Roy Pitt was going, the band was not as enthusiastic about the material.

'I don't really know, it's a bit of a nothing song, to be honest,' says Keith. 'We basically did what we were told, I think. We rehearsed it, performed it and – when Roy thought it sounded good enough – we went and recorded it. We just did it, and he thought it might be a hit. You've got to put your trust in somebody, I guess. Again, it didn't get a lot of interest.'

For Keith West and Steve Howe fans, the B-side of The In Crowd's single holds, once again, much more interest than the A-side; on this occasion, they would be credited with the songwriting (alongside their bandmates Simon Alcot and Ken Lawrence, as the song is credited to The In Crowd). *You're On Your Own* is more sedate than *Things She Says* but features two excellent fuzzy solos from Steve and a soulful vocal from Keith. Sadly, once again, it is cut short just as it starts to take off in the closing seconds.

Thinking back, Keith says, 'I don't know who worked out the melody on that... it was probably split between the band. They used to put any sort of name they liked on the B-side. You might not find my name on it; I don't know who gets the credit for that song. It might say Hopkins or something?'

Far from being despondent at not breaking through with their second single, Keith gives an insight into the mind of a working musician at the time. When asked about the lack of success of *Stop! Wait a Minute,* which was released on the 10th of September 1965, he explains, 'We were still working a lot, so we didn't really care. We weren't too worried about it, to be honest. We were working, we were earning money, and we didn't really worry about the charts. We just liked playing live, basically.

'We loved the whole live thing, so that was the main interest at the time, definitely. Plus, it was all new territory. We didn't know how long it was going to last. You thought you had a couple of years and then you're gone. That's when you would need to start thinking about doing something else, getting a proper job.

'There's a classic story about Paul McCartney when he was asked, in 1967, about the future for the band and he replied, 'Oh, it might all end next year and John and I will probably just write songs or something.' Nobody knew. Careers were quick in those days. You were in, and flavour of the month at one point, and then the next month you were gone.'

A decent insight into the sort of living that groups were making in 1965 can be gleaned from Bryan Morrison's autobiography, *Have a Cigar*. Keith would have some history with the Bryan Morrison Agency in the fullness of time, but before that, Morrison tells of being offered a year's contract of £250 per week as live agent for The Pretty Things. His 20% management cut of £50 per week was viewed by him, at the time, as a huge sum. The In Crowd would be on similar money, and certainly their weekly wage would be well in advance of what their peers (or their parents) would be earning.

Entering the studio in October 1965, for what would turn out to be their final single, the band were once again presented with a song by Roy Pitt. *Why Must They Criticize?* written by George Bean, was an attempt to change tack and hitch an early ride on the freakbeat and jangle pop bandwagon that was emerging with bands like The Byrds from the USA. But, having acquiesced to Roy's wishes in their previous records, this latest pick met some resistance. As Keith says, 'That was again a strange choice. All of these songs just weren't representative of us. When we played live, we weren't anything like that, so I couldn't really see the point of doing this stuff. We weren't like that, and so it all went horribly wrong.

'We did *Why Must They Criticize?* under protest. It was sort of a folk song. There was a line about growing your hair, that kind of stuff, and by that time I think they were more worried about us getting a hit than we were.'

The flipside, true to form for The In Crowd, was a closer reflection of who they were as a band. While, on this occasion, it was not an original composition, their cover of James Brown's *I Don't Mind* is skilfully done with solid backing vocals and a fine soothing guitar solo from Steve to support a passionate, soulful vocal performance from Keith.

Reflecting on The In Crowd's recordings and their time with Roy Pitt, Keith wishes that he and the band had been more forceful with their own ideas. 'Maybe we should have had more balls and been more upfront about the whole thing,' he says. 'Roy came in as a big fan but, with the benefit of hindsight, he's chosen three stinkers as singles and we've created some fantastic original material on the B-sides at a time when it's becoming apparent that the world's turning in the direction of bands creating their own songs.

'You've got The Who and The Kinks who are echoing McCartney and Lennon [in writing their own material] and myself trying to create original songs for the band. I can remember being frustrated and disillusioned about making records. I remember I asked Roy, once, when we were recording a B-side, whether we could focus on it a bit more, as it was more like us as a live act. But he, and the powers that be at Parlophone, just told us to forget it and said we didn't know what we were talking about.

'Yeah. The people that Roy Pitt was selling the product to were going along with it as well. They must have done, because selling records takes time, money, and effort, so they'd have had to be behind it.

'I don't understand it, I never did. The band, though, never complained. I never complained. We just got on with things and were busy working. It never really entered our minds to kick up a big fuss or go against their decisions.

'It would have been better to have *Things She Says* as a single. It gets the most airplay out of all those songs, and has become a freakbeat anthem. It's got some real power in it.'

Released in November 1965, *Why Must They Criticize?* failed to enter the charts. The band, though, were seemingly unworried by this and simply got back to doing their job of playing live – helping to meet the vast appetite the nation's youngsters had for music delivered with skill and passion. As Keith explains it, 'If the record part is 10% of what we're doing, and the live part is 90%, and that's going great then well – you know – it's not too bad, is it?'

Throughout 1965, and the first half of 1966, The In Crowd was a much-in-demand live attraction playing on bills across the UK with the likes of The Who, The Hollies, Donovan, and The Small Faces as well as venturing out into Europe for dates in Holland, Germany, and France. Travelling abroad with the band was something of an eye-opener for Keith as, at this time in the UK, working-class people would rarely travel abroad for holidays and the package holiday boom was still a little way off. He remembers travelling to Jersey as a child, 'It was a bit strange. I remember the airplane. It was something out of *Thunderbirds* as the cars went in the front. I don't know how many you could get in there, but it was bizarre. That was the furthest I'd ever been until the band started going to Europe, which I thought constituted a very jet-set lifestyle.'

Amongst the hundreds of club gigs that the band played in this period, there was also a slew of private gigs booked through a burgeoning London business called, For Fun Ltd. The company boasted 'the first mobile discotheque in London', and was run by the man who accompanied Keith on the fateful night he had his musical socks blown off, on Eel Pie Island, by Steve Howe. Enter Lord Antony Rufus Isaacs, son of the Marquess of Reading, and brother of the model and socialite Jacqueline Rufus Isaacs.

Effortlessly proving his top-level connections by working out of Lord Snowdon's studio at 20 Pimlico Road (Lord Snowdon was, at that point, married to the Queen's sister, Princess Margaret), Antony Rufus Isaacs had, through his high society connections and amiable disposition, cornered the market in providing entertainment for Debutante Balls.

Deb Balls were originally conceived to show that a young woman was available to be married, and their purpose was to display her to eligible bachelors and their families. But, in the mid-60s, with the Queen having abolished the tradition of Debs being formally presented to her in 1958, Deb Balls had become something of an anachronism, and an excuse for high society debauchment.

These balls, with the removal of royal patronage, became rock and roll, hedonistic events with Antony charged, and more than willing, to provide the music. 'I was organising Deb parties three times a week,' he said in 2020, 'two events during the week and then one big one at the weekend. You never got out of your dinner jacket. Firstly, Four + 1 and then The In Crowd came onto my radar, and we booked them a lot. They were incredibly popular, as they were just what the girls wanted.'

Adding more, by way of context when speaking to *Flashback* magazine in 2012, Antony Rufus Isaacs said, 'In the mid-60s, you could still get a top band to play at a private party relatively cheaply – The Kinks played at my 21st birthday in 1964, for example – and the musicians liked the work… they would earn more than they got at a club.'

Aside from the money, there were other benefits to playing these events as Ken Lawrence recalls, 'We'd turn up at these country estates, I mean we are talking absolutely mammoth places, and all the Debs and Hooray Henrys would be there. We used to send them up a bit and take the mickey out of them somewhat, and give stupid answers to their silly questions.

'I remember telling them we had done a gig in a street and plugged into the electric lights to power the amplifiers and they would believe us; they weren't the brightest.

'I was always jealous because Keith pulled the best ladies, [at the Deb Balls]. He always pulled the best-looking women, and there were some fantastic society girls there who were absolutely barmy about him. I was so jealous. I did get my share, as the drummer, but he got the best because he's a real ladies' man with the gift of the gab and everything.'

Keith takes up the story, 'Antony Rufus Isaacs, whose nickname was Fluke [because he always ended up dating pretty girls which, in the view of his peers, was a fluke], appeared on the scene and started getting us some gigs at the Deb Balls which he was running. He was also involved with Dandie Fashions, which was a clothing emporium in London and really hip and trendy, The Beatles and everybody shopped there. He basically took us over.

'He got us some gigs at the Deb parties, and they were raucous, mad affairs. These people were more rock and roll than you can imagine. Knocking back champagne all day long, absolutely trashed. These great big houses. They would be worth £15 or £20 million today, and they all came with grounds and everything.

'Loaded families and their daughters were coming out to party. It was all going on, having sex in the gardens, skinny dipping in ponds and swimming pools; it was all going bonkers. We would typically play for a couple of hours, and there would also be a DJ, but often they threw money at us to keep playing and at the end of the night they would say, 'Can you do another hour? Here's a couple of hundred quid', so of course we would. They loved it.

'The more raucous it was, the better.'

Following their engagement at a good many For Fun Ltd events, Antony became increasingly friendly with the band and with Keith in particular, showing him the finer side of life in the form of great restaurants and society parties. Keith's burgeoning friendship with Lord Antony, a man whose background and education couldn't have been more different than his own, is an example of a continuing theme in Keith's life which is his ability to get on with anyone (Les Jones being, perhaps, the exception; but Keith does not seem to be alone in that camp).

By his own admission, Keith does not like conflict and always attempts to smooth ruffled feathers. But that is not to say he is a passenger and will sit back and let things drift on by. As Ken Lawrence relates, 'I rated Keith as a singer and we were pretty good friends. He liked to be the boss, though. He installed himself as the boss and no-one challenged him.'

As friendships developed, Antony Rufus Isaacs became increasingly involved with the band. In Keith's words, 'He started getting us gigs in Holland and managing us, and looking after our career in an organic way. I don't think it was formalized. I don't remember him getting involved in records or anything like that. Just live work.'

Looking back on his part in the history of The In Crowd (which would extend all the way through to the band becoming Tomorrow), Antony has mixed feelings. 'Not about the people,' he says, 'I took Keith under my wing because he was a lovely chap and they were a lovely group of people, but the great tragedy was that we never got that big hit, that breakthrough song.

'I was good friends with Bobby Wace who managed The Kinks, and I was trying to get them to write a song for Keith and the band. Essentially, though, I didn't know what the fuck I was doing, but I thought these guys are brilliant and he [Robert Wace] agreed.

'One of my recurring thoughts, if not quite a regret, is 'Did I fuck up their careers?' It was a plaything for me, I tried to look after these guys, and to bang their fees up, but I was more of a consistent supporter and a facilitator than a manager, and they needed professional, experienced management, which they didn't get – as history proves.'

5. Feminine persuasion

As you would expect from any rock star's biography, women play a major role in the story; they fill multiple roles: as influencers, as inspiration, and – not quite as elegantly – as short-term distractions.

For women in the UK in general, the 1960s represented great change at a great pace. In all strata of society, transformation was taking place, from the Debs Balls which evolved from glorified cattle markets into fun events that celebrated a girl's evolution; to the middle class where an increasing number of women were attending University; to the working class where more women were entering the workplace and exercising newfound financial power.

This is not to say that the expectations on women to care for children – and carry out the household chores – had disappeared, but more that a woman's role could be extended to include other avenues and opportunities… as long as she kept her end up at home! Not exactly a fair division of labour or total emancipation, but progress at least from the home and family-focused drudgery of their mothers' lives.

With more women entering the workplace came economic freedom, and the ability to spend on socialising without having to rely on being 'taken out' by their husband or boyfriend. Hence the popularity of the clubs and bars which sprung up and which did great business at the time. Girls wanted to have fun, and they wanted to dance, and they wanted to drink, and they wanted to meet boys, on their own terms. Dancehalls, clubs, bars, and nightclubs have always operated on the same principle: if they can attract a female audience, to dance, then they will attract a corresponding male audience. Thus, it was the job of the band to attract girls to dance. Keith – with his good looks and charm – and the rest of the band with their combination of good looks, hip image, and musical ability proved very attractive. It also meant Keith met a large number of young women, some of whom were keen to explore the newfound sexual freedom which the contraceptive pill offered.

The role of women in the story of 1960s pop music is, when viewed some 50 years later, somewhat broad-brushed as screaming girls or groupies. These stereotypes show an unflattering image of women as deranged, hysterical creatures. It portrays them as having as much influence on the music and the culture of the time as in-season cats. The reality is, as ever, somewhat more nuanced.

Ken Lawrence, drummer in Four + 1 and The In Crowd gives a glimpse into the dual personas of some female fans as hysterical teenage spectators *and* sexually forward adults. 'We had a van,' says Ken, 'and when it was parked outside the venue we were playing at, girls would write messages to the band in lipstick on the side.

'Normally it would be innocent stuff about us being the best, or them loving us, or blowing a kiss to a particular band member. But often the messages were pretty graphic and came with telephone numbers and address details, and were open sexual invitations.

'To give you an example of how, for the time, near the knuckle the messages were, is the story of the night when we were on the way back from a gig, and were driving back through a village where we filled up with petrol. Some old chap or old dear must have read the messages on the van and called the police. We were pulled over and threatened with being charged with obscenity if we didn't clean it off!'

Similarly, Keith remembers a close encounter with the hysterical frenzy that was a Beatles gig at the time, where girls simply lost control. 'The first time I saw the Beatles,' recounts Keith, 'was at a Beatles Christmas show [which ran from the 24th of December 1964 to January the 16th 1965 at the Odeon Hammersmith].

'Jimmy Saville was part of the line-up and performing presentation duties, and he was big mates with the band. Also on the bill were The Yardbirds and Freddie and The Dreamers and, during the course of the run, guests would appear like Susan Maughan doing *I Want To Be Bobby's Girl* and all that.

'Jimmy was fronting it and asked me if I wanted a ticket, and as I hadn't seen The Beatles before, I went along and was backstage with Jimmy next to The Fab Four and all the rest of them.

'Before the gig, I went down into the audience, and it was mostly screaming girls. I saw The Yardbirds, complete with Eric Clapton, and they were great. Then, the Fab Four came on, and did a short set, and you couldn't hear a fucking thing. They were screaming from the minute they started playing. I've never experienced anything like it in my life.

'I went back upstairs afterwards, and I met the four of them. I was pretty nervous, but I can remember it. John, he was quite… sort of ... well, he wasn't fat, but he was a lot bigger than you'd imagine. Well-built is probably the right term. Ringo was the friendliest, and was very relaxed and quite funny.

'I can remember John being a bit cynical and asking me something like, 'So, you're in a band, are you?' I could see they were a tight little pack, those four. Together they'd take the piss out of you something terrible if you did or said the wrong thing, so I was just very polite and said that I was in a band, and then changed the topic of conversation to the fact that the girls were screaming so much I couldn't hear them playing.'

Keith continues, revealing something not heard before.

'The Beatles used to come on and do a short spot – bang, bang, bang. And the girls, they used to pee all over the seats. They would get so excited that they literally used to urinate all over the seats. People would have to come and clean the seats off between the first and second shows [nightly shows were 6.15 pm and 8.45 pm] – a horrible job.

'They used to get so fired up, even before the band had come on. It was unbelievable. I've seen screamers before but I've never seen anything like that. *She Loves You,* whatever number they did, it was just drowned out by screaming. I think it's quite well-documented that they hated it. You just couldn't hear anything; it was just a racket. They weren't there to listen to the music at all; they just wanted to scream their heads off for 25 minutes.

'I've never really understood the screaming thing. I wanted to listen to the music. I went twice, and the second night was exactly the same thing.'

While the teeny boppers were still evidently losing their marbles to the mop-top cherubs from Liverpool, other women viewed themselves more as musicians' peers rather than just adoring foot soldiers.

Pat Stebbings was one of those women.

As part of her job as a waitress at Blaises, and as a dancer, Pat would have been well used to being in close proximity to the stars of the day. Blaises itself was a small after-hours, members club, located in the basement of the Imperial Hotel at 121 Queen's Gate in Kensington, West London (which has now been demolished). In its mid- to late-60s pomp, it was a mecca for musicians, agents, managers, and writers from The Beatles, The Stones and The Who to Bob Dylan and David Bowie.

Among the musicians that both played at the club, and used it as a watering hole, were the members of The In Crowd; for a short time, Keith and Pat dated, and feelings were intense. However, about-to-be divorced Keith was keen not to be tied up by any relationship, no matter how strong the feelings, and the relationship drifted and stopped. Shortly afterwards, Steve

Howe started to date Pat, and they would eventually marry in 1969.

Another of the women that could more than hold their own was Dana Gillespie who was Keith's girlfriend for a few months. Dana's place in rock and roll history is assured by the fact that Davy Jones (or David Bowie as he later became known) had a long relationship with her romantically, sexually, and artistically through the 60s and the 70s. Indeed, Bowie wrote *Andy Warhol* for her. She also appeared on the *Ziggy Stardust* album, and her 1973 album *Weren't Born a Man* was produced by both Mick Ronson and Bowie.

Despite only turning 16 in 1965, Dana (who came from an upper-middle-class background, and curiously was the official British Junior Water Skiing champion in 1962) was a fully-formed artist and woman when Keith encountered her. She is something of a force of nature and would have been one of the 'It' girls of the time.

Keith remembers their first meeting. 'Tom Jones and the Playboys, The In Crowd, and Dana were all on the same bill. That's where I met her. She was a very fit girl, pretty and with a great figure and long legs. Tom Jones was after her all the time.

'This sounds a bit egotistical, but girls would come over to me and say, 'Can you pretend you're my boyfriend because he's driving me up the wall?' That happened on this occasion, so I knew that she fancied me.

'She was only young at the time, 16 or 17, but then again I was only 19. She had a load of nerve as she was writing and singing her own material. She used to get up on her own, with just an acoustic guitar, and perform.'

Keith says, 'I would say Dana was my first serious girlfriend. She was smart, confident, and a talented performer and singer already, at 16-years-old. When we went out together, she would turn heads everywhere. Guys would stare at her with that big mane of hair and she always dressed beautifully. She also seemed to know everyone around the London scene. You could tell she was a very sociable person.'

Dana also remembers those heady days remarkably well and, rather unbelievably at the time (aged just 16), she was already ensconced and living alone in a basement flat under her parents' house in South Kensington. 'The flat was only one minute from The Cromwellian and three minutes' walk from Blaises,' Dana recalls, 'so that's where one went to pull, to be seen, and to have fun basically.

'After the clubs shut, we would inevitably land up at my place, and various musicians such as Brian Jones, Ronnie Wood, Twink and Syd Barrett would crash on one of the sofas. I also had a full range of instruments there so we would jam. I cannot remember doing anything musical with Keith there... we were probably busy doing something else,' she says with a throaty laugh.

'Keith was great looking with jet black hair, and he was tall and slim-hipped. You could never count on or expect fidelity from a musician. I know what fun they can be, but I know what they get up to on the road. We had a lot of fun, and I liked him a lot. Even hearing his name makes me smile.'

Dana was not the only glamourous encounter that Keith had at Blaises. He remembers one remarkable evening, during the period, when The In Crowd had a Thursday night residency, and Murray Head (a singer and actor who would later go on to have worldwide success with the song *One Night in Bangkok* from the musical *Chess*) escorted the film stars and international sex symbols Brigitte Bardot and Ursula Andress into the club.

Murray knew Keith quite well and liked the band, so he positioned the stars at a table directly in front of them, which Keith remembers as being both disconcerting and distracting at the time. After their performance, Keith was introduced to the actors and above all remembers how petite they were. At one glorious point (when Murray had either gone to the bar or nipped to the loo), Keith found himself gamely protecting the honour of the two ladies with one safely positioned on each arm. 'I wish someone had taken a picture of that!' says Keith. 'I'd kill for that now. *Dr. No* is one of my favourite Bond movies, and meeting Ursula had quite an effect on me; she was so sweet and was exactly as I imagined her to be. My first long-haul holiday was a trip to Jamaica solely because of that film's location.'

Blaises was not the only place where Keith was meeting and mixing with a range of women; the Deb Balls and other gigs were taking him to places – both geographically, and from a lifestyle point of view – that he had never been before. One such encounter was with Suzie Ravenscroft, step-sister of the DJ John Peel (who was born John Ravenscroft but changed his name to more easily distance himself from his public school roots), who he met at a society event. Keith and Suzie could not be superficially less well suited, and Keith remembers being both intimidated and overwhelmed when he visited the Ravenscroft family home on the Wirral Peninsula to attend a lavish family picnic complete with lobsters and champagne.

The two embarked on a passionate relationship that finished when a bemused Keith, when trying to contact Suzie, was informed curtly and without further explanation that she had gone away to finish her studies abroad. Confused and hurt, Keith managed to put the relationship behind him but received a mysterious letter with a picture of a baby in a pram inside. On the back, it simply read 'Yours'. While not having any clear evidence, Keith contacted John Peel (who he knew reasonably well, having done a few radio programmes with him), to see if what he suspected was categorically true. Keith recalls that John was essentially sympathetic to his plight and confirmed

Keith's suspicion that he had fathered Suzie's child with a sardonic 'Congratulations'.

But, Peel seemed neither overly concerned that Keith had fathered a child with his step-sister, or in putting the two back in contact, and that's where the matter rested… for 25 years until, in the early 1990s, Keith was contacted by a young woman who could prove that he was her father and that Suzanne Ravenscroft was her mother. She said that she would like to meet. Not going into any detail when he spoke about it, Keith remembers the meeting as being wholly unsatisfactory all around; two people with no history and no shared interests simply not finding any chemistry. It would be their only ever meeting.

Back in the 60s, while Keith was busy going through the natural process of both breaking hearts and having his heart broken, (something which he wishes had happened before he got married and which probably explains why Norma was granted a divorce in 1967 with Keith cited as the guilty party for abandonment), other members of the band were having greater success at establishing mature relationships. Steve Howe, for example, married Pat Stebbings with whom he would have a son, Dylan, in 1969. Dylan would grow up to be a professional musician and bandleader who has enjoyed a long career notable for playing with The Blockheads and Wilko Johnson, re-working Bowie's *Low* album as well as playing on many of his father's projects.

Speaking in 2019, Steve said, 'The fact that Keith and I were married to the same woman makes our friendship even more remarkable. We went through a love triangle, but everyone was as sensible as could be about what happened, and in the end we maintained our friendship, which says a lot about Pat.

'There were problems that came later, but if you look at the three people involved it just kind of came about. I didn't like it at the time but took it for what it was, and moved on.

'The important thing is I believe we all feel that we have bettered ourselves since then, and not made more of a mess of it since it happened. But, you have to accept that things change and on that count, Keith, Pat, and I worked through the situation and came up with the best we could.'

As Steve reveals, Keith would also marry Pat, in 1978, following her divorce from Steve in 1971, and she and Keith would go on to make a life and have three daughters of their own together. They are still happily married and live in a beautiful house in a private road near Weybridge. The saga is understandably delicate, and one which arouses a certain amount of natural curiosity, but, despite numerous requests for an interview with Pat, she has maintained her silence.[1]

[1] The closest we came was when, on hearing that I would want to talk to her, she told Keith, and I quote verbatim, 'If some person calls me up and tells me he wants to ask me about the 60s, I will tell him to **** off!' A strong woman, and a proud wearer of the hard won right to live her life as she pleases, even if it is mildly inconvenient for her husband and his biographer!

6. 1966 and changing times

As we know from the *World in Action* documentary *The Flipside,* The In Crowd (or Four + 1 as they were known when it was aired) were 'one of 10,000 beat groups trying to make it in the UK', and the landscape was competitive, to say the least.

Peers of The In Crowd, at the time, were a group which hailed from Colchester in Essex called The Fairies. They had relocated to London in 1964 and signed a contract with Decca Records recording and releasing three singles which did not chart. The driving force behind The Fairies was their drummer John Adler or 'Twink' as he was known to everyone (after a hair product at the time which was a home-brand perm lotion; a nod to his brilliant mop of curly hair).

Twink, on his re-location to central London from the relatively provincial East Anglian town, set about embracing every aspect of life that the Capital had to offer. He was now unencumbered, as many musicians on the circuit were, by living at home or having to placate parents as to his whereabouts, earnings, prospects or hours of business.

He began to move in rarefied circles and at one point was sharing a flat with the artists Nigel Waymouth and Michael English who would go on to define – through their imprint *Hapshash and the Coloured Coat* – what the counter-culture and psychedelia would look like. He also spent time with the leading lights of *Granny Takes a Trip,* the most famous counter-culture clothes shops on London's Kings Road, plus people such as John Pearse and Sheila Cohen.

These people, through their clothes and associated artworks, were starting to move the look and feel of the time away from the mod look – with its deliberately conservative cut, and colour palette – into a much more flamboyant direction. They were also pushing the boundaries of how people thought and behaved; they would drop methedrine into their tea, and stay up all night talking and plotting about how to change the world and the people around them.

Twink recalls such sessions as being incredibly influential; he was learning about counter-culture thinking and politics, as well as clothes, art, and LSD!

Playing out against this colourful background of discovery and change, things – sadly – were not progressing at all smoothly for The Fairies. As Twink recalls, 'The Fairies and The In Crowd were pals and we used to hang out together around Denmark Street and go to the pub and The Giaconda.

'The Fairies were on our last legs. We had experienced a lot of trouble in 1965 when our singer, Dane Stephens, had a car accident in which there were fatalities involved and we lost him for a year; he went to jail.

'He re-joined us, but it was never the same, and the scene was changing. I remember that Steve and Keith came down to a gig we were playing at the Café des Artistes, on the Fulham Road, and at the end of the evening, both Steve and Keith asked me if I'd like to join The In Crowd. I jumped at the chance. We had been through a lot, and we were like brothers [The Fairies], but I had to earn a living and it really wasn't going anywhere whereas I had seen The In Crowd at Club Noreik, and I knew they were fantastic.'

Similarly, but for dramatically different reasons, things were also happening within The In Crowd camp which would significantly impact their line-up and progress across 1966. Recruited into Four + 1 at the same audition as Keith West in late 1963, Simon 'Boots' Alcot had remained a strong presence within The In Crowd. 'He came across on stage as Mr Moody,' remembers Ken Lawrence, 'and he smoked Russian black cigarettes and said he had a knife down his boots… which I am pretty sure he didn't.

'As far as I was aware, he came from a good background, but he created a 'persona' of the temperamental artist, which was difficult to deal with sometimes. We used to tack the mickey out of him because he took himself so seriously – he thought he was the star of the band.

'Having said that, in other ways his feet were on the ground, and I recall he had a Greek fiancé who he planned to open a hotel with once he finished with the band.'

Ken's comment about 'Boots' having created a persona is more accurate than even he knows. The full story about Simon Alcot – and how he came to leave The In Crowd when they were on the cusp of leaping forward with Steve Howe amongst their number – is one that has not been fully told until now. Born in May 1944, about six months older than Keith, Simon Alcot's birth name was actually Robert Alcock and he was an adopted child with no siblings.

He grew up in Kilburn and attended Salisbury Road Secondary Modern where he made two great friends – Roger Hammond and David Hugman. On leaving school, Robert tried his hand as a printer, porter, and postal clerk before falling in with Four + 1 at the end of 1963 and pursuing the life of a professional musician. Despite not all being in the music business, the three friends would remain close and were out in central London, on Monday the 25th of April 1966, to celebrate Roger's 21st birthday with an all-day pub and bar crawl.

During the course of the revelry, the three friends came across a sex joint called The Spent Penny at 23 Lisle Street, in Soho (now the site of Beijing Dumpling), where sex workers used the private flats on the upper floors, and the first floor was a clip joint.[2] The three friends entered the establishment and Roger handed over £5 (more than £100 in today's money) for what he thought would be an experience befitting his landmark birthday. However, the very definition of clip joint is centred on disappointment; after a short time, the three men conceded they had been 'had' and left. All that is except Roger who, in his relatively inebriated condition, had something of a set-to with the manageress and got some of his £5 back.

The three friends then re-grouped and planned and enacted some fairly schoolboy-like revenge by emptying a dustbin bag full of rubbish onto the stairs that provided access to the club. The police were called, but due to the low-level nature of the disturbance, and the absence of the alleged perpetrators, nothing further was made of it.

If only the three friends had left it there; the course of their lives would have been so very different.

At around 7.30 pm, having drunk some more in the couple of hours since their previous visit, the three friends returned to Lisle Street and emptied another bag of rubbish onto the stairs. This time, however, they exacerbated their misdemeanour by setting the rubbish on fire before pouring half a gallon of petrol onto the flames. In doing so, they ultimately set fire to all four floors of the building.

The girls working in the club were forced to climb through a window to flee the blaze, and to call to passers-by for help. Tragically, when the fire brigade investigated the charred building's remains, after the fire had been extinguished, they found a man's body. A civil servant named Reginald Gordon West had, with the darkest of ironies, entered The Spent Penny

[2] A clip joint is a strip club in which customers are tricked into paying excessive amounts of money for low-grade goods or services—or sometimes, nothing—in return.

shortly before the boys made their return visit and – before availing himself of any services – used the club's small toilet cubicle. It is likely that he was overcome by smoke when the fire started and he ultimately perished.

The national newspapers covered the fire and death of Reginald in the morning's papers of April 26th and one week later, after a police identikit picture was featured on the TV crime programme *Police 5.*

The three friends handed themselves in.

At their trial on June the 3rd, all three men pleaded guilty to manslaughter, and not guilty to murder, which the jury accepted. On the 17th of July, Roger and Robert were sentenced to two years imprisonment, and David to 21 months, which began immediately, and they were taken down to Wormwood Scrubs.

Gita Renik, who was working at the time at The Bryan Morrison Agency (of which more later) recalls there being an 'awful atmosphere' at their office on the day after 'Boots' was found guilty of manslaughter. She remembers a workplace that was usually the epitome of 'upbeat' as having a dark shroud hanging over it; 'real life' had suddenly made an unwelcome visit into their lives.

Steve Howe and Keith, to their credit, both visited 'Boots' in prison with Steve remembering the visit as, 'very sad, but he had committed a very serious crime and was lucky not to get a more severe sentence I suppose.'

Keith also recalls the visit, 'I've got only bad memories of doing it. It was terrible. He was just a victim of circumstances, which is what his lawyer said. He just happened to be there, but they were going to do the whole lot of them, basically, because the victim was a civil servant.'

With the loss of 'Boots' on bass guitar, a re-shuffle was needed for The In Crowd to keep working and fulfil their gigs (and earn their living). Therefore, allowing for the fact that Steve Howe's addition to the band was akin to recruiting several guitar players, John 'Junior' Wood was able to move from rhythm guitar to bass and soon established a driving style which laid a foundation for Steve's creative guitar work. Sadly though, in the middle of 1966, while the whole of England was caught up in a wave of euphoria which would eventually lead to them winning the World Cup at the end of July, The In Crowd would lose another of its formative members.

One of the pleasures, but also one of the frustrations and harder aspects of researching and writing a biography, especially one whose central participants are now in their mid- to late-70s, is that memories fade, perspectives differ, and – in some cases – scores are settled. It is your job as the biographer to balance the evidence. Mostly, it is the case of memories fading when it comes to explaining why Ken Lawrence's departure from The In Crowd has been recently attributed to drug-taking affecting his performance – as told in magazines like *Flashback* and Steve Howe's autobiography.

Drugs certainly played a part in Ken's life as a member of Four + 1, and The In Crowd and, if you recall, one of his favourite moments with the band was during the recording of *Things She Says* when he was 'full of beans and high as a kite on blues.' Keith takes up the story, 'Ken was a lovely guy, but he was taking too many pills and started imitating Keith Moon on the odd night, because his head was gone completely. We all told him to calm down.

'That was a period when we all took a bit of speed because sometimes we were doing two gigs in one day plus all-nighters. I didn't really enjoy it as much as Ken did, but we did take them just to keep us going on a long night. Probably about six, seven months, we were taking pills; the whole band was.

'All the rock bands were doing speed; little pills to keep you going. But after a while, you need more and more and more.

This is what happened to Ken. I remember one night, we started a number up and we were like, 'One, two, three', and he was half speed. He was completely wrecked. He had to go, basically.'

Steve Howe has similar-ish memories. 'We were all getting experimental and dropped a few things, and Ken was getting weirder on stage until, one day, he fell off his stool. We just thought, oh my god, I guess we are going to have to get a new drummer. He was a little bit out of it, and I guess the group was starting to get the determination to forge ahead.'

As always with conflicting versions of the same story, the truth most often lies somewhere in the middle. In a lengthy interview, in 2019, Ken Lawrence offers a more mundane, less memorable (and less rock and roll) version of events which others could be forgiven for losing track of, over time. Essentially, Ken left The In Crowd because his parents didn't like his behaviour and suspected he was taking drugs. They heartily disapproved and forced him to quit.

Ken recalls, 'It was horrendous, I was living at home and my parents were running a few businesses and expected me to take them on, which I didn't want to do. Since the age of 11, all I wanted to be was a professional drummer, but my parents were going crazy about my lifestyle as they had paid for me to go to a number of private schools such as Compton House for Young Gentlemen. They expected me to progress to be a doctor or a lawyer.

'For years, though, I had been bombing out of school and going to listen to music at the 2i's coffee bar in London, knowing that music was my life and I didn't want to do anything else. But, I was living at my parents which was probably the biggest mistake of my life, and they were always asking, 'What are you going to do in two years when rock and roll doesn't work out for you?'

'I remember the guys dropping me and my drums off at the house, and I was distraught because I didn't want to leave. In fact, I remember Keith trying to talk me into staying. I regret that decision and I should have stuck with it, but at 18 years of age or so, I didn't really think about going off and getting my own flat and being independent.'

So while Ken's drug-taking was a problem for the band (and for his parents), in all likelihood it only indirectly led to his departure from The In Crowd although, as Ken recalls, 'I did sit in for Twink on a couple of occasions later on and auditioned for The Searchers not long after leaving the group. But, following that, I put my drums away and didn't play for almost 20 years.'

As well as changes in personnel, 1966 also saw an important change in the behind-the-scenes organisation as Antony Rufus Isaacs began co-operating with the Bryan Morrison Agency (BMA) as live date bookers and management. BMA and their bookers, Tony Howard and Steve O'Rourke, would both wittingly and unwittingly have a big effect on the careers of Keith and the other band members and their roster was building up all the big acts in what would become the heart of the UK psychedelic scene. Chief amongst them, of course, was Pink Floyd but they also had Soft Machine, The Pretty Things, Donovan, and now The In Crowd.

With a five-days-a-week professional booking agency behind them, who had venue contacts across the whole of the UK and in Europe, The In Crowd started to work further afield. Checking the band's gig list for 1966, it can be seen that they visited Holland in October and December of that year, and memorably spent two weeks in Milan as the 'band in residence' at a newly opened nightclub. Steve Howe in his autobiography recounts the tale of the band driving all the way across the Alps to Milan and then experiencing an uncomfortable two weeks in the northern Italian city as the object of some horror and ridicule; the general Italian population were unaccustomed to brightly dressed, young English musicians amongst them.

During this time, the face of the music scene was starting to change once more, and the newly-formed power trio behind Keith – Steve Howe, Twink, and John 'Junior' Wood – was starting to push the boundaries of what they were playing. Extended musical experiments were inserted into what had been core parts of their traditional set, songs such as *Why* by The Byrds, and *Shotgun and the Duck* by Jackie Lee.

'For the first time,' recalls Keith, 'The In Crowd started to jam on stage, and in rehearsals, and we started linking the numbers and let Steve do his own thing. It worked really well with the audiences.

'We were all listening to West Coast stuff by then, The Doors, that kind of stuff. I was a big Doors fan and Steve liked all the jazz records we used to play together in his bedroom; the whole thing was getting all kind of improvisational and extended, and the middle sections could go on for minutes. We had this thing called *Shotgun and the Duck* which we'd been doing for years; it was a club favourite that went into a psychedelic sort of thing which, strangely enough – if you listen to the live version of it – is manic. I mean, it's completely manic.'

As part of the band's association with BMA, they had secured a residency at Blaises and, indeed, Steve and Keith were sharing an apartment at the hotel above the club. Being in such close proximity to Blaises had great benefits as not only did blues legends such as John Lee Hooker play the club, but also new acts from the USA, such as The Byrds, did so too. Chief amongst these new acts to visit the UK and completely change the musical landscape was Jimi Hendrix and all the members of The In Crowd were in attendance at his first UK show at Blaises, on December 21st 1966, where he was introduced to the band. He became something of a friend and cheerleader for them.

Unbeknownst to the band, and to Keith, one final thing took place in December 1966 that was going to have a remarkable impact on him and indeed them all in the following year. A young German musician named Mark Wirtz, recently relocated to the UK and working as an in-house producer for EMI, had experienced an incredibly vivid dream about a grocer named Jack who is taken for granted by his village…

7. Band on film

The history of music on the silver screen, and musicians acting, is something of a mixed bag. It covers the sublime, the ridiculous and everything in between. For every triumph such as Lady Gaga in *A Star is Born* or Prince and *Purple Rain*, we have the films and acting careers of Sting and Roger Daltrey to consider.

Keith West and his bandmates' film careers also cover a wide spectrum of quality and success. While a keen cinemagoer, Keith's professional relationship with the film industry had extended only as far as The In Crowd playing at the glitzy premiere of the James Bond movie *Thunderball*, in late December 1965. However, through their association with Antony Rufus Isaacs, the band came into the orbit of firstly the star – and then the director – of *Blow-Up*, now considered a classic movie. It's a film that revolves around a hip London photographer who thinks he has taken pictures of a murder.

Reflecting on the circumstances around this unlikely pairing, Keith says, 'The In Crowd were playing at a club called Tiles that Jeff Dexter used to DJ at, and David Hemmings came down one night and saw us and thought we were brilliant. He'd won the lead role in *Blow-Up* which featured a band.

'Michelangelo Antonioni, the director, originally wanted the Velvet Underground – who couldn't do it because of visa problems – and then he wanted The Who, who didn't want to do it. So, David recommended us to Antonioni, and the request went forward to my publishers, Ian Ralfini and Martin Wyatt at Robbins Music. They commissioned me to write two songs for the film, which I did, *Blow-Up* and *Am I Glad to See You*.

'I ended up playing those songs on acoustic guitar to Antonioni during an audience at a posh hotel near Hyde Park, and I can remember that he liked the songs, so I thought it was all going well. They took us down to Dandie Fashions, which

Antony Rufus Isaacs had some investment in at the time, to get some outfits; we went to another shop called Hung on You, where we got some garish polka dot shirts.

'We got fitted out in jackets and trousers which we were going to wear in the film. We even recorded demo versions of the two songs at a session produced by Tony Howard, and the film company then mocked up the Ricky-Tick club in Windsor in the studio, and we did some rehearsals.

'But, for one reason or another, we ended up getting replaced by The Yardbirds. Lots of explanations for our replacement have been put forward over the years; from Steve's reluctance to ape Pete Townshend's guitar smashing antics, to the whole bands' larking about on set, but one thing I know happened was that they made up several cardboard replicas of Steve Howe's beloved Gibson ES-175. It's Steve's replica guitar that Jeff Beck smashes up in the movie, but it's a very small scene, a couple of minutes, and it's all over. It was much ado about nothing really.'

Despite their cruel elimination from the final movie (which would be released in the UK in March 1967, and go on to make $20 million on a $1.8 million budget), the experience of writing songs to order was an interesting one for Keith, 'I talked the role through with David Hemmings who plays a photographer, so I linked it up to his whole lifestyle and wrote the lyrics around his role.

'But, on reflection, the whole meeting with Antonioni was weird. We were in his hotel, but he could speak hardly any English at all, so he had an interpreter. So, every conversation started with, 'Mr Antonioni says this ... Mr Antonioni says that ...'

'It looked like he was on a slightly different planet, as well, Antonioni, but he didn't say too much, didn't give too much away. Yeah, it was hard, and when they were auditioning for extras and stuff, he used to line them all up and he'd walk down one by one, look at them and say, 'No, no.'

'He was a strange character. We were told he didn't think the grass was green enough for one of the shots in the park scene, so apparently, some poor minion sprayed it with some kind of dye. The whole thing was a weird experience for us anyway.'

Another frustration for Keith was that the two songs he wrote for the film were not featured on the official soundtrack album, which was composed and played by Herbie Hancock. Inclusion on the soundtrack, as well as being potentially lucrative, would at least have been some compensation for the time and effort the band – but Keith especially – put into the project. It wasn't until 1995, when RPM Records issued an excellent compilation album of Keith's work from 1965 to 1974, that the tracks finally saw the light of day. Ironically enough, when listened to today, the tracks would have sat reasonably well within both the movie and its soundtrack; it does not take too much imagination to visualise a montage of David Hemmings zipping around London while Keith's *Blow-Up* plays in the background.

More interestingly, *Am I Glad to See You* contains some neat production tricks and the outgoing coda, with handclaps and Keith's howling vocal, works particularly well. The 7" single of the two tracks is worth tracking down on Munster Records.

While the band's first foray into the movie business had eventually yielded nought, at least they could take comfort in the fact that to even be associated with a film which would stand the test of time, and come to epitomise the era, was worthwhile. Sadly, this was not an epithet that could be attributed to their second film, *Smashing Time,* which was released at the end of 1967.

As Keith, somewhat uncomfortably, recalls, '*Smashing Time,* was a cheesy '60s movie with Rita Tushingham, Michael York, and Lynn Redgrave. It's about swinging London and was intended to be a satire but didn't really work. We were in it as a band called The Snarks. There's no music in it; we were just there to act as popstars hanging out in nightclubs or with all the '60s heads.

'We worked on it for quite a few weeks though, and it's tough I've got to say; lots of early starts and then sitting around all day and not doing too much.

'We were in about five or six different scenes, and there was a silly scene where the Post Office Tower – which was the big new thing at the time – was revolving, and somebody pulls a lever and it starts going too fast, and we were all clinging up against the wall – it's very cheesy.'

Released on the 29th of December 1967, the film performed poorly at the box office (with takings of $290k against a production budget of $630k). As Alexander Walker, the *Evening Standard*'s film critic noted, the film arrived, 'too late to parody swinging London as by the time of its release the fad was already dead'.

While hammering a nail into the coffin of the band's film career, their appearance in *Smashing Time* is notable for one other reason. Astute observers[3] can see that a certain member of the band was not able to make the filming and was replaced by John Pearse, who was the bespoke tailor at Granny Takes a Trip and a friend of the band. John 'Junior' Wood was, in fact, in hospital at the time with jaundice which the doctors linked to his use of alcohol and amphetamines. While he did rejoin the band after filming had concluded, he did, according to Twink, 'Settle down a bit, as essentially he had experienced a nervous breakdown.'

[3] The whole film is available on YouTube for anyone who *really* wishes to see it.

8. The song that defines an era

The labelling of a song as 'era-defining' is a subjective affair, particularly when the song in question didn't enter the charts when it was released. But such an argument could be made for *My White Bicycle,* which was recorded when Keith and the band were still The In Crowd in March 1967 (although it was not released until May 1967, by when the group had changed their name to Tomorrow).

So, do the song's credentials support the era-defining description?

It was unarguably inspired by a counter-culture movement; it was recorded using innovative 'psychedelic' recording techniques; it was laid down at the same studio in which The Beatles were recording *Sgt. Pepper's Lonely Hearts Club Band* (with various Beatles dropping in on the sessions) and it was adopted as an anthem by the most influential psychedelic venue, the UFO club, during The Summer of Love. Plus, it was later recorded and released as a single by actor Nigel Planer in his guise as Neil, 'the hippie', from the anarchic 1980s TV show *The Young* Ones. Could there be stronger supporting evidence of its significance?

Looked at with the benefit of historical perspective, what becomes evident is that *My White Bicycle,* and indeed its B-Side, *Claramount Lake,* represented a huge leap forward in the songwriting of Keith and Ken Burgess.

As Steve Howe recalls, 'With *My White Bicycle* and *Claramount Lake,* we had gone away from how standards were written with basic chords and all that 'Moon in June' crap. [*Claremont* Lake, near Esher in Surrey, is where Keith sat stoned one day and wrote the song. It didn't sound right when pronounced as Claremont – the phrasing was wrong – so Claramount won through.]

'In the main, at that point,' Steve continues, 'the subjects of popular music were fairly trivial, and we had managed to fashion something a bit more concrete, *My White Bicycle*... it's about a bicycle, *Claramount Lake*... it's about a lake, but there's something to grab on to, something with relevance that was a bit more spaced out, but was also something important.

'This all came from Keith and I being fed up with playing covers and having the idea that we could do something different. That gave me my first opportunity really to invent the whole thing about the guitar. A great opportunity, as we had to be guitar-driven, but not a responsibility that I felt loaded with. It just felt natural for me to open out and be more of a guitarist of my own making.'

The idea for *My White Bicycle* had come to Keith following a trip to Holland at the end of 1966. 'We were in Amsterdam, and one of the girls at the club asked me what I was doing after the show and invited me to go along with her to an art gallery.

'I went down to the art gallery, which was just an excuse for us to spend some time together, I think. Anyway, she came back to the hotel where we were staying, and was telling me about these Dutch provos that had provided people with free bicycles that you'd get on and then drop off somewhere. They'd painted them all white.

'It was when she said 'white bicycle', it just triggered something off in my head, and I thought that I should write a little story about it. In five minutes, probably, something like that, I scribbled some lyrics down. I was always scribbling things on bits of paper.

'When I got back to London, I got my guitar and wrote it out, only using two or three chords; it was in D, I remember that. I remember the D chord is pretty much the whole song, it's just one chord, basically, and a little bridge in the middle.

'I didn't think much of it, but I took it down to rehearsal, and I remember thinking that Steve would not go for it as it wasn't musical enough. But, we started playing it and he liked it, and when he started to improvise around it I told him that he needed to stay on the D chord, and then you could see him thinking about the possibilities.

'Then Twink started doing something with the hi-hat, doubling it up to 16s, and all of a sudden it just started to drive; it sounded like a car driving or something motoring along. It just clicked, and I banged in the lyrics, and that was it. I had the intro down, it was just a simple sequence – it's very simple, anybody could do it – and I had the bridge worked out; three chords in the bridge. I didn't know whether they were going to work or not, but they did, and it was that simple; we made it up on the spot!

'I didn't know what Twink was going to do on it; it could have been completely wrong, but whatever he did was dead right. Then John, as bassist, pretty much doubled up on what Steve was doing, the sort of driving sound. Then Steve worked out the sitar-type piece which follows the melody. It was really clever what they'd done to it, and we started playing it immediately in the set. They were good enough to do that, they really were.'

Keith remembers the basic elements of Amsterdam's White Bicycle story but, in fact, it was a community bike-sharing programme that industrial designer and inventor Luud Schimmelpennink – a member of the radical Dutch Provo counter-culture movement – instigated in the Dutch capital during the mid–1960s.

After gathering 50 bikes and painting them white, the anarchic Provos, who focused on drawing a reaction from the authorities through pranks and non-violent action, parked them unchained all over the city, so that they could be used, then left on the streets, by anyone who needed them. The aim of the programme was a forerunner of today's environmental schemes to eliminate all motorised traffic in the city centre and improve public transportation.

In Amsterdam, though, the police impounded the bikes because municipal law forbade them to be left unlocked. The Provos then retrieved the bikes, equipped them with combination locks, and painted the combinations on the frames. Even though the White Bicycle Plan received no support from local authorities at the time, it has served as the model for similar programmes that operate in major cities around the world, from London to Singapore.

Writing a great song, however, is still a long way away from getting the chance to record it at a world-class studio, and releasing it on a major record label. For this, The In Crowd needed some record label attention, and it would come in the form of the newly installed in-house production whiz at EMI, Mark Wirtz. Wirtz accompanied Norman Smith – the fabled Beatles engineer and Pink Floyd producer – at the invitation of The Bryan Morrison Agency, to a Pink Floyd show, before they carried on to Blaises where The In Crowd caught his attention with their newly-written song.

Speaking to *Sound On Sound* in 2014, Mark Wirtz confirms his excitement at first hearing the group, 'I thought they were terrific, and right off the bat we got along great,' says Wirtz, who began working with the group soon after that first encounter. 'We just clicked; definitely a case of kismet. One of the reasons I loved working with them was that the rhythm section was a trio, and so there was never a clash between the instruments.

'They would come into the studio, and I would ask them what material they had, and then Steve and Keith would get together to work out an arrangement for the song they were going to do. Steve would play the guitar, Keith would sing, and they would play me the tune while Twink and Junior would listen.

'I was always like the fifth member, sitting in on keyboards for all of their stuff, and I'd make myself fit in with the concept of their ideas. This was not about Mark Wirtz, it was about them, and so it was never a case of me auditioning, approving, or selecting the material; it was just them really having it together, to the point where all I had to do was agree.

'Having an idea of the song and the structure, I'd just add myself into the arrangement as a keyboard player, we'd record it, and three or four hours later we'd have a track. It was incredibly self-contained; they were very much on top of it. Working with them was fabulous.'

Pretty soon, The In Crowd would find themselves in the enviable position of being at their first EMI recording session at Abbey Road, tracking in Studio Three where, sitting alongside Mark Wirtz, was Geoff Emerick, then-involved in engineering the Beatles' *Sgt Pepper's Lonely Hearts Club Band* in one of the next-door studios.

Keith remembers Geoff especially fondly. 'He was lovely. He was a working-class guy, so I got on with him like a house on fire… a really nice bloke. The rest of them were all quite middle-class, and Geoff was just a normal street guy. Plus, he was a genius engineer; I mean he was probably the fifth Beatle as far as I'm concerned. He could make any sound that they wanted, and I don't know how. He was amazing.'

Keith also remembers being distinctly underwhelmed by the Abbey Road experience, saying, 'I don't think we thought too much of it. I didn't anyway. It's a stuffy sort of place to work.

'There's men in white coats walking around taking measurements, where you could put the microphones and stuff like that. They had big German Neumann microphones which looked alien to me. I was used to using a short mic where you'd grab hold of it and sing close to it. You couldn't do that; you couldn't touch the microphones at all, that sort of stuff, it was a little bit different.

'They actually gave me a dummy mic once to hang on to when I first started recording. I didn't get on with it, being in a booth with the door shut... and they're all up there behind a glass window looking down at you.

'The Red Light goes on, and it's 'Take one'; it's a horrible sort of atmosphere – headphones on, great big headphones – and you've got to perform so that they are satisfied. I didn't enjoy that very much at all; I'd have rather been with my boys, a semi-live sort of situation, but that was never going to happen. You pretty much did as you were told, I guess, in those days.'

Mark Wirtz, too, recalls feeling that Abbey Road was trading on its past glories and not looking to the future, 'In Studio 3, at that time, we had old consoles which had four huge faders in the middle that looked like the levers used to switch the direction of a train. Let me tell you, back then Abbey Road was a horrible studio, not only because of the union-type mentality where you couldn't move a mic an inch without somebody in a white coat being called down from upstairs to do it, but also because the equipment was antiquated.

'The console had one master EQ switch that could be set for classical or for pop, and that was a problem for someone like me who was a fan and disciple of Phil Spector whose sound was more random than by design.'

Aside from the restrictions of the studio itself, it seems as if the musicians and their newfound producer had as good a time as possible while recording the main track and the B-Side. It was all concluded within three sessions. Mark Wirtz recalls, 'I remember, it was 10 o'clock in the morning when I listened to the demo of *My White Bicycle*, and then we began recording it. It didn't start off as a particularly exciting track, but we were all into it and really enjoying ourselves while smoking a couple of joints. What's funny is that, for the part of the record where you hear a police whistle, Keith went outside and actually got a policeman to come in and blow that whistle. There were joints everywhere and the place stank of marijuana, but the policeman came in and he was all excited, he blew his whistle, and then left.

'Whereas Nazareth's hit version of *My White Bicycle* is distinguished by Manny Charlton's slide guitar and Dan McCafferty's high-pitched vocal, the Tomorrow original is altogether different and sonically far more interesting. Right from the start, we hear backwards guitar and backwards hi-hat, together with Junior Wood's pulsating bass and Twink's driving percussion, punctuated by Steve Howe's edgy guitar licks.

'The backwards hi-hat that runs throughout the entire song was my idea,' claims Twink, while Wirtz recalls the excitement of experimenting with backwards guitar. 'That wasn't an orchestrated part,' he explains, 'we just recorded a regular solo and turned it around. It was totally random.

'In all, three hours were spent on recording the instruments and maybe an hour doing the vocals. As for the mix, that may have taken a while, but altogether we're probably talking about three sessions lasting a total of nine hours.'

Keith remembers the sessions, and also remembers the frisson of excitement the band would experience on being in close proximity to The Beatles. 'There was no security in those days; you just walked in the front door,' says Keith harking back to a more innocent age. 'We normally tried to get more than three hours of studio time, because that's what you were allotted – three hours.

'Since The Beatles were so successful, they could do pretty much what they liked, so they stayed on longer. We used to go into their studio late at night when everybody had left and were amazed that they had their own lights in there as well, coloured lights to get the right atmosphere in the studio. You could see all kinds of fish and chip paper laying around… all sorts of debris, cups of tea, and the like.

'We would even go and touch their instruments. Junior got Paul McCartney's Hofner bass out; all of their instruments were just lying around in the studio, they used to leave them there overnight.

'On one late-night session, we had some hippy girls, friends of ours, come down, and visit us in the studio. One of the engineers was being a little uptight, so I can remember these girls taking his shirt off and body painting him while he was on the desk. We would have all got the chop if they'd been caught. I think he secretly enjoyed it.'

Twink also recalls a close encounter with the Beatles, 'I remember sitting outside Studio Two with Keith because we knew The Beatles were in there. The doors are like those on a bank vault; you can't hear anything that's going on inside. The red light's on, and we couldn't hear anything; we were just sitting there giggling excitedly, waiting to see somebody.

'Then the front door opens, and Ringo comes in, and he walks down the hallway towards the studio, 'Evening lads', he says, and as he opens the door to go in, you can hear *Being For The Benefit of Mr. Kite* being remixed by John Lennon who's sitting there in his caftan and granny glasses. Lennon just looked around, gave us a nod and went back to the desk. Ringo goes in, and the door closed. Magical.

'We would mainly work in the afternoon, as we were gigging, so we didn't get up too early, but we did do some evenings,' remembers Keith. 'I was living in Walsingham Mansions at the time, which is over by Chelsea Football Club, and it would take me about 40 minutes to get to Abbey Road with just some notes and my harmonica in my back pocket. The other guys, especially Twink, had to drag their instruments over there every day, which was a bit of a pain.

'But, it was very quick, a few three-hour sessions; two tracks done, mixed, and out. Everybody was playing live regularly, so you didn't need to rehearse; you'd just get used to the feel of it by going over and over it again, and as long as they got the sound right, which they did, they'd mic up the drums, get it all set up, and bang you'd go.'

With a great central premise, a superb recording, some original sounds that had not been heard before, plus a little sprinkling of 'Beatles-proximity' dust, *My White Bicycle* seemed a surefire hit when it was released by Parlophone on the 12th of May 1967. It garnered some excellent reviews from the music press and music industry figures with *Melody Maker* deeming it, 'One of the most exciting and commercial and catchy records to have come out of the new school of pop music since the word 'psychedelia' first made its presence known.' *Disc and Music Echo* said it had a 'Byrds-gone-mad intro', and that it 'bowls along with urgency, but the thing that really endears it is the Pete Townshend quality in the lyric.' John Lennon, himself, asked for the song to be played at The Speakeasy.

Even today, trying to explain its lack of chart success has everyone a little baffled. 'It did end up being an anthem,' says Keith. 'Everywhere that it got played, it went down really well, but it wasn't a hit, unfortunately. We thought it was going to be top 40 at least, and it didn't do anything at all. It was bizarre.

'I don't know what happened there, it was quite commercial-sounding as well, a big hook to it, and compared to some of the stuff that was around at the time – like *See Emily Play* by Pink Floyd, which made the charts – I didn't really understand. Everybody blamed it on the record company not promoting it, but I don't think that's anything to do with it, it's just something that didn't click on radio at the time. Eventually, though, the strength of the song was seen when it was covered by Nazareth in 1975, and went top 10, which was some compensation at least and confirmation that we weren't completely deluded at the time.'

Despite the fact that the original record did not hit the heights in the charts, the song has gone on to have a long shelf-life and still enjoys regular radio play both in the UK and Europe and always features in polls of 'Best Psychedelic Tracks' or 'Soundtracks to the Summer of Love'. Plus, Joe Boyd himself (the storied first producer of Pink Floyd and the only producer to work with Nick Drake), when speaking in 2019, talked about the influence of the track and why it proved to be the perfect title for his bestselling book *White Bicycles – Making Music in the 1960s*.

'The reason I used it as the title of the book is a combination of two things,' said Joe, speaking in his Little Venice flat surrounded by a huge collection of vinyl records, music books, and posters. 'What happened was, I finished the book, I gave the manuscript in, but I didn't have a title. So, we're getting towards the deadline where the sleeve design needs to be done two weeks from now or whatever. Then the publisher starts emailing me with some ideas for the title such as *Memories of a Record Producer*, ideas that are really, really horrible. So I'm thinking 'fuck', I have to find something better, and I've been wracking my brain and I just said 'okay, I'm going to clear my head and start reading the book for inspiration.'

'The opening chapter of the book is about that night at UFO when Tomorrow are singing *My White Bicycle*. Then, at the end of the chapter, I wrote, 'By the end of the summer, the white bicycles in Amsterdam were being stolen and repainted.' So it was like a symbol; it was a combination of the fact that the song had been played that night, which I describe as the apex of the 60s, and then I used that as a symbol of the falling away of the idealism.

'So, it's the fact that there's a symbol of hippiedom, the white bicycles in Amsterdam, and that the song had been performed that night. It dawned on me that I should call the book *White Bicycles* and I immediately knew it was a really good title. I think it has been absolutely essential to the success of the book because I think it means that somebody who's not a balding, bearding, male, 50-something nerd might buy the book.

'A woman might even want to buy the book with that title, whereas, in the main, books on the history of music are not something that women read. But you feel optimistic that two or three of them might because of that title. It gives it, at least, a chance.'

Another unexpected offshoot that the song created came with the commissioning of a striking advertising poster by Nigel Waymouth and Michael English, who'd recently gone into partnership as Hapshash and The Coloured Coat. Antony Rufus Isaacs gave his friends Nigel and Michael the commission and remembers paying them £100 for it (roughly £2,000 today). However, despite the beauty of the design, when EMI saw that it incorporated bare breasts, they declined to have it distributed. The duo, therefore – in an act of sneaky revenge – came up with a second design which had an obviously phallic mushroom contained within it; this snuck past the powers that be and was distributed.

The *My White Bicycle* poster was one of the first in a long line of commissions that the two artists undertook for the most influential bands of the day such as Cream, Jimi Hendrix and Pink Floyd. Their silkscreen printed poster designs are now recognised for their cultural value and have been the subject of numerous exhibitions and retrospectives; indeed, some of the pair's work from the time is on permanent display at the Victoria and Albert Museum in London.

My White Bicycle's significance, for all the rock and roll folklore that surrounds its creation, and its afterlife as a cultural beacon is perhaps best summed up by Steve Howe. '*My White Bicycle* did us almost us much good as an album. It was a very popular song, and it felt like it was going to be a hit. Indeed, it was a hit with everyone in the music scene and industry… but not so much in the charts.'

9. Darlings of the psychedelic underground

While The In Crowd's music was changing direction naturally, the recruitment of Twink, in August 1966, brought someone into the band who was not only interested in the wider ideas of the counter-culture, but who was also connected to a few of the leading lights of that movement.

As Keith acknowledges, 'Twink was into the whole hippy movement, probably a little more than Steve and I were, although we had a different take on it.

'Our thinking was that we had developed a good fanbase and we were conscious that we wanted to take them with us, and not alienate them. Superficially, his [Twink's] image made it more obvious that he was into the whole thing. His playing style was energetic and when Steve used to go off on his improvisations, Twink and Junior would follow him. I don't know how they did it; it was like there was telepathy in there somewhere. They never rehearsed it; they just went off on these crazy experiments.'

It was certainly the case that – as powerful a personality as Twink was – him arriving and completely changing the dynamic and direction within the band was not going to happen. Keith had grabbed hold of Four + 1 by necessity, and The In Crowd was very much seen as his band, and he organised the hiring and firing. While there was obviously some synergy of thinking in terms of musical direction, and the band members were all being influenced by what was happening on the West Coast of America, change would not be instantaneous.

Steve Howe relays the thinking taking place within the band at the time. 'Rather than copying Steve Cropper, or covering a song from America, we started to believe we could open out with our own ideas. That was a nice challenge and something we really liked and the effect it had was that, when we went on stage, we indulged in getting high on hash and creating an atmosphere.

'No-one could have predicted the way my guitar, my 175, my wah-wah, and the Vox amp – the way that combination produced a really rounded and satisfying sound; a big sound. Plus, Twink brought a more stylish kind of drumming because of his experience and professionalism, and the excitement inspired everybody to raise the bar.

'The sound I was developing on the guitar was allowed to grow and that showed in the drone improvisations that we would become known for, where I would steer this strange ship with percussion and people dancing. It was part of a growth in musical freedom which was included in Keith's new songs and added to the old songs through improvisation.'

While Tomorrow would eventually hitch themselves firmly to the counter-culture and psychedelic bandwagon, it's important to recognise that, as 1966 came to an end, this was still an extremely small cultural force (albeit one that would gather pace with incredible speed in 1967 and pretty much burn itself out by the end of that year). Its influencers, too, were concentrated among a small number of people and locations in London, predominantly within Soho and the King's Road.

Foremost in the tale of Tomorrow and this movement is the UFO club, which began its life in December 1966. The circumstances that led to the opening of the venue are covered fully in Joe Boyd's book *White Bicycles,* but the club was in an Irish dance hall, The Blarney Club, located underneath a cinema at 31 Tottenham Court Road; it would run from 10.30pm to 6am every Friday night.

UFO was the brainchild of John 'Hoppy' Hopkins and Joe Boyd, who wanted to provide an outlet for like-minded people and give them a place to gather. 'We were really excited about the UFO club,' says Keith, 'we'd been down there to see Pink Floyd, and we thought this was our sort of club because they're all smoking dope.'

Both 'Hoppy' and Joe were already building a reputation in the counter-culture community, and Joe particularly credits 'Hoppy' with helping to set the intellectual and political agenda of the entire movement. This agenda was articulated through his activities that centred on the *Indica Bookshop* in St. James (including the London Free School movement which would eventually morph into the Notting Hill Carnival).

Joe himself was an American who had fallen into the music business through his passion for the blues, and then stumbled into the folk genre which would ultimately lead him into the path of Pink Floyd. Joe was, according to Keith, 'A smart guy: sharp, American, hustler, boyish-looking – the girls loved him.'

Joe himself says, 'Looking back, I think people who are involved in the rave scene today would say that between February and August 2011 everything happened. Everything changed. I'm sure people who are young and involved in any scene in history, experience intense periods where things seem to be moving really fast.

'If you look back, for me that period from the summer of '66 to the summer of '67 was unbelievable. It was so intense and creative. I was fortunate; I had met John Hopkins when I first came to England with the Blues Tour in '64. He took pictures of Muddy Waters and stuff like that, and we became friends.

'When I was living in London, in the summer of '66, there was all this stuff starting to happen. The London Free School, Pink Floyd at Powis Square, and I had worked for Elektra Records, and we had our office in Soho. I met a number of people who became the axis of that scene, The Move, Joe Cocker, Procol Harum, and all that. I had secured a little foot in the door of the pop world. Fundamentally, my world –

before the summer of '66 – was folk; I went to folk clubs and had produced The Incredible String Band.

'But the other part of my world was Hoppy and the underground. I was very political; I adored Hoppy and that whole scene. A lot of people around Hoppy I was much more sceptical of; I didn't really like a lot of the anarchists. Hoppy was practical; he wasn't doing crazy shit for the sake of doing crazy shit. He wanted to get something done.

'He was fantastic and a skilled politician so I started going to these events at Powis Square, and I heard Pink Floyd. I was looking to start my production company, so I said to the Pink Floyd guys that I would get them a record deal and I got them an offer from Polygram. We had the deal, the lawyers were drawing up the papers, and in my book I described this terrible moment when Peter Jenner, their manager, brings down the new agency guys. Bryan Morrison, Steve O'Rourke, Tony Howard, they walk in and I go, 'Oh shit, these guys are serious trouble, for me.''

As well as appearing out of nowhere to snatch Pink Floyd from Joe Boyd's grasp, the Bryan Morrison Agency was also becoming a more powerful force within The In Crowd's world. From an initial informal agreement with Antony Rufus Isaacs, to a contractual arrangement where the band were now among a number of strong bands which the agency acted for.

Central to this relationship and a key part in the rapid evolution, which would soon see the band both change their name and find their audience, was Tony Howard. Spoken of warmly by everyone, Joe Boyd remembers him as, 'A real visionary. He was an East End Jewish guy whose uncle was the trumpet player and bandleader Eddie Calvert. He had a little bit of music business knowledge, and so when he went to art school he ended up organising concerts, and he was right there at the beginning of the Bryan Morrison Agency.

'He was smart and funny, and he changed my life. He's one of those behind-the-scenes people; he managed Marc Bolan, T-Rex. He tour-managed Pink Floyd for years. He wasn't as aggressive financially as Bryan and Steve, but he did okay, and Tony was really key for Tomorrow; he was really close to them.'

To understand how Tony Howard changed the life of Joe Boyd, and in turn helped to create the legend of Tomorrow, we must first explore a number of interconnected matters that were taking place concurrently, and coming to a head, in April 1967.

The first of these involves Joe Boyd, UFO, Pink Floyd and The Bryan Morrison Agency. As Joe Boyd rightly thought, in March 1967, the Bryan Morrison Agency taking on Pink Floyd as a client was bad news for him on two counts. Firstly, his proposed record deal with Polygram would be replaced by an EMI deal (costing him a substantial windfall); secondly, his headline act at the UFO [Pink Floyd] was now looking to expand its horizons as a live act… and that did not involve £50 gigs at UFO. The price would increase to £75 as a one-off to fulfil a commitment, and then be a minimum of £100. The economics of which would ruin the UFO as a profit-making enterprise.

As Joe recounts, 'Bryan Morrison didn't give a shit. He was very happy to just take the deal away and give it to EMI, to be the hero and get the advance. Tony understood how devastating all of this was for me, and for the whole burgeoning underground scene. To have this thing taken away from us in that way, and at this point, would have caused severe problems.

'He called me up and suggested I go for a drink with him, during which he explained to me that while I saw Pink Floyd and the Soft Machine as my only options – because they were the two groups that represented the underground to me –

everything was changing. Then, the next time I saw him, he took me to Blaises as I had never been. Then he took me to The Speakeasy (located at 48 Margaret Street, London) and he was my door opener into this world.

'Tony maintained that every group would work cheaply to get their names associated with UFO, to play UFO. He told me not to worry about the fact that we'd lost the Floyd. He told me that if we appointed him as the agent for the club, he would split the commission with the other agents for the different groups, and that we would be sorted. He promised that he would get groups, every week, that would fill the club.

'Initially, I was very sceptical,' says Joe. 'We hadn't worked with anyone except the Floyd and Soft Machine and the only other artists and musicians that would play were things like Sun Trolly, who was a sax player that Hoppy knew, people like that. We had Mick Farren and The Social Deviants, acts like that, begging to play the venue but I had refused them, and that was it.

'We didn't have anybody else. So, Tony, in that context, took me to Blaises to see The In Crowd and, when Steve Howe would go off on a solo, I could see how my crowd would like it; the UFO crowd would dig it. So okay, Tony, you made your point; get me The In Crowd, we'll have them.'

There was, however, one stumbling block to be negotiated before this marriage could take place, and like most marriages it involved one of the parties changing their name. Plus, if we are to extend the analogy somewhat, this was something of a shotgun wedding which would move the band from being a benevolent dictatorship to being a democracy which, as Steve Howe notes, 'Was like a new adventure with the same group of people – which is an interesting twist to try to pull off.'

The haste of the decision around the name change can be gleaned from the fact that Gita Renik, who worked at the Bryan Morrison Agency, celebrated her 21st birthday at Blaises on

Thursday the 20th of April 1967 where her favourite band, The In Crowd, were performing. By the Friday of the following week (the 28th of April), The In Crowd were no longer, and the band's short but legendary career as Tomorrow would begin.

In truth, the name change to Tomorrow was a mixture of luck, pragmatism, and inspiration. Joe Boyd had been won over by The In Crowd's charms from seeing them at Blaises, but he knew that 'Hoppy' would not countenance having a band play at UFO whose name and image were so linked to the mod movement. The In Crowd's overtones of exclusivity were at total odds with UFO's message of inclusivity.

Keith remembers the circumstances that led to the change. 'Joe Boyd had come down to see us at Blaises and wanted to book us, but he wasn't sure about The In Crowd name. Did it fit in with the hippy sort of thing?

'Tony Howard told us that Joe wanted to book us, but that we were going to have to change our image slightly. He believed it was dated, what we were doing; the mod thing had finished. He told us that our music was changing, what we were doing was changing, and that the old name didn't really fit and that we were better off changing the name.

'We'd done it before [in changing from Four + 1], so it wasn't an entirely alien idea.'

Keith recalls that the band were rehearsing at Blaises and took a break to decide on a new name. 'Various ideas and thoughts were bandied around until suddenly Junior blurted out, 'How about Tomorrow?' Everyone went silent for a second or two and then unanimously agreed it was a perfect choice. I have to say, that's the only time in all my career that a band name decision has happened that fast; it's been known to drag on for weeks sometimes – which it did with Bodast– and even with my own band, Moonrider, we argued for at least a month.'

If the forces of pragmatism, with a sprinkling of creativity, had come together to inspire the band's change of name, a large slice of fortune would now enable them to play the UFO sooner than they might have imagined. But what was it that made the UFO so special? Joe Boyd provides some context and insight during an interview in 2019.

'All-nighters on weekends were something of a tradition in London already. When I first came in '64, I went to a little basement club near Leicester Square to a Ken Collier trad jazz all-nighter. There were folk all-nighters too, at Bunjies Folk Club on Litchfield Street and places like that.

'It was a response to the fact that everything closed so early, and it was frustrating for people because there was also no transport. There were no night buses. So, the idea was that you just went in somewhere and stayed and you left when the tubes and the buses started running at 5.30-6am.

'Hoppy and I really liked the location [UFO]; we liked the size. They charged us fifteen quid, but it was right under the Continental Cinema which was showing French art movies and stuff like that. They had their entrance and then, next door, there was a door with stairs going down and the Blarney club was right underneath the cinema.

'Mr. Gannon, the landlord of the Irish club – when we told him we were going to have amps and drum kits and stuff like that – was afraid he was going to get in trouble with the landlord. But, we talked to the manager of the cinema and asked him how late his films ran, and he told us they would be done by 10.30pm at the latest. I was sort of dismayed, like maybe this means we shouldn't really rent this place, this place doesn't work, but Hoppy was adamant that it would be great, and that it would be an all-nighter.

'He improvised immediately, and from the very start, that was the understanding – that we couldn't have people shouting and loud music going on before 10.30pm. We were not sure people would buy it. On the first night, I wondered who's going to turn up? But, in fact, it was pretty crowded, and it was a big success straight away.

'It was Hoppy's domain, and there was a lighting tower where whoever was doing the light show for the group would come up and do their thing. Hoppy would do projections using a 16mm projector and he also had a turntable, so he would play whatever records he wanted to play.

'We played Indian music, we played jazz, we used to play rock. We used to have the main group play twice; I think it was around 11.30pm or midnight for an hour, and then another set at 2.30am or three. In-between, we would have other acts.

'We sometimes had this group that Hoppy would book that had a sitar player, or Sun Trolly would play. We had the People Show, which was a theatre company, and they would do little plays right in the middle of the audience. Somebody would just start saying something really loudly, and it would be a drama or some kind of weird thing like a confrontation between people or a funny thing that plays out right in the middle of the audience.

'We had Yoko Ono, too, and we invited The Alberts down, who were a surreal comic act. They had Bruce Lacey who built robots, and so he would turn the wheels and a robot with flashing lights would suddenly come out into the middle of the floor, stuff like that.'

A curiosity about the club was that it did not have an alcohol license.

'It was dry; there was no alcohol. That was part of the deal. Mr Gannon got to sell the soft drinks and they were the cheapest, worst, synthetic, garish orange and green bottles. The thing that Irish teenagers would buy when they went to see a show band.

'We had tables where people would get handed leaflets about cool things like *The International Times*. People would pass buckets to raise money for causes, stuff like that. After the second set by the main group, if they didn't want to stay around until dawn, they'd get in their van and go home. We would show a movie, sometimes we'd show a Kurosawa movie at 5am, or we'd show W.C. Fields shorts, and people would be sprawled out on the floor as a lot of them were tripping or stoned or whatever.'

Having changed their name following their gig on Thursday the 20th of April, the newly-named Tomorrow were aching to establish their credentials as part of the counter-culture movement. In April 1967, this meant two things only; firstly, playing the UFO, and secondly, playing the *14-Hour Technicolour Dream* – a 'happening' organised by Hoppy and some other promoters that was due to take place at The Alexandra Palace on the last weekend of the month.

As it stood, with seven days to go, they were not scheduled to achieve either of these ambitions, yet fate would intervene and – by the end of the following week – they had played both and established themselves firmly at the heart of the psychedelic scene.

Getting to the bottom of how this fabulous 'double' was achieved by the band has taken some detective work. Joe Boyd's listings of who played at UFO were published in his book, but they do not show Tomorrow as appearing at the club until the middle of May 1967. But Joe himself had no explanation as to how Tomorrow appeared, unbilled, at the *14-Hour Technicolour Dream* if they had not played at UFO previously. It was Twink who finally unlocked both mysteries.

In Joe's records, and in the adverts which were taken in the music press of that week, The Smoke were booked to be the headline act at UFO on Friday the 28th of April 1967. But, as Twink recalled, they had to pull out, and the timing was perfect for Tony Howard to get Tomorrow to stand in for them. It was to be serendipity for all concerned.

UFO at the height of its popularity and energy must have been an assault on the senses for all that attended. Antony Rufus Isaacs remembers 'the lights' – which were under 'Hoppy's' charge – which included oil lamps throwing psychedelic shapes onto every surface. Twink, meanwhile, recalls, 'the smell of incense, with Joss sticks burning all the time.' [Presumably to cover the smell of hash as well as to create a chilled out vibe.]

Keith remembers the band's first appearance at the club. 'They were a different audience as they *really* listened to our music and they liked us from day one – some bands they didn't. The Move played there, and they hated them. They didn't boo them off, but they got no response at all. They just took to us immediately and I remember coming out of the second number thinking, 'Wow, they're digging this. They really are.''

Tomorrow made sure that they made an impact on the UFO crowd from the start of their set, while also establishing their left-field credentials (and the incredible talent of their lead guitar player), with an arrangement of *Jesu, Joy of Man's Desiring* by Johann Sebastian Bach before ripping through a set which included original material such as *My White Bicycle* as well as covers that would resonate with the audience: *Strawberry Fields Forever* by The Beatles and *Why* by The Byrds.

The band also placed themselves firmly in the affections of their audience by playing material which made the connection between themselves and drugs. Chief amongst them was *Three Jolly Little Dwarfs*.

'It's quite a mad story, and they all loved it at the UFO Club,' says Keith. 'It's a crazy song based on the time I came out of John Lord's flat [later to find fame as the keyboard player in

Deep Purple and Whitesnake] having taken acid. It was like Disney World out there.

'When I got home, I couldn't sleep so I started scribbling stuff down. I literally saw all this, it wasn't real, obviously, but I saw this Disney setup, and it had dwarfs running around. It was mad.

'It's a bonkers song and a bonkers night, and I said I'd never do it again after that. That was it for me. I only took acid once or twice; I just found it a bit scary. Some people had some bad trips on acid. Syd Barrett was a prime example, and I'd seen it at first hand.

'I didn't know that at the time, but I thought that it was too out of control for me. I liked to keep a certain amount of control. But, it's a bonding thing; you take acid, you're all in it together, and you have to look after each other as well, in case anybody's getting a bit scary.

'Another issue was that everything we were taking was undiluted at that point as well. It was a lot purer, and the brand of hash we were smoking was mostly called Red Leb [short for Lebanese]. You didn't have any problems with that, at all, just a mild sort of ... it chilled you out, you know.'

While playing the UFO was a rubber stamp for a band's psychedelic credibility (as Tony Howard had rightly convinced Joe Boyd), the venue offered very little by way of comfort for the musicians themselves.

As Keith recalls from his times playing the club and as a member of the audience, 'You walked in, down the stairs, and it was like nothing you'd ever seen before in your life. There was a big light show going on, semi-pornographic images on the walls. It was very art house with lots of people with long hair and a chilled out, relaxed atmosphere.

'We had a little room out the back that you got changed in, and our friends used to come in there and everybody was smoking dope. We'd smoke a bit of dope before we went on, most nights, as we had stopped drinking alcohol then, because we knew that was bad for us when playing. You can experience awful hangovers.

'Steve had a little hubble bubble pipe, I think he bought it from Holland, and we'd all take a hit on that before we went on stage. It became something of a bonding ritual.

'Once the call came to go onstage, you'd access it via a stepladder, though it wasn't very high, and there were curtains either side and there'd be oil light shows going on, and all that kind of stuff. Then we'd hit it, wearing our favourite clothes; the Granny Takes a Trip gold jacket for me, Steve wore a blue jacket, Twink could be wearing a big floppy hat, velvet trousers, and Junior wore whatever he felt like on the night.'

As Keith has said, the UFO crowd took to Tomorrow immediately, perhaps because they were a little friendlier, or more down to earth and approachable than either the University-educated Pink Floyd or the Soft Machine. Looking back, Joe Boyd shares this opinion. 'Of all the groups we tried in the spring, searching for the answer to losing Pink Floyd, Tomorrow was the favourite. The crowd just loved them. Tomorrow was such a weird-looking thing; their energy was incredible. In some ways, the nights they played were just as memorable nights at UFO as the Pink Floyd nights.

'Steve would go off on these long solos, and it was what the crowd were used to. They were used to the way the Floyd would sing and Rick would go on these journeys, and ten minutes later they'd come back with the verse and chorus again from the song.'

Steve Howe confirms that the admiration was mutual. 'We loved to play UFO; it was the most exciting gig we could play. It seemed like you were playing to the cream of the crop of the hippies. The UFO kind of came out of the ground and it wasn't anything much as a venue, but there was a sense that this was the place where psychedelic music was explored. There was nowhere better than the UFO. You were compelled to go on and do your best as these were the people most likely to enjoy it.'

In his book, *All My Yesterdays*, Steve confirms the night of the 28th of April as Tomorrow's debut at the UFO. For him, the date sticks in the memory for another notable reason. Steve says, 'We were playing our set and improvising when suddenly Jimi Hendrix gets up and gets hold of the bass guitar, which Junior has laid down while he was doing some dancing. He got up and played, and I had no idea what was going on. Things like that happening at the UFO were not uncommon.'

In a photograph, taken on that night you, can see Junior on his knees and praying in the direction of Hendrix while Keith is energetically frugging away in the background on the tiny UFO stage. Hendrix had taken advantage of what was to become a regular occurrence in Tomorrow's sets, which was Junior dancing and performing while not actually playing his instrument, leaving Twink and Steve to carry responsibility for the music. As these performance elements developed during the Summer of 1967, they would become something of a divisive point among the band members.

The appearance and association with Hendrix, as if appearing at UFO wasn't enough, gave Tomorrow even more credibility among the trendsetters and music critics of the scene; their association with him was to be one of mutual support and admiration. Twink was best friends with Mitch Mitchell and, like Keith and Steve, attended many of the early Hendrix shows. He even helped Mitch provide drum lessons to Pink Floyd's Nick Mason at one point. Due to these friendships with both Jimi and his sidemen, Tomorrow would play on many bills with Hendrix over the next year.

In the course of just one remarkable night, Tomorrow had placed themselves right at the centre of the zeitgeist, something which must have given them a huge confidence boost. Although, as both Steve and Keith confirm, they weren't shy in that department already. Keith says, 'The band was very solid together, the four of us, and we thought we were pretty good, so we were a little bit arrogant actually, which you needed to be. When you're touring, as we did later, with Hendrix and with Steve Winwood you've got to believe in yourself. Otherwise, you're screwed. So we did, we always thought we don't care who we play with; we'll take them on. Basically, that was our aim, and it was a good attitude to have. We were pretty confident in our abilities at that time.'

Steve confirms this, 'We saw other great bands, but we started to get an ego. Not as individuals necessarily, but as a collective about how good this band was. It was our secret weapon, how confident we were; we were kind of cocky and a bit flash and a bit 'follow that'.'

The band would need all the front they could muster if they were to take what they – and the witnesses of their UFO performance – saw as their rightful place among the elite performers of the psychedelic movement. There were only three small problems standing in their way. Firstly, the *14-Hour Technicolour Dream* – the event which they (quite rightly, as history proved) viewed as being the zenith of the counter-culture movement – was taking place that evening on Saturday the 29th of April; secondly, they were not on the bill; and thirdly, they were already booked to play a show 90 miles away from the Alexandra Palace action, in Hampshire.

Tomorrow's gig list records them as playing The Birdcage, Eastney, in Hampshire on the night of the 29th of April (where actually they were billed as The In Crowd due to their late name change), and indeed they fulfilled this commitment before embarking on a bold adventure. Twink explains, 'What happened was, we had already done a gig that night and I said, 'Come on guys, I've done this before.'

'For example, when I was with The Fairies, we did a gig and then we went to the Scene Club and just turned up and asked to play because we wanted that exposure; we wanted to play there. I said come on guys, let's go down to the *14-Hour Technicolor Dream* because we should be on the bill.'

While bombing from one club to another in central London is one thing, embarking on a two-hour drive and arriving past midnight at the Alexandra Palace is another, but fortune was with them.

'When we got there, the security guard looked at us questioningly through the window, and we just fibbed and told him we were on the bill and he let us through. We pulled up around by the stage door and there was a band coming off, and the roadies just started to set our gear up on the stage. So we went on straight away. It was that simple; it was meant to be. In fact, Barry Miles, one of the promoters, said to me later when I told him my story, 'Twink, you would have been welcome anyway, you didn't need to crash it.''

History records that 7,000 people bought tickets for the Alexandra Palace event (at £1 per ticket) and that Pink Floyd headlined (arriving on-site at 3am as they had also played another show that evening… in Holland), sharing the bill with acts including the Crazy World of Arthur Brown, the Soft Machine, The Move, and The Pretty Things. Twink's memories of the night are rather limited, 'All I can remember is I went on stage wearing a fur raccoon coat that I used to wear sometimes, and I had on a big top hat as well. We played our set with John Lennon in the audience looking up at us.'

Clips of the event on YouTube focus on Lennon's attendance and indeed that of Yoko Ono, who presented her 'The Happening' piece (which consisted of audience members cutting clothes from a model perched on a step ladder until she was naked). The ambitious event, and the film clips of it, demonstrate the difference in what the promoters were trying to achieve, with theatre troupes mingling with the crowd and performing in the middle of the audience, and a wildly eclectic bill which comprised poetry, art, drama, politics, and music.

While no footage of Tomorrow's show exists, there is an audio clip of *Three Jolly Little Dwarfs* being played as the camera crew films elsewhere and Steve Howe's Indian-tinged main guitar lick sounds both terrific and entirely within context as a background to the event.

If the *14-Hour Technicolour Dream* represented the apex of the counter-culture vision – in that it was a pure in spirit event motivated by more than capitalist ideals – then it can also be viewed as the beginning of the end too. As Joe Boyd, who attended the event recalls, 'I didn't get there until one o'clock in the morning, but it was still full of people and there was all this shit going on. I remember, after the Floyd played, I'd taken something that I was told was mescaline, but wasn't really, so I was a little bit high but not very.

'I was with this girl and we went out to lay on the grass, and we saw these hundreds and hundreds of people pouring out of Alexandra Palace, dancing, whirling down the drive, down the hill to the bus stop. I thought at the time, this whole thing is getting pretty fucking big. This is really going to change the world. The underground was becoming the mainstream.

'Tomorrow, in my memory, is central to that moment. They were a perfect symbol of working-class kids who wanted to be stars and somehow got deflected by the counter-culture. By drugs, by the scene, by the zeitgeist, whatever.'

Keith holds an alternative view. 'Joe has that wrong. We didn't think about being stars; we just wanted to be successful and grow as a band.'

As has been intimated, following the Alexandra Palace event the ideals of the counter-culture movement were diluted by those wishing to cash in on what they saw as a trend. Steve

Howe observes, 'When Zoot Money's Big Roll Band changed their name to Dantalian's Chariot, it seemed contrived. The way Tomorrow emerged from The In Crowd seemed more natural to me, but eventually, there would be many who would join that club [Zoot Money's].'

Confirmed as bona fide members of the psychedelic movement's elite, Tomorrow would go on to play the most high profile 'hippy' events of the Summer of Love including the *Love-In* at Alexandra Palace at the end of July, and the *Festival of the Flower Children*, Woburn Abbey, at the end of August. These events were largely unremarkable save for criticism of the quality of the staging and the sound equipment at the Woburn event.

Tomorrow's shows at these events were memorable though, as not only was the band's improvisational musical theme well-established, but Junior was adding to this with improvised dance routines alongside a nubile American dancer known as Suzy Creamcheese. The original Suzy was a character played by a number of women who worked with Frank Zappa and The Mothers of Invention, while Tomorrow's Suzy was Suzy Zeiger, the girlfriend of John 'Hoppy' Hopkins. Observing the band at the time, Chris Welch wrote in *Music Maker* magazine, 'One of their best numbers is a nameless freak-out in which Suzy Creamcheese and bassist Junior dance a modern ballet, while guitarist Steve Howe plays some remarkable guitar. The whole effect is rather like a psychedelic mime show.'

Having sadly passed away in 2016, Junior was not able to be interviewed for this book, but when questioned by *Flashback* in 2012, he said this of the band's stage show, 'We were always very visual in our performance. Our live performances were much more exciting than our records – there was a buzz on stage that wasn't transferred to disc. Suzy and I were the main exhibitionists. Things got a bit over the top in Wales one night, and we were ordered off stage for being too raunchy! But that's Wales for you!'

Indeed, photos of the two performing their dance generally show Junior in an advanced state of undress with a painted face, and it doesn't take a great deal of imagination to see that, on occasion, the two might have pushed the boundaries of what was perceived to be decent at the time.

Another show, which the band played at Jimi Hendrix's personal invitation, was the *Bank Holiday at the Saville* event (held on the August bank holiday Sunday) with the Jimi Hendrix Experience. As Keith recalls, 'When we did it, Robert Stigwood was in charge because he used to always come down and say hello and bring down a tray of drinks for everybody. There were bottles of scotch, vodka; he would load up the stuff. He'd put it on there and we'd do the show.

'We used to close the first half and then we'd go upstairs afterwards and watch Hendrix. I remember being up there with Lulu and Maurice Gibb, who was a good friend of mine at the time. He was a lovely guy, Maurice, he really was. I felt a bit sorry for him; he got overshadowed by his [Bee Gees] brothers completely.

'He loved Hendrix, he liked rock, he liked all that stuff we were doing. He wasn't really into the music that they were doing, in particular. I think he wanted to experiment and do other things, but he wasn't allowed to, obviously.

'While we were there that day, the Bee Gees were rehearsing along with Tim Rose [writer of *Hey Joe*]. We were standing around, and they got up and did *To Love Somebody,* and *New York Mining Disaster* which was their hit and we just thought they looked wrong, old fashioned, and then – when they started to sing – we all stopped and thought 'fucking hell'!

'Those harmonies were spot on. It was a bit like when The Beatles went on the *Ed Sullivan Show,* and Ed Sullivan thought they were just another rock band. He then heard them when they were rehearsing *This Boy,* with its three-part harmony, and he said he was blown away by it. Same sort of thing, these guys, their voices just blended perfectly and it was class.

'Another thing I can remember is Lulu telling us that we were great, but that we needed to tell our guitarist not to turn his back on the audience. Being a pro, Lulu thought you should never turn your back on an audience. Steve used to just turn around and go off on one of his magical solos; she didn't understand it at all.'

The review of the performance, by the *NME's* Andy Gray reads, 'I liked Keith West's futuristic act, in which he combines his torrid singing and the playing of his Tomorrow group with a ballet dance, in which the drummer kills the bassist with the bass-man's instrument, while the sensuous fifth member of the group, a mini-skirted erotic dancer, waves her luscious body around with the grace of a snake.'

10. The eye of a perfect storm

Joe Boyd's book *White Bicycles* begins by saying: 'The sixties began in the summer of 1956, ended in October 1973 and peaked just before dawn on the 1st of July 1967 during a set by Tomorrow at the UFO Club in London.'

Indeed, this quote was pretty much the starting point and inspiration behind this book. Who were this band Tomorrow that were responsible for this pivotal moment, and what happened to them? Who was it that wrote their songs?

To write a song that defines an era is one thing, but to be credited with delivering the performance that saw all the separate strands of the storied 1960s come together is another. It is quite some legacy.

It can be argued that Tomorrow found themselves through a mixture of luck, judgement, talent, and bravado at the eye of a perfect storm. As Joe Boyd also says, 'Everything was accelerating: new drugs, clothes, music and clubs. The psychedelic underground and the pop scene were starting to overlap. The UFO crowds were bigger each week and it was hard to maintain the original atmosphere. It was also difficult to ignore the increased attention from the police.'

Establishment disapproval of the central tenants of the counter-culture movement, and a clampdown from the authorities on its higher profile leaders, was becoming a real problem in the weeks that followed the *14-Hour Technicolour Dream*. John 'Hoppy' Hopkins had been busted for drug possession and sentenced to an incredibly harsh eight-month prison sentence, while Mick Jagger and Keith Richards (along famously with Marianne Faithfull, a fur coat and a Mars Bar) had been the subject of a police sting instigated by the *News of the World*. Jagger had been sentenced to three months in prison for the possession of just four amphetamine tablets, which he had bought legally in Italy and of which his GP was aware, but had at least managed to remain free on bail pending an appeal.

To say that passions were running high on the night of Friday the 30th of June, when Tomorrow arrived at the UFO (for what would be the third of their five appearances at the club), is to downplay how under-attack the small community felt. They believed they must defend their principles and they were outraged by the collusion between the police and the typically hypocritical *News of the World* (with its sex and drugs headlines and the pretence of defending the moral integrity of the nation, while at the same time splashing as many titillating details as it could get away with). As the UK's highest circulation Sunday rag, it held enormous influence.

As Joe Boyd recalls, 'I told the band that I wanted them to do a set at eleven o'clock and then we were closing the club and taking everyone on a march down to the *News of the World's* offices. They agreed and said that they'd also play when everyone got back.

'It was exciting because you felt like, whatever it was that had been going on six months earlier in Notting Hill, the London Free School and *The International Times,* it seemed like that was a real corner of society, a tiny little corner. Now, you felt *wow,* this is everywhere; this is big. And we'd already had the Alexandra Palace event [*14-Hour Technicolour Dream*].'

Even though the march itself comprised only a couple of hundred people and was ultimately something of a damp squib (as the newspaper's offices were closed when the protesters arrived well after midnight), there was still a sense of euphoria among them as they made the half-hour walk back to UFO. Once back at the club, Tomorrow attacked their set with a ferocity fired by indignation.

As Twink recalls, 'That was the first time we played *Revolution,* which wasn't even a song at this point, but a spontaneous jam. I was repeating the phrase, 'Revolution... now! Revolution now!''

Observers at the time recall Twink abandoning his drum stool and walking around the audience and getting them to join him in the chant of 'Revolution...Now!' But reports of him rolling around on the floor with a microphone, and of Skip Spence of The Pretty Things jumping in on drums are – according to Twink – embellishments on the truth.

Keith remembers, 'It was very late when we finally went on, and all that waiting around got us fired up. There was an expectation in the air that something different was going to happen, even for the UFO club, and we were all inspired by that feeling. We had our sound all worked out; we knew it could fly if everything came together, and it did. We went full out. I was screaming my lungs out even though pretty tired. Steve was in heaven, fingers speeding across his guitar neck, and Junior's Bass was positively roaring, pushing us all on as Twink flailed away on his kit. An unforgettable performance.'

Joe Boyd describes Tomorrow as 'tearing into *My White Bicycle'* and that there was a 'unity of spirit' between the audience and the musicians on that night. 'I wasn't completely unprepared for the phenomena that Tomorrow represented because I had already been there with The Move. They had already started to go psychedelic, while still drinking beer a year earlier, and that had fascinated me because they were a real pop group, but Roy Wood was listening to The Byrds and Jefferson Airplane. They were picking up on what was going on in San Francisco, but they weren't so tuned in to what was going on in Notting Hill. I don't think they really knew what to make of Pink Floyd.

'Roy Wood was a fan of Roger McGuinn [of The Byrds] and all that west coast stuff, but the idea was that you could still be a working-class pop group with those ambitions in England [to make a decent living], and yet have this other [hippy ideals] element. So, in a way, Tomorrow was a repetition of what I'd already been intrigued by.'

While the heady feeling, which the UFO protesters conjured up among themselves, revealed a glimpse of a change that would never come to pass, it was a strange coincidence that *The Times* newspaper – printed and distributed on that very same morning, Saturday the 1st of July 1967 – carried an article about the treatment of Jagger. '*Who breaks a butterfly on a wheel?*' was the title of William Rees-Mogg's famous lead article, and it would prove a powerful weapon in ensuring Jagger was ultimately set free. The establishment was correcting itself after an over-reaction, but that would still not save the UFO from being forced to move from its Tottenham Court Road home following a *News of the World* exposé. In it, the paper printed a blurry picture of a bare-breasted girl supposedly taken at the UFO; the article claimed she was only 15-years-old and demanded that the club be closed.

The 30th of June would ultimately be the peak of the counter-culture movement, a moment when music, drugs, and people would all come together and attempt to change society through political action (the march). Ultimately, though, the passion and energy of that evening would be attenuated.

Joe Boyd would eventually summarise the experience as, 'Beneath the surface, the progressive sixties hid all manner of unpleasantness: sexism, reaction, racism and factionalism. It wasn't surprising, really. The idea that drugs, sex, and music could transform the world was a pretty naïve dream.

'As the counter-culture's effect on the mainstream grew, its own value and aesthetics decayed. The political setbacks of the coming years grabbed the headlines while the dilution of ideas happened more quietly, but none the less vividly for those who noticed.'

As this energy started to fade, and the moment began to pass, Tomorrow had not even got an album out.

11. Tomorrow sessions, bootlegs, and on record

It must have been a frustration to both the band and their fans that during the peak of the Summer of Love – when the band were playing all the important festivals of the day as well as the UFO and other London clubs – that the only record Tomorrow released was the 7″ single *My White Bicycle,* with *Claramount Lake* on the B-side.

Comprising one studio album, two 7″ singles, and two BBC studio sessions (plus a bootleg recording of a festival-type Christmas gig), the band's recorded history is relatively small. Frustratingly, all members of the group agree that their recorded output rarely captures their live intensity and the big sound for which they were known.

The two BBC sessions demonstrate how well thought of Tomorrow were among the arbiters of taste at the BBC, especially John Peel. The first session was recorded in September 1967 for the inaugural *Top Gear* show, which was broadcast on the 1st of October 1967 (and co-presented by Peel and Tommy Vance amongst others). They then cemented their place as being among John Peel's favourites by becoming the first band to record a 'Peel Session' when they again entered the BBC's Maida Vale studio, in January 1968, to record for the opening show of *John Peel's Top Gear*.

Keith recalls, 'We were really happy to be asked to appear on *Top Gear*; John was a fan of Tomorrow and he was, of course, influential in breaking my *Teenage Opera* single on his radio show. His audience was definitely our audience too.

'I have to say, I can't give enough praise to all the guys in the band; they were always so professional, super-tight, and nailed the takes really fast. It gave me enough time to add my vocals with the odd harmony on tape. Studio time was always a problem at the BBC sessions.

'All the work we did together as a band – be it TV, film, radio or whatever – we all pulled together and performed at 100%.'

Twink recalls the sessions well. 'I can remember John Peel coming in and just letting everybody get on with it. He didn't try to control the sessions. He'd just come in greet everyone and say, 'Great, love your stuff', and then he'd disappear and leave us with the engineers to work out the recording. That was it.

'He must have done that with all the bands because I recorded for him later with The Pretty Things and the Pink Fairies and he did exactly the same thing. He'd show up, say 'Hello lads, great. Get on with it.' Then he would disappear into the control room. But, he was quite a fan of Tomorrow, a big supporter.'

The band recorded four songs for each session with *Real Life Permanent Dream, Colonel Brown, Three Jolly Little Dwarfs,* and *Revolution* comprising the first; *Blow-Up, Strawberry Fields Forever, Now Your Time has Come, and The Incredible Journey of Timothy Chase* made up the second.

Notable from the first session are the various DJs that introduce the tracks, one of whom described *Three Jolly Little Dwarfs* as 'a song for baby hippies'. The rawness of Steve Howe's guitar sound then gives listeners some idea of how the band might have sounded live. The Maida Vale sessions were themselves an unfussy affair with Keith remembering, 'Just one or two vocal and guitar overdubs.'

Also of note is the episodic nature of the tracks. *Revolution,* for example, breaks down into individual segments from the spoken word intro, into the straightforward verse, and then the main guitar riff guides the chorus and leads into the repetitive, but powerful, main refrain. It's this breaking up of songs into segments which would be Tomorrow's enduring legacy.

The second BBC session, broadcast on Sunday the 4th of February 1968, leads off with *Blow-Up* which seems an obtuse choice given that it was a deliberately mod-sounding record and was not on the soon to be released album. You cannot help but think that the band would have been better served to include *Am I Glad to See You*; at least its extended outro would have allowed more musical improvisation from Steve, Junior, and Twink. The band's cover of *Strawberry Fields Forever* is strong (and perhaps, as Steve Howe claims, a forerunner of the grunge guitar sound which would dominate the early 1990s), but again an odd choice for the band. Keith thinks it was chosen by the band because it was a popular element of their live set.

'Our version was guitar-driven and arranged by Steve, unlike the original,' says Keith. 'I remember walking into rehearsals one day and hearing Steve play the song, which sounds like he's playing two guitars at once. I just jumped in on vocals and it came together immediately.'

Now Your Time has Come at least has the advantage of being new to listeners and contains typically inventive guitar work from Steve Howe. *The Incredible Journey of Timothy Chase* offers a pleasant change of pace with its stretching of Keith's vocal range, its strong harmonies, and the band's ability to stop and start at the drop of a hat. Plus, it was on the studio album which would be released the following week.

Unfortunately, the provenance of these BBC session recordings is somewhat questionable. While versions exist both on unofficial CDs and on YouTube, *Record Collector* magazine maintains that only two of the live-in-the-studio tracks – *Revolution* and *Three Jolly Little Dwarfs* – remain in the BBC archive, surviving on a Transcription Disc that was pressed for use on the World Service.

Accordingly, it's difficult for the listener to judge exactly what they are listening to. Are they recordings that have somehow been saved from the BBC sessions? Or are they the same tracks culled from other sources and passed off as the fabled session tracks?

Similarly, the live recording of the *Christmas on Earth* gig from the 21st of December 1967 is 'unofficial' and only recorded via a single ambient mic (and not from the sound desk). It does, though, capture the raw power of the band and the bootleg includes *Caught in a Web* which the band recorded and never released, as well as muscular versions of *My White Bicycle, Revolution, Real Life Permanent Dream* and an excellent, impassioned *Hallucinations*.

Aside from the above-discussed curios, it's near impossible to give a fair assessment – once you are aware of the trials and tribulations involved in its production – of Tomorrow's one studio album which was released on Friday the 9th of February, 1968.

The album opens with the original 7" single *My White Bicycle,* a great recording and a brilliant song. Starting the album with it is a poor example of sequencing though as – at this point – the song was nearly a year old and would have been familiar to the fans. Strong singles normally reside at the close of an LP's A-side or kick-off the B-side.

The album's second song *Colonel Brown* is one whose inclusion would be argued about in the future. One of a number of character pieces written by Keith, some feel, as Steve Howe does, that 'They were a bit twee.' Keith's view, however, is that 'These songs were very popular played live, and were taken up with the whole band's approval.

'Also, songs of this type were very much in vogue at the time. If you think *Colonel Brown* is twee, then you also have to brand *Yellow Submarine, Itchycoo Park, Hole in my Shoe,* and *Little Piggies* with the same label.' Also, in Keith's view, these types of songs are quite dark in their subject matter. In this instance, the number of hooks and sheer charm of the song would probably still merit its inclusion.

Real Life Permanent Dream is, sadly, an example of where the studio recording has managed to pull the intensity and life out of the song somewhat. Keith's vocal sounds clipped and precise as opposed to passionate and inflamed as he records the end of a relationship. 'At the time, I was having a brief fling with Syd Barrett's girlfriend, Lindsay Korner, who was unhappy with Syd's strange behaviour.

'I felt uncomfortable with the situation, though, as I knew Syd quite well. Lindsay and I met on a plane as we were playing at the Paris Olympia, and she and a friend were dancers on the show. I saw her a couple of times back in England, but it ended soon after.

'Apparently, after we ended the affair, Syd was walking around dressed like me in a copy of a black velvet suit I had made for me from Granny's.'

Real Life Permanent Dream is an example of a truly great Tomorrow song which only those who heard them live would really think was a classic of the time.

Track number four, *Shy Boy, is* a song of Keith and Ken Burgess's that Mark Wirtz had placed with Kippington Lodge in October 1967. They released it as a single [before they achieved their footnote in rock history when Nick Lowe joined their ranks], but it failed to chart. It's a strong song and it hums along readily enough, with a cheesy end-of-the-pier organ sound, and is a story about an office boy too shy to ask out the object of his affections. Again, it's a complicated song with a dark subject matter, masked by the sweetness of the tune.

Things get back on psychedelic track when *Revolution* kicks in, but the production might be viewed as overblown, compared to the guitar-led version which was heard on the

BBC sessions and with which Tomorrow's audience would be familiar. The sentiment and excitement comes across clearly in the song's climax but, having failed to chart as a single when released in September 1967, how it was viewed in early 1968 is anyone's guess.

Opening side two of the album is *The Incredible Story of Timothy Chase* which is both dreamy and trippy while being – at its core – a sardonic attack on Bryan Morrison. Following on, in a similar vein, is *Auntie Mary's Dress Shop,* which is a pastiche on the success of clothes shops such as Granny Takes a Trip and Dandie Fashions. 'Hiding behind their counter-culture vibe,' says Keith, 'was a focus on money and business which is highlighted when the lyrics mention dress shop number two.'

The inclusion, on the second side of the record, of *Strawberry Fields Forever* is understandable given the fact that the band had mastered the song upon its release; it had become a staple of their live set, and it was an excellent way to demonstrate the guitar prowess of Steve Howe. Again, the way in which listeners would receive this version of the song in 1968 is questionable given that, while rawer than the original, the structure was the same as The Beatles version which had been a hit 12 months previously.

Track nine, *Three Jolly Little Dwarfs,* is stripped of most of its Indian guitar vibe that marked it out so clearly on the *14-Hour Technicolour Dream* snippet. In the early part of the song, Keith's vocals are even delivered in a style akin to Anthony Newley (an observation which could also be levelled at David Bowie's *The Laughing Gnome* from the same year).

Track 10, *Now Your Time Has Come,* has also, more recently, had its provenance called into question. The 1999 CD re-issue of the album includes, in the cover notes, evidence which prompts the question, 'Was the title really intended for this song, or was this track slipped in to replace the original song which was – very late in the day – deemed unworthy of inclusion?' Whatever the actual, original title of the song, it's a fine tune – stripped of a little energy perhaps by the production – but including a really punchy guitar instrumental section.

Now Your Time Has Come #2. The original track of this name (included on the 1999 CD re-issue) is a straightforward boy meets girl tale. It's not easy to see why it was removed from the album where it would have sat solidly as an album track. It includes Howe's signature guitar and Keith's strong voice. If there is such a thing as a 'typical' Tomorrow track, then this is it.

None of the band members can recall why and how this switching of the songs took place; it will remain an unsolved mystery. So will the decision not to include *Caught in a Web* on the album which had been recorded but would never be released. It still languishes in the EMI vaults.

Closing the album is *Hallucinations* which – in this version – sounds uninspired when compared to the live version captured at the Christmas gig. Keith believes this was due to a lack of available studio time more than any other reason and this 'easy-listening' version might also be explained by the fact that Mark Wirtz had recorded a lightweight cover of the song, and released it under the name of Steve Flynn, in the final months of 1967. This version more closely represents his previous recording, and the song peters out as opposed to reaching a definitive climax.

Keith comments, 'When Mark and the band first started recording, it went very well. We had a great engineer in Geoff Emerick and we were very pleased with the mixes of *My White Bicycle* and *Claramount Lake*. But we all agreed that, as we went forward, Mark was running out of ideas and thought to be too straight. His background was in arranging Europop-style background music, so we figured he needed to get in touch with what was going on in our world.

'One evening, we all met up at his small flat at the GPO Tower. We turned him on with some hashish and were having a little party, playing music, bonding... We ended up at the Speakeasy Club, and when the waiter came over to take our order, Mark hid under the table giggling out of control. I looked over at Steve and thought this was not such a good idea after all!'

Clearly, the 11 songs that were released on the original album in February 1968 did not capture the hearts and minds of the record-buying public, but nor did they satisfy the band members who had written and recorded them. All involved have their opinion on what the problems were.

Steve Howe's reflections are that 'The first things we did, *My White Bicycle* and *Claramount Lake,* they were really successful recordings that included the use of leading-edge technology and a huge amount of imagination, but they came out in a different era.

'When it came to the album, it was felt that the group didn't have enough [psychedelic style] material that would go into this record. Keith and Mark, for their own reasons, could imagine some of the other songs being on the album, but they were a little bit twee compared to *Real Life Permanent Dream,* for example.

'There was a little batch of songs that we did that filled out the album. Maybe they were not representative of the group, but perhaps reflected more of Keith and his talent and his writing style. I have no gripes about it; we obviously didn't have more material. The ones that have that authoritative approach – such as *Revolution, Real Life Permanent Dream, Hallucinations, The Incredible Journey of Timothy Chase* – do have energy, but still did not capture quite how energetic we were on stage.'

Steve's point about a dearth of original material is an interesting one as the band chose to leave *Claramount Lake* off the record, as well as the original version of *Now Your Time Has Come* and the recently-recorded *Caught in a Web*. Live staples such as *Why* and *The Shotgun and The Duck* were also excluded. A differently sequenced album with *Shy Boy* and *Auntie Mary's Dress Shop* removed, and the inclusion of the omitted tracks, might have provided a more cohesive record.

One of the reasons, potentially, for the album's lack of cohesiveness is because it was not recorded within a specific time frame and in a single studio. While sessions for *My White Bicycle* and the second single, *Revolution,* were conducted at Abbey Road, subsequent sessions – lasting until December 1967 – took place at a number of studios including De Lane Lea in Kingsway. This unhappy situation was the product of EMI's lack of faith in the group. The reason the album was allowed to limp to completion by EMI was probably more based on the solo success Keith was having, as opposed to any long-term belief that the record label had in the group.

As Keith remembers, 'We did *Revolution,* and then we started doing the album, which didn't go too well. I think they wanted us to write all our own material and some of it wasn't even written. We should have, looking back, put our foot down a bit more and put some of the live set in, songs like *Why*. But it just trailed on and we were busy working all the time, so the right decisions weren't made.

'Even the sleeve wasn't what we wanted, and there was all kind of problems with it. It was in and out [of studios] pretty much. I even ended up mixing a couple of the tracks as well. Mark was away or something, and it had to be finished.'

It is possible to highlight many elements of the album as being responsible for its lack of commercial success at the time – from the flat production, to the sequencing and choice of tracks, to the black and white album cover, and the bizarre sleeve notes by Roger Fennings. Mostly, of course, these are historical criticisms as the album is now regarded as one of the finest psychedelic albums ever made. What really killed the record at the time was none of the above elements but, simply, timing.

When the album finally emerged, in February 1968, to very little fanfare from the record company, Tomorrow's time at the heart of the psychedelic movement – indeed the psychedelic movement itself – had all but faded away. If we think about how quickly the participants in this scene say things moved on at the time, then songs that were up to a year old when they were finally released must have seemed out of step and behind the times. A big record, with significant record company promotion, released by Tomorrow in August 1967, would undoubtedly have given the band the hit they deserved.

As it was in August 1967, the band, their lead singer and songwriter, their agency, and their record company were all looking elsewhere. They had a chart smash on their hands...

12. Teenage Opera, 'the' soap opera

The idea for the song that was to define Keith West's professional career, in the mind of the general public at least, supposedly came from a dream which Mark Wirtz had in December 1966. 'I saw this grocer named Jack, who was taken for granted by his village,' said Wirtz in an interview in 2008. 'He was only appreciated when he died – mostly by the children of the town who had taunted him when he was alive, but who loved him dearly and now missed him.'

As Keith points out, as gently as possible, 'I wrote all the lyrics and, therefore, many elements of his inspired dream simply weren't there at the beginning, especially the children's section. But Mark, over time, and probably through telling the story repeatedly, has increasingly taken ownership of the entire narrative of the song.'

In reality, the involvement of both Keith and Mark in *Excerpt from a Teenage Opera* would be equally as important. Their combined strengths of lyrics and music, hip profile and classical training, a great singer and a killer hook, lots of studio time and a certain 'throw it all at the wall' approach to production, all combined to create a unique chapter in pop history.

As rock and roll ideas go, on the surface it was not the most promising concept. Still, Wirtz had got himself into a position where he was an in-house producer and arranger for EMI, and therefore had a certain latitude to pursue his own projects, without necessarily seeking the permission of his paymasters.

The antecedents of the song, and indeed Wirtz's professional standing, go back to early January 1966 where Wirtz, a German musician with wide ambitions and interests from classical music to pop and rock, experimented with his vision by writing and producing *A Touch Of Velvet - A Sting Of Brass* under the name Mood Mosaic. His vision sounds simple, 'To create movies on record', but when explained, the concept becomes more nebulous; this lack of clarity would eventually cause problems for both Keith and Mark further down the line.

Never one to undersell his 'genius', Mark Wirtz's explanation of his vision [in his own words] takes some swallowing: 'Sonic, sensually graphic movies which, projected on the big screen in the listener's mind and heart, would touch the audience into an experience as seen through the eyes of their own imagination, viscerally interpreted by their own unique emotions.

'*A Touch Of Velvet* [the musical portrayal of a lovemaking event] was the original, primitive prototype of what I aspired to. A recording which, much like making a movie, made the musical experience the star, rather than a featured artist whose image and typical style would limit the freedom and possibilities of instrumentation and sound concepts.

'My idea was to select all participants in my movies on record, just like casting actors and technical crew in a film.

'My vision didn't stop there. In order to have the same freedom which you have in moviemaking by shooting different segments in varying locations, with different characters, I implemented a method by which I recorded my movies on record in separately recorded scenes that I would later edit, cross-fade and ultimately melt together into a seamless whole. This method drove musicians and sound engineers crazy at first, until they heard the finished result – which they were so impressed by that they changed from being indignant opponents to enthusiastic fans and partners.'

Keith cuts through the pomposity of Mark's statements saying, 'Mark's opinion of himself and his vision is somewhat overblown. Many things Mark professed to invent were not new either. Phil Spector, The Wall of Sound, The Shangri-Las,

The Leader of the Pack, Brian Wilson, Pet Sounds, and the wonderful Jimmy Webb, had all been doing it for years.

'Also, how is it possible to create a movie into a recording format? Asking the record-buying public to imagine pictures, or actual scenes, whilst listening to a piece of incidental/background music is where he was heading until the penny dropped and he had to change tack.

'Honestly, I was not too impressed with most of his work. The two songs I wrote with him stand out by a mile as being the pinnacle of his production and arranging skills. We fell out eventually, and it came to a head with the track *Sam*.

'It was my face on the record. I was the artist with the sole task of promoting the song. Listening to the original mix being played back at Abbey Road, I was thinking to myself it's over 30 seconds before I start to sing, there is no chorus, so when I finish the last verse I have to wait approximately two minutes until the fade. That is a very long time in TV-land as anyone will tell you but, as it happens, the record was over 5 minutes long and no radio station or TV show would give it that much air time back in 1967. So, I hardly ever performed it.

'Another bone of contention was the B-side, *A Thimble full of Puzzles.* As I was the artist, I expected to perform on both sides of the record and had written a couple of songs with Ken Burgess. It was not to be, sadly. I was railroaded. Even worse, when I listened to this track, I couldn't believe how awful it was; it's elevator music at best. I made up my mind instantly that I had to jump ship.'

A Touch of Velvet was accepted and released by EMI and achieved a decent amount of airplay as well as becoming the theme song for Radio Bremen's show *Musikladen*. It was also used by some radio stations and DJs in the UK as idents, notably Dave Lee Travis on Radio Caroline. This small success gave Mark the opportunity to work on other projects and allowed his work to be heard by a wider circle of industry figures, one of whom was Kim Fowley.

Enshrined in rock folklore as the exploitative Svengali figure behind 70s all-girl group The Runaways, Fowley (in reality) has an extended pedigree as a publicist, songwriter, and producer. His credits include working as a publicist for P.J. Proby as well as writing songs for Frank Zappa, Warren Zevon, Kiss, and Alice Cooper, and producing albums for The Runaways and Gene Vincent.

Mark Wirtz remembers Kim, 'He was taken with my production and arrangement of the Beach Boys' tune *I'm Waiting For The Day* for the female artist Peanut. He not only hired me to produce and arrange several tracks for him but quickly became my champion and tutor as much as my hero. I was mesmerised by Kim's flamboyance, unique thinking, reckless courage and utter disregard for music business convention, or protocol.

'To me, Kim was the eternal, paradoxical commuter between the gutter and esoteric supremacy – a pig and a saint, a fool and a genius – he truly personified the ultimate spirit of Rock'n'Roll.

'One of Kim's many idiosyncrasies was his habit to preface virtually every noun with the adjective 'teenage'. He would catch a 'teenage' taxi to a 'teenage' restaurant where he would order a 'teenage' steak before making his way to a 'teenage' studio to cut a 'teenage' record.'

It was an idiosyncrasy that would have a dramatic effect later in Mark and Keith's collective history.

While planning to join Fowley in the USA, Wirtz was contacted by EMI's product manager Roy Featherstone, at the behest of their head of A&R, Norrie Paramor, and offered a contract to join EMI as a producer with virtually unlimited creative freedom. Unable to resist, he accepted and cancelled his plans with Kim Fowley.

EMI's offer to Mark came with a £30.00 a week wage, a 1% royalty, plus basic arrangement and conducting fees in accordance with musicians' union terms. Soon afterwards, he signed an exclusive publishing deal with Tony Roberts and Ian Ralfini at Robbins Music as a composer/writer… not realising that his contract with EMI had included all of his publishing rights! This mistake would have more than a few ramifications in the next few years. Complicating matters further was that Mark had already signed a publishing agreement with Ardmore and Beechwood.

While the creative licence Mark had been granted at EMI was ahead of its time, his frustrations with the antiquated technology and working practices at Abbey Road (which have been covered in the *My White Bicycle* chapter of this book) remained. He recalls, 'All in all, for better or worse, no matter how many grievances and frustrations I initially felt working at Abbey Road, there was no point in complaining, let alone attempting to seek refuge in another studio. Abbey Road was the only game in town for us – all EMI producers were contractually bound to work there exclusively. In terms of history, that curse turned out to be a blessing. Because of all the prevalent challenges and limitations, and our experimentation and inventiveness in overcoming them, the resulting music was among the most creative and profound in pop music history.'

Upon arriving at EMI, Mark soon became friends with Geoff Emerick and even shared with him the contents of his dream and his plans to create a record around it. Mark recalls, 'I took Geoff aside and shared my *Grocer Jack* dream with him. Geoff said it was interesting as a fairytale but had doubts about it as a rock record.

'I was confident though and said that it was not going to be just a rock record but a rock opera. A movie on record. It would be widescreen and technicolour with special effects and a cast of hundreds.'

'Hmmm...' responded Geoff, 'with which artist?'

'I don't know. Doesn't matter,' I stated blithely. 'We record all the music first, and then we decide whom to cast as a soloist.'

'EMI will never approve a budget for a recording with no artist,' said Geoff, [who knew EMI's working practices better than Mark and was being realistic].

'True,' I agreed. 'So, let's make it officially part of the Mood Mosaic project. Mood Mosaic is all orchestral and background singers and has no featured artist.'

'Then, I proceeded to explain to Geoff my plan of recording the work in separate scenes at the end of regular sessions, taking advantage of the varying orchestras and bands, as well as the boundless options of varying sound configurations.

'Geoff was enthusiastic and said that it sounded exciting and then asked me what we were going to call it as we needed a title, for the paperwork.

'Teenage – Kim Fowley's catch-all adjective – flashed to mind. *Excerpt from a Teenage Opera* I suggested, adding that if the single was a hit, then people would want an entire LP of the whole *Opera*. Geoff just grinned and asked when we would start.'

Exactly how Keith came to be involved in the project has become a little blurred over the years, but Steve Howe was certainly the catalyst. Following his work with Mark on the recording of *My White Bicycle*, he was doing some session work at EMI and contributed the lead guitar part to what would become the B-Side, *Theme from a Teenage Opera*.

'Do you know anyone that writes lyrics?' is how Steve Howe recalls Mark Wirtz pulling Keith West into the project. But, having already worked together on *My White Bicycle* and *Claramount Lake,* it seems unlikely that Mark would need reminding of Keith's lyrical talents. More likely is that Steve, when hearing that lyrics were required, volunteered his friend for an easy payday.

Keith's memories are a little different. He recalls Mark saying to him, 'You've heard the instrumental which Steve has done? I've got this other backing track,' and he played me this piece of music.

'It wasn't really my thing at all. But I liked the intro and bits of it, so I agreed to write some lyrics for it. Mark had liked my character-based songs like *Shy Boy* and *Colonel Brown.'*

While the exact details of how Keith got involved, through who, and why, is up for debate, what we do know is that section by section, scene by scene, the music for *Teenage Opera* was being put together at Abbey Road and that EMI were not aware of it.

As Mark recalls, 'The biggest challenge was the recording of the famous children's' segment, which I cast with kids from the London Corona school. There was no way I could hide the expense of the children's fees in regular, official session paperwork. To prevent arousing suspicion, or stirring the political waters, I simply made a deal with Corona and paid for the kids' performance out of my own pocket. Best money I ever spent.'

While Keith did, of course, accept the commission to write the lyrics for *Excerpt from a Teenage Opera,* he initially had no desire to be its featured artist and vocalist. Keith recorded, what he believed to be, a demo of the song which also included Herbie Flowers on bass, 'Big' Jim Sullivan on guitar, Clem Cattini on drums, and The Flowerpot Men, as well as the Corona children on backing vocals!

It seems though, for the very reasons that Keith did not wish to be the face of the record, Mark Wirtz was a few steps ahead in his thinking…

'Did I ever consider performing *Grocer Jack* myself? No way,' he maintained in an interview.

'I was shrewdly aware that due to the project's heavily-orchestrated concept which, at the time, was regarded as very uncool and likely to be condescendingly dismissed as old people's music, I needed a performer whose image was hip and seductive to rebellious and anti-establishment rock fans. Keith fitted the bill perfectly.

'Not only did he look and act like a hippie, without being so far out that he would put off the more mature audience sector, but he had already established himself as a cult icon in the underground rock community and, by association, would validate *Grocer Jack* as a bona fide rock record.'

Keith's take on this is, 'A little credit at last; as long as I didn't turn off the more mature record buyers, eh?' While Keith remembers that his work on the *Teenage Opera* tracks was an example of EMI putting their foot down, and him just having to get on with it, the lyrics themselves are remarkable.

'I wrote the top line of the song, the actual melody, and the lyrics. I'd received a backing track with just a load of chords on it. I went round to Mark's flat, he set me up with a tape recorder, made some coffee and went out for lunch, and I worked the lyrics out to *Teenage Opera* in about an hour.

'It sounds a bit arrogant, but sometimes things are easy to do. A story is quite a flowing thing. Here's an idea, write a story around that. The darker side of me came out, with the people standing around a grave. I didn't think I was going get away with that, but it worked. It gave it an edge. It could have sounded a tad cheesy, otherwise.

'I must say, Mark backed me up with all my ideas. I initially thought he would think them too subversive for a pop song, but he went with it all the way, to my great delight.

'It was my idea to get those kids in and sing the chorus; I didn't want to sing it. It was too cheesy for me. I didn't want to do that part of the song, 'Grocer Jack, Grocer Jack, Is it true what Mummy says?' and 'oh no, oh no'. So, I was thinking what could be done to get me out of it.

'Anyway, I went to see my publisher, Malcolm Forrester, one afternoon and when I walked into his office, he was playing a children's tape. Malcolm, at the time, was looking at acquiring various music catalogues and delving into the theatre and also classical music for long-term income streams.

'That's where I got the idea from, the sound of these kids singing triggered something and I came up with the idea to put them on the record. To this day, I still honestly believe that without those children singing the chorus, my record wouldn't have charted so high; those lyrics combined with the natural kids' voices had us all going in the control room, and when it was unleashed on radio the effect was 'reach for the Kleenex'.

'It was that simple. I didn't think they'd go for it. I put forward my idea of having children sing the chorus, and then somebody researched it and found the Corona School and they all came down with their mums and dads. It was a 'happening', as they called it in those days. Everyone in the studio was excited.'

Despite having been written with – what most lyricists would consider to be – indecent haste, the lyrics for *Teenage Opera* merit consideration in isolation. The first verse especially, which sets the tone for the song, is remarkable in the way it immediately conjures a tragi-comic tone and creates the character of Jack.

Count the days into years

His eighty-two brings many fears

Yesterday's laughter turned to tears

His arms and legs don't feel so strong

His heart is weak, there's something wrong

Opens windows in despair

Tries to breathe in some fresh air

His conscience cries: "Get on your feet

Without you, Jack, the town can't eat"

There's something of the English pastoral characters that Coleridge and Wordsworth created in *The Lyrical Ballads* about the way Keith conveys the physical frailty of Jack, as well as his sense of civic pride and duty. Before we get too above ourselves, and hail Keith as a genius and place him among the pantheon of great English poets, we must remember that writing in this way was also being explored by Ray Davies of The Kinks, Lennon and McCartney, and Pete Townshend of The Who at the time. Keith's lyrics, though, are certainly an elegant example of this trend among the most celebrated of English pop lyricists.

The main chorus is a great example of catchy simplicity with its repeated refrain of:

Grocer Jack, grocer Jack, get off your back

Go into town, don't let them down, oh no, no

While the first half of the next verse is a straightforward telling of the story:

The people that live in the town

Don't understand

He's never been known to miss his round

"It's ten-o'clock", the housewives yell

"When Jack turns up we'll 'give him hell"

The rest of the verse returns to the more wistful vision of middle England with its cooked breakfast and the particularly evocative use of 'marmalade labels' as a metaphor for something which, if it was to be gone, would be missed.

Husbands moan at breakfast tables

No milk, no egg, no marmalade labels

Mothers send their children out

To Jack's house to scream and shout

The final verse, once the refrain from the chorus has been repeated again, establishes the idyllic place in which the people live before switching into the darker element of the story where the townspeople and their bewildered children have to come to terms with their behaviour.

A Sunday morning bright and clear

Lovely flowers decorate our marble square

People cry and walk away and think about the fateful day

Now they wish they'd given Jack more affection and respect

Little children dressed in black don't know what happened to old Jack

If the fate of Jack is still being alluded to at this point, then the listener is left in no doubt when the chorus with subtly-changed lyrics is sung repeatedly through to the end.

Grocer Jack, grocer Jack, is it true what mummy says

You won't come back, oh no, no

The genius of the song and its lyrics are tied up in the lines 'Is it true what mummy says, you won't come back, oh no, oh no'. At this point, the fact that Jack is truly dead and that a child realises this (and the listener is getting confirmation) comes crashing through, giving the song a final emotional kick as it moves towards its conclusion. It's this element of the song which separates it from being viewed as a pure novelty record and probably accounts for its continued popularity and importance.

Keith recalls being in the studio when the children's choir recorded their vocals and recalls the 'lump in the throat moment' when the wobbly tuning of their closing refrain was captured. Lightning had been bottled.

The element of pathos, which is present throughout the song and crystalised at the end, allowed the song to speak to all the different audiences that Mark Wirtz had identified from teenage pop aficionados to journalists and DJs and older listeners. A perfect pop record that subtly explores a [deathly] serious subject within a catchy tune and easily memorable lyrics.

With the demo version safely in the can, now came the make or break moment for Mark Wirtz as he prepared to present his work, and to reveal what was calculated as a £2,000 bill for studio time, to the powers that be at EMI.

Mark remembers, 'A delegation from EMI's Manchester Square head office assembled at Abbey Road's Studio 3 in curious anticipation of my mystery project's unveiling.

'Headed by product manager Roy Featherstone, the crew consisted mainly of promo and marketing execs, all of them music pimps, not one of them true music lovers. Sadly, missing from the gathering was A&R chief Norrie Paramor, not only my strongest Manchester Square supporter but himself a distinguished and highly creative music maker who would have been the only one capable of appreciating my vision and courage.

'Nevertheless, I felt such an inner confidence about my work, certain that its sheer power of originality and grandiosity would melt through any prejudice or reservations, that I fully expected fireworks of excitement and applause.

'On my cue, Geoff hit the play button and the studio monitors burst into the bombastic sounds and music for the studio premiere of *Excerpt from a Teenage Opera*. There was dead silence when the playback concluded, each member of the executive staff incredulously staring at the other for a reaction clue. None of them had ever heard anything like it, and none of them dared to speak for what seemed like an eternity. 'Children?' Roy Featherstone finally gasped. 'Have you gone mad? You think anybody out there is going to buy a Rock record with children on it?'

'Roy's appalled comment burst the dam of silence and released a flood of condemnation from his colleagues: 'Four minutes long?'; 'Classical music merged with Rock?'...

'The ultimate consensus was not only that of rejection but outright condemnation, 'Absurd record'; 'Would never sell a copy'; 'Radio would never play it'; etc., etc., etc.

'The bottom line was that the audition of *Teenage Opera* was a dismal bust. Instead of rewarding me with applause and accolades, the committee's unanimous verdict was uncompromisingly final – to can the tape and kill the project.'

It's interesting to speculate what would have happened to Keith and Tomorrow if this had indeed been the end of the matter. Keith assumed this (rejection) is what would happen to the record when he agreed to provide the lyrics and to provide a guide vocal for the demo version. Something of a payday and the experience of working on an inventive project with Mark and keeping the twin beasts of EMI and his management at the Bryan Morrison Agency happy.

But, as the *Teenage Opera* would subsequently prove time and time again, the genie – once let out of the bottle – is not so easy to get back in. Its saviour turned out to be a man already familiar to Keith, and one whose uncanny ability to distinguish the truly original from the derivative, and to champion it regardless of trends, would establish him as a kickstarter of careers and a maker of hits for the next 35 years – enter John Peel.

Mark says, 'That would have been the end of it, had it not been for one man – Radio Caroline's pirate Disc Jockey John Peel.

'I was introduced to him by Tony Roberts of Robbins Music who really liked the song. We played John an acetate and before the record had even reached its bombastic ending, John – with a big grin on his face – opened up the microphone, promised the listeners a marvellous surprise, then put the needle back to the beginning of the groove and played the record over the air.

'Within moments of *Grocer Jack's* final bars travelling through the ether, Radio Caroline's phones lit up, from listeners calling in to request the record to be played again, and again, and again. EMI had no choice but to rush-release the single.'

Having been persuaded by Bryan Morrison and EMI that it would be both in his and his band's best interest to be associated with a hit single, *Excerpt from a Teenage Opera* was released on Friday the 28th of July, 1967. The song obviously tapped into something that record buyers and listeners in the UK (and further afield) were looking for and the single entered the charts a week later and kept on climbing, finally peaking in the UK at #2 on the 23rd of September. The song was only kept off the #1 spot by Engelbert Humperdinck's *The Last Waltz* (Keith was in select company as the same fate had also befallen The Beatles' double A-side of *Strawberry Fields Forever* and *Penny Lane* earlier in the year with his monster hit *Release Me*).

What the record tapped into among the record-buying public would be a matter for much conjecture for a long time afterwards. Mark Wirtz, at the time, focused on the sentimental element of the song.

In an interview with *Melody Maker*, published on the 30th of September 1967, Mark is quoted as saying, 'I want to exploit this idea of bringing drama to records and develop it further and further. But it has to be done very slowly, or else it's in danger of sounding sick or contrived. You can do so much with musical instruments. They can sound happy or sad or very happy or very sad.'

With the benefit of 50 years of hindsight, looking back and trying to pinpoint the exact reasons for the song's success are as fraught with peril as they always were. Distilling the elements of a hit record into a formula has eluded every record company and artist that ever attempted it. But what the record *did* have in its favour was a whimsical English-language lyric which, having won the World Cup only a year previously, seemingly appealed to an English audience currently in the thrall of all things Albion.

Also, for a European audience, the orchestration, balalaika, and brass instruments, and fairytale element, played into the regard they had for this brand of traditional music and values. Plus, there was the extra ingredient of a hip and handsome young singer who, even when lip-syncing on German TV show, *The Beat Club,* managed to look genuine, moody, and intense.

A lot of ticked boxes.

From the moment that John Peel and a host of other DJs started to play *Teenage Opera,* Bryan Morrison himself became more involved with Keith and his career in the role of official manager. While Bryan had been content to allow Tomorrow to be handled by Tony Howard, while he looked after his first love The Pretty Things, Keith's record had given him what he truly craved, a big hit record and a potential star on his books.

In the annals of rock and roll history, the late Bryan Morrison (save for in his own memoir *Have a Cigar*) does not fare very well. Joe Boyd is virulent when he talks about the stealing of Pink Floyd from him: 'Bryan Morrison didn't give a shit – he was just after the money' and there are numerous other examples of people pouring scorn on his abilities and artistic integrity.

To be fair to Bryan, he was in the music business and had the responsibility for paying peoples' wages. He was simply more focused on the business element than some artistic types would have liked or valued.

But, at this particular moment in Keith's career, what he needed was experienced, clear-minded, and well-funded management (not needing or chasing the revenue from a single hit). Management that had been through the mangle of overnight pop success and had come out of the other side wiser and prepared to provide a clear, long-term view and a solid strategy for their client who was just about to be drawn into a whirlwind. Sadly, the relatively inexperienced Morrison would provide none of the above and proceeded to work with Keith and Mark on a strategy that can best be described as 'off-the-cuff', or 'make it up as we go along' at worst. It was an approach which would, ultimately, serve none of them well.

Mark Wirtz is another who holds a low opinion of Morrison's professional competence. 'Morrison attempted to get involved in Keith's *Teenage Opera*-related affairs but, beyond being well-intentioned and acting as a cheerleader, Bryan was utterly in over his head when it came to the maze of complications and challenges surrounding a project of *Teenage Opera*'s magnitude.

'As such, Bryan was indeed a cliché example of the blind leading the blind. What we desperately needed was an experienced, shrewd leader, and protector, who could serve as the political architect of *Teenage Opera*'s ultimate completion and success.'

When defending Bryan Morrison, despite his protestations to the contrary, one could argue that Mark's entire vision for the *Opera* had a certain 'nailing jelly to a wall' element to it, and was difficult to communicate and understand. Even when articulated in his own words, it was a bit… woolly.

'*Teenage Opera* was never intended to be performed on a stage, and a musical was exactly what it was not. Most significantly and quite contrary to the biggest misconception of all, *Teenage Opera* did not have a traditional plot or story. A theme? Yes. A dramatic frame? Yes. But a story? No.

'It was, in fact, a kaleidoscope of stories, a bouquet of allegorical, tragi-comic tales about a variety of characters and their fate, all related to each other by the common thread of living in the same imaginary turn-of-the-century village. Each character distinguished him or herself by rebelliously pursuing a dream or lifestyle against all odds and in defiance of conformity; their ageless celebration of youth and individuality embodying the very spirit of Rock'n'Roll.'

Given the above explanation, when viewed through the prism of history, Mark and Keith should perhaps be credited with the invention of the concept album as opposed to what they were often credited with, the invention of the rock opera.

Its complex influences and rationale aside, the release of the record was a dizzying time for all involved. Mark recalls, '*Teenage Opera* was released internationally and made it to #1 in 16 countries. The global infatuation with *Teenage Opera* triggered an international Blitzkrieg of frenzied publicity and hype, triggering speculations, rumours, expectations, fabricated reports and a Pandora's Box full of questions. In particular, what was the story and when would it be completed and released in its entirety?'

'What had started as crackling sparks of curiosity soon ignited into a bonfire of mystery, intrigue, and hoopla. The circus was in town, and Keith and I were the main attraction, me up on the high wire, only my profile showing; Keith in the centre of the ring, all lights upon him, rockin' and rollin'. We were having a blast, bathing in the glory and excitement of *Teenage Opera*'s runaway success.'

The calls on Keith and Mark's time (but mainly Keith as the singer and face of the record) were many and various. From appearances on *Top of The Pops,* to flying to Germany and Holland to appear on various pop shows, to featuring on the BBC's twice-weekly chat show *Dee Time*. All the while appearing regularly at gigs with Tomorrow and giving innumerable interviews to the music press from across Europe as well as various Girls' magazines, such as *Jackie,* for whom he was 'Pin-Up of The Month'.

As Mark touched on previously, the main line of the media's questioning was around the possibility of the full rock opera – what was the story, and when would it appear? All good questions and ones which Mark's rather loose explanation of his vision did nothing to provide the answer to. Therefore, the strategy was, if not formally agreed upon then certainly embarked on, between Mark, Keith and Bryan to accept that every possibility was on the table, be that a film, a stage play, a concept album, or an animated movie. Any number, type, or style of musical collaboration could be involved in the project. It was a throw it at the wall and see if anything sticks approach which would ultimately fail dismally.

As Mark recollects, 'Little did we suspect that the success would soon hurl us upon a runaway train of confusion, conflicts, and dilemmas, turning a dream into a nightmare.'

However, and to continue the locomotive analogy, while the *Teenage Opera* train was running, it was decided that the best thing to do was to keep riding it which meant producing a second single to capitalise further on the success and to – in Mark's mind – convince EMI that his plan to create movies on record was plausible, feasible, and commercially viable.

As Mark says, 'To begin with, EMI shocked me with the unthinkable – despite all evidence to the contrary, and ignoring the public's keen appetite for the complete *Opera* – company management was convinced that *Teenage Opera* had merely been a novelty hit, and stubbornly refused to green-light recording the entire work. Instead, EMI insisted on a further hit single from the *Opera* before being willing to give their bureaucratic blessings to the expense of an entire album production.

'With no choice but to swallow my disappointment and follow EMI's mandate, I became determined to not only give my very best shot to another excerpt but to make it even bigger and better than *Grocer Jack*.

'Geoff Emerick, Keith, and I commenced work on *Sam*, my most ambitious and challenging work yet. The stakes were as high as the expectations were overwhelming. After all, *Sam*'s success would either vindicate *Teenage Opera* as a viable, credible work of importance, or, in its failure, condemn it into oblivion. If making a hit record on command is an absurd proposition at the best of times, to pull another *Grocer Jack* success out of a hat, from a work as complex as *Teenage Opera*, was ludicrous.

'By far the most worrisome problem, however, which led me further and further into a quagmire, was the public's fixed expectation of a conventional story. For fear of disappointing the public by the absence of such a story, inviting their rejection altogether, I felt increasingly torn between sticking to my original concept, or surrendering to the pressure of obligation and giving them one, thus completely bastardising my original vision and intent.

'Another shock to the system was a complete change of policies and upper management at EMI's Manchester Square headquarters. A&R chief Norrie Paramor, not only my champion and most loyal ally, but also the only executive of note who understood music, was replaced by a new creative head, a Mr Beecher-Stevens, whose resumé of corporate management was impressive, yet lacked any previous association with, or even interest in, music and records. Producers and other creative staff were stripped of their individual freedom of creative decision-making, which was taken over by a committee that gathered in a weekly A&R meeting to deliberate and decide upon all project developments and new artist signings.

'Though feeling concerned and threatened by the events and changes, I felt secure enough about the importance of *Teenage Opera*. to believe its fate to be safe from any detrimental interference. Surely the BBC would play *Sam* and – assuming its success – surely EMI, out of sheer self-interest, would happily leave me a free hand in completing and releasing an LP as soon as possible?

'Finally, the day arrived when, shortly before its public release date, the finished *Sam* recording was presented to the industry and press in a studio premiere. It was an awesome event. Abbey Road's Studio 3 was packed wall-to-wall with people, and the air sizzled with electricity as everybody awaited the big moment. And when the moment arrived, it became the spectacular highlight of *Teenage Opera*'s life.

'In contrast to *Excerpt from a Teenage Opera's* premiere, *Sam* was greeted with breathless applause and accolades, hailed as brilliant and sensational. The sentiments expressed during this premiere were reflected in the media's subsequent frenzy of reports and rave reviews, predicting *the Opera's* ultimate triumph.'

Keith's lyrics for *Sam* were another example of his creative ability. As he says, 'The words for *Teenage Opera* were the only time I have ever written anything that didn't truly mean anything to me from an observational point of view. *Sam*, while ostensibly being about a train driver character, was also a comment upon the decimation of the railway industry that was happening at the time because of the Beeching Report. It recommended that out of 18,000 miles of railway in the UK, 6,000 miles should be closed entirely, and that some of the remaining lines should be kept open only for freight. A total of 2,363 stations and many rural lines were to close, cutting communities off from their lifeblood, both financial and cultural.'

The track *Sam,* itself, was another enormous production, although Mark played down rumours that it had taken 80 hours of studio time, whilst publicists [presumably Bryan Morrison] played up the fact that EMI were again worried about the huge cost. *Sam* features roughly the same history and musicians as *Teenage Opera,* but session recordings indicate even more percussion overdubs, which were later mixed down or totally removed. The track features the heavy use of percussion (a Wirtz trademark since 1964) and sample edits of the backing tracks show that the sections were originally considered to be in a different order.

There were rumours that Wirtz had covertly recorded train sounds at railway yards but he did, in fact, record the church bells at The Dom in his hometown of Cologne, Germany. The 4th Central Holloway Brownies Pack sings the children's chorus on the record because, according to Mark, The Corona School was not interested in participating. The issue may have come down to money, with the children getting a flat fee for their contribution to the original and not benefiting from the large amount of money it generated in both record sales and publishing royalties from radio airplay. Lyrics printed on the promotional picture sleeve show a spoken word section with a young girl (singer Penny Gold) asking Keith if Sam 'will come back?' Promo copies also contained a note, warning DJs of the track's length, and Wirtz later hurriedly returned from a holiday to produce a truncated radio edit of *Sam* when it became evident that its length was reducing its radio play by DJs.

As Mark says of the EMI playback, 'Alas, as it turned out, this moment in time was not only *Teenage Opera*'s pinnacle, but also its final hurrah. Upon release, despite the initial hype and promotion, the BBC played the record only rarely. Consequently, even though enough people heard and bought the single to make it a [minor] hit, the sales figures paled in comparison to *Teenage Opera*'s.

'EMI, instead of getting the message and giving the go-ahead to completion of the *Opera*, insisted on yet another random single to make up for what *Sam* had failed to achieve, to validate the expense of a complete LP. That meant more delays, more pretensions, more excuses, and more deceptions in the upkeep of *Teenage Opera*'s promise.

'From hereon in, what had started and evolved as a wonderful dream, sank further and further into a steady decline.'

Sam was issued on November the 17th 1967, and did chart at #38, but many things worked against it in matching the success of *Teenage Opera* not least of which was the fact that those crucial supporters of the original single – the airwaves-ruling pirate radio stations who were operating illegally from boats in the British channel outside the legal jurisdiction of the British Government – were suddenly shut down. As Mark comments, 'Overnight, the BBC, with only a few weekly hours of programming time dedicated to a limited playlist of rock and pop music, were once again in total control as Britain's sole musical output with the dictatorial power to make or break a record.'

Keith also remembers the feelings of deflation around the time, 'As long as you were having hits, you'd make an album. If you weren't, then you wouldn't be making any albums. They bottled out. *Teenage Opera* was costing too much money.

'Again, we didn't know what the actual bills were, because Mark was being a little bit shady, doing it all off studio time. But it would have been quite an expensive record to have made, as far as they were concerned. So, by the time *Sam* came out at a similar budget, they were getting cold feet.

'*Sam* only got into the top 40, so that was pulled. That whole project was pulled, basically, to my relief, I've got to tell you. I didn't want to do it anymore. *Sam* is a good record for that genre of music, and it lends itself to a children's book and that kind of stuff. That's the way my manager was trying to develop me, taking acting lessons, doing this and that. I didn't want to do that. I wanted to do *Lost Highway* [an Americana-themed track, written many years later by Keith], to be honest.'

By the time *Sam* was released, and with it achieving only moderate success, Keith, as you can tell from his words, was completely disenchanted with the project and to a certain extent the entire music business – as we'll address in the next chapter.

The reason for this disenchantment has much to do with the media's constant speculation about *Teenage Opera*'s future and neither Keith, Mark, or Bryan Morrison ever being able to give a straight answer to this question. As has been said previously, the strategy from the three principal spokesmen was not to confirm or deny any rumour and to see what happened and therefore be open to any opportunity that arose. This led to Keith saying, at one point, that EMI was prepared to spend £30,000 on the forthcoming album and also to continual rumours that Cliff Richard would be starring alongside Keith in a film version of the *Opera* (this story ran on the front page of the *Melody Maker* on September 16th, 1967).

Picking up on just three instances of coverage provides a flavour of the insanity which surrounded the project and the variety of rumours which the public were being presented with.

On the 26th of August 1967, *Melody Maker* ran a story headlined, 'Keith West Switch – More Teenage Opera' which read: 'Keith West will be releasing a follow up to Excerpt from a Teenage Opera. Last week Keith told the MM that no more Teenage Opera singles would be issued, but now the situation has changed. Producer Mark Wirtz, who co-wrote Teenage Opera told the MM on Monday 'We start recording the rest of the Opera on September 5th until the 8th but I shouldn't think the follow-up will be released until November. In fact, I think two more Opera singles will be issued before the album comes out.''

On September the 9th 1967, *Melody Maker* again ran a story about the project with the headline – 'West to re-write Opera for a film'. 'Owing to the enormous success of Keith West's Excerpt from a Teenage Opera single, he has now cancelled all his engagements for solo TV and radio appearances and work with his group Tomorrow, for the whole of November.

'This week Opera moved to number four in MM's Top 30 and film offers for the world rights to the complete Opera still poured in. Said a spokesman for Keith on Monday Teenage Opera originally started as a new venture in sound. As the whole scene was experimental we had no idea it would become so popular so quickly. But, now we have realised that the public are ready for such a venture and therefore Keith has decided to take November off to re-write the Opera as a film score – not just an album thing.

'West will be working with choreographers among other people concerned with producing the film of the *Opera*. It has been rumoured that MGM have made an offer.'

By October 7th, in an interview with the *New Musical Express,* the cracks in Keith's energy and enthusiasm started to appear. The journalist points to the fact that Keith is 'sniffing and sipping an orange juice' and Keith will later blame his poor health on 'too much travelling' as he had just returned from trips to Germany, Belgium and Holland in fairly short order. While he again talks up the next excerpt from the *Opera,* he is in a most 'un-Keith West-like' mood for the interview, and instead of his normal upbeat self, he is critical of a great many things.

On the rumour of Cliff Richard joining him on the *Opera,* he says, 'All that business about Cliff appearing in the *Opera* is not likely to happen. Having an old artist like Cliff in the production would be like going around in circles.' Ouch.

About Alan 'Fluff' Freeman and Pete Murray, he says, 'One thing I am beginning to learn is not to worry too much about what people say about you. They did not like *Revolution,* which I actually wrote for Tomorrow, well that's OK. I didn't write it for them but for the few thousand people that did buy the record and understand it.'

Even one of Keith's heroes gets a broadside, 'Pete Townshend said my *Opera* was badly done. I used to know Pete years ago when he was in The High Numbers, and we were called Four + 1. They used to come and listen to us because we were the up-and-coming sound. He wanted to write a pop opera, but it turned out to be a beat version on one of his LPs. Anyway, I am not upset about what any of them say.' Clearly.

With Keith's spirits dipping and his involvement in the *Teenage Opera* project spluttering to an unsatisfactory conclusion, his mind started to return to his first musical love: his band. Had his exposure as a pop star been the spark that they needed to fulfil their obvious potential and to break down some music industry doors? Or had they been unavoidably sucked into the *Teenage Opera* typhoon, which had now blown itself out, leaving all involved stranded on a barren shoreline?

It was time to find out.

The A team - Keith's parents Annie and Sidney Hopkins.

Shy Boy - Keith with his sisters; Anne on the left and Mavis on the right.

A first family holiday to St. Osyth in Jersey with Sidney Hopkins, Mavis, Anne, and Keith (on the left). Keith's Uncle Bert, Aunt Aggie, and Annie Hopkins (on the right).

John 'Junior' Wood who started the whole adventure via a 'musicians wanted' ad in 1963.

An early promotional shot for Four + 1.

Four + 1 on the road with their trusty van - Left to Right: Ken Lawrence, John Wood, Les Jones, Keith West, Simon Alcot.

Club Noreik bill, April 17th 1965.

The In Crowd strut their stuff at a Radio London promotional show in 1965.

Sporting a smart mod image following Roy Pitt's influence in 1965.

About to cut their debut single, The In Crowd at EMI's Manchester Square office, London.

Promotional shot for the 'That's How Strong My Love is' record sleeve. Left to Right: Ken Lawrence, John Wood, Simon Alcot, Steve Howe and Keith West.

Tomorrow photoshoot on Antony Rufus Isaacs' family estate near Reading, April 1967.

Tomorrow photoshoot on Antony Rufus Isaacs' family estate near Reading, April 1967.

Not a care in the world. Tomorrow photographed on Friday 28th July 1967. The day *Teenage Opera* was released.

Captured at the height of the Summer of Love, in July 1967, Tomorrow wear the latest clothes from Granny Takes A Trip and Dandie Fashions.

Leading Tomorrow's sound - Steve Howe at the Windsor Blues and Jazz Festival, August 1967.

Junior and Suzy Creamcheese add a theatrical element to the Tomorrow stage show.

Keith and Steve escape the English winter in
December 1967, in Montego Bay, Jamaica.

A picture of Keith outside the flat he shared with Steve Howe, in Highgate, in 1968.

Keith and Ken Burgess head down to Marshwood in Dorset, in early 1969, to write songs.

On holiday in Spain with his lifetime's love, Pat, in 1971.

My White Bicycle in Spain, on holiday, 1971.

A scratched polaroid from 1977 shows Keith and John Jessup discussing maternity and Masterswitch.

Antics with Keith and Ken Burgess at Rockfield Studio, 1980.

Time for work with The Rockolas, 1984.
Left to Right: Mike Read, Paul Foss, and Keith West.

Keith's daughters pictured at Mahon Harbour in Minorca.
Left to Right: Carrie, Shelley, and Jodie.

Keith back out front and rehearsing
with The Detours in 2016.

The Keith West Band, 2019.

13. Confusion reigns supreme

If we remind ourselves what Joe Boyd wrote in *White Bicycles* when looking back on 1967's 'Summer of Love', he said, 'The idea that drugs, sex and music could transform the world was always a pretty naïve dream. As the counter culture's effect on the mainstream grew, its own value and aesthetics decayed.'

These sentiments also apply to what befell Keith and Tomorrow as the phenomenal success of *Excerpt from a Teenage Opera* started to make the future uncertain for the band in the second part of the year. Just as commercialism diluted the counter-culture message and philosophy, so this narrative played out at the very heart of the band.

In many ways, Keith's story, Tomorrow's story, and the story which surrounds *Teenage Opera*, can be viewed as a tragedy of Shakespearian proportions which ran from the 28th of July 1967 (the day of the song's release) until the 5th of December 1967. If we define a Shakespearian tragic hero as 'a good man who comes to a bad end through the force of his own ambition' then Keith is our tragic hero. However, that would be a superficial reading of events which were much more nuanced at their heart. Keith sums up the dilemma at the heart of the tragedy.

'I had to decide what I was going to do – go on with that career [as a solo artist] because Bryan Morrison was trying to fit me out in three-piece suits and get my hair cut and telling me I can make my fortune, or go on with the band, who were all telling me that they didn't want me to leave. It was terrible. I didn't really want to be a solo star and when I think back, it screwed it all up – it screwed my own career up, and it screwed the band up.'

Just as the future for *Teenage Opera* had become messy and confusing, due to the multitude of rumours and ideas that were running concurrently, and EMI's continual prevarication, so this lack of clarity spilled over into Keith's work with Tomorrow. Just a look at the band and Keith's work schedule at the time provides an insight into how fast-paced and frenetic everything must have been, and how and why the future path for Tomorrow became so horribly unclear.

Following a Seaside Summer Special package tour in late June and early July – where Tomorrow supported Billy Fury, The Move, The Nashville Teens and Amen Corner (before being thrown off the tour for being too loud) – their diary of engagements reads:

Friday, July 21st – Tomorrow play UFO.

Friday, July 28th – *Excerpt from a Teenage Opera* released.

Saturday, July 29th – Tomorrow play Love-In Festival at Alexandra Palace.

Wednesday, August 9th – *Excerpt from a Teenage Opera* hits the charts.

Friday, August 11th – Tomorrow play 7th National Jazz & Blues Festival at Windsor and UFO on the same night.

Thursday, August 24th – Keith West appears solo on *Top of the Pops.*

Saturday, August 26th – Tomorrow play the Festival of the Flower Children, Woburn Abbey.

Sunday, August 27th – Tomorrow (Billed as Tomorrow 'featuring' Keith West) play Sunday at Saville's with Jimi Hendrix.

Tuesday, August 29th – Keith West appears on the BBC's *Dee Time* TV show.

Friday, September 1st – UFO festival at The Roundhouse (Tomorrow played the Friday night with Pink Floyd and Arthur Brown).

Saturday, September 2nd – Tomorrow Play 5th Dimension, Leicester.

Saturday, September 9th – Tomorrow (billed as Keith West 'with' Tomorrow) play Corn Exchange, Chelmsford.

Wednesday, September 13th – Keith West on location in Devon and Cornwall, making a solo film for *Top of the Pops.*

Thursday, September 21st – Tomorrow record their first session for BBC Radio at Maida Vale.

Friday, September 22nd – Tomorrow's *Revolution* single released.

Sunday, September 24th – Tomorrow fly to Belgium for promotional duties.

Tuesday, September 26th – Keith flies to Germany to appear on *The Beat Club.*

Thursday, September 28th/29th – Keith in Holland for TV appearances.

Sunday, October 1st – Tomorrow's BBC Radio session aired.

Sunday, October 1st – Tomorrow - Billed as Tomorrow 'featuring' Keith West play Sunday at the Saville – with Pink Floyd and The Incredible String Band and special guest Tim Rose.

October 1967 – Tomorrow (billed as Tomorrow 'with' Keith West) embark on a UK 'package' tour with Traffic; Vanilla Fudge and The Flower Pot Men. Dates are: 04 - London (Finsbury Park Astoria); 06 - Chesterfield (ABC); 07 - Newcastle (City Hall); 08 - Liverpool (Empire); 10 - Croydon (ABC); 11 - Birmingham (Town Hall); 12 - Bristol (Colston Hall); 14 - Wolverhampton (Gaumont); 15 - Leicester (De Montfort Hall); 17 - Ipswich (Gaumont).

Friday, October 27th – Tomorrow fly to Ireland for four dates.

It's no wonder that Keith was left feeling schizophrenic at the end of this schedule, and you could forgive his band member friends for not being pleased at having been relegated (in the main by promoters as opposed to anyone connected with the band) to mere sidemen when gig posters began to be printed as Tomorrow 'featuring' Keith West, or Tomorrow 'with' Keith West.

As Keith recalls, 'The band were really supportive; on the surface, they didn't seem to be too upset by it. I was embarrassed more than anything else because the record was flying in the charts, going crazy, and everywhere we were being booked they were using my name to get more people in. It was bound to happen.

'They never really said too much about it. I don't know what they thought behind my back, but obviously profile is great when you're trying to grow a band.

'Steve took it the best; he was very supportive. For everything I've ever done.

'I said to him recently, I couldn't have done some of that without his support. He's always been like that; he's my wingman, you know. The other two, I think Twink and Junior didn't take it that well and looking at it I don't blame them; on the posters, it does stand out like a sore thumb, it's Tomorrow *with* Keith West – it's really clunky.

'I couldn't take it off [the bastardised name of the band on the posters] because it was out of my control, so we carried on working through the dates that were already in the book with these new names. But it was getting impossible because people expected to hear the record [*Excerpt from a Teenage Opera*], so that had to stop. It had to stop right then and there, but it was difficult to work, it really was.'

According to Steve Howe, 'As Keith was having his success, I was closer to him than Twink or Junior. I felt part of the

Teenage Opera record as I played on the B-side and had obviously got Keith involved with writing the lyrics in the first place, as we were mates.

'It was frustrating that while people wanted to book the band, it was more because Keith West was a name; but when we went out, we were Tomorrow really. Then the thing became Keith West *and* Tomorrow, or Tomorrow *featuring* Keith West which we saw as a plus at first, but didn't realise it was going to get so confusing.'

There were, seemingly, many potential benefits to the band for one of their number to become a star. More bookings in new venues and higher fees were immediate benefits, and the band were also trying to think of how to use Keith's overnight fame to their advantage.

'At the time, Mark Wirtz was saying that we were all going do something in his [*Teenage Opera*] project,' says Keith. 'Steve Howe would do something, and Twink was going to do something. I don't know if that was a reality at all, but that got bandied around quite a bit. Obviously, in hindsight, it was never going to fly.'

Twink, too, remembers this particular plan, 'We had a meeting at EMI just before *Excerpt from a Teenage Opera* was due to come out: Mark, Steve, Keith, Junior and myself. It was suggested at the meeting that we should all have a single, which Mark thought was a great idea and lots of bands picked up on this and did this later.

'The plan was that this record, *Teenage Opera*, should be released as Keith, Tomorrow. Steve should have a single as Steve, Tomorrow; Twink, Tomorrow; Junior, Tomorrow – and that was kind of agreed.

'But, as we know, the single came out as Keith West and shot up the charts, and that's when the shenanigans began. All the stuff going on in the background, with music publishers and managers.'

Keith comments, 'I have no recollection of this meeting; it may have been discussed, but this proposal wouldn't have been taken very seriously by EMI's hard-nosed A&R department at the time. Mark was already causing problems by hiding the cost of our ongoing opera project.'

While Twink and Keith don't agree on everything, on this point they are aligned. 'It was a real mess, it really was,' says Keith casting his mind back with a pained expression. 'This thing was selling like crazy, I was a pin-up and getting stacks of fan mail. I was off doing TV and all that. Plus, you had to do it, it's in your contract, you've got to do it – interviews, TV, it was all day long. Then there was the pressure to come up with a follow-up, and all that.

'I thought you could pull off a one-off and just get away with it; I didn't think it was ever going to be a hit, obviously. Everyone told me not to think too much about it as in all probability it would not be a hit, but management was to blame for that. Bryan Morrison should have told me not to do it. He should have told me to forget about it.

'But it was a huge hit. So, from their point of view – from a professional point of view – it was a great decision. It was just sad for me that my voice suited that particular song. I wasn't supposed to sing it. I'd written it, I'd written part of the music and the lyrics, the top line of the song, the hook, and I thought I'd give it to somebody else to do. I was being told somebody else was going to do it.

'And then, I went in and sung the demo, and they all liked the voice on it. So, that was it.

'I was under contract already, and it was just out of my hands really. Again, with the benefit of hindsight, I should have put my foot down and said 'No', but EMI… they didn't care. All they were concerned about was that they'd got a hit on their hands.

'There was no right decision at the end of the day. You're caught in a whirlwind. All of a sudden your record is in the charts and has sold 40,000 copies in a week, and you are being told that you need to follow it up. I mean, what do I do now? Then suddenly you get informed that you're doing this, you're doing that, and you've got a diary full of promotional work.

'I was missing some of the appointments because I was so knackered. I remember that for some interviews with the NME, stuff like that, I used to have to call up and say that I couldn't do it because I've just got back from Holland or wherever. I was doing this, doing that, it was too much. At one point, I just thought, whoa, I need to back off.

'I was still gigging with Tomorrow at this point, as well. But when you do a TV show it's an all-day thing; you're at the studio all day. *Top of the Pops*, you had to be there all bloody afternoon to get up and mime for three minutes. I fell out with *Top of the Pops* once because I was flying in from Holland and they expected me to be at the studio by two o'clock to do a mime at 7pm so I informed them I would be late and they said they wouldn't make an exception for me. I assured them it wouldn't happen again, that it was just a one-off, but their attitude was totally belligerent. Their attitude was simply – do you want to do it or not?

'All the television companies, in my experience they always thought they were doing you a favour; they put you up there, and they get a show for nothing. That was the kind of attitude; they'd be doing you a favour putting you on there, so you better be well-behaved.

'That was the sort of attitude at the time; you daren't let anybody down. To turn up late to a TV recording session or a *Top of the Pops* slot, you'd be finished; you'd be out.

'But it wasn't all bad, obviously. It was tremendously exciting, it was all kicking off – but elastic bands can only stretch so far. Management should have known that if I did the single and it's a hit, then the band's had it. That's what they should have said. I would have then had the attitude that I'm not going to do it.

'Nobody ever sat me down and did that. Of course, hits, success, and money – that's all they care about. It's the music 'business' and you have got to realise that.'

The height of the confusion around where Keith West stopped and Tomorrow started (or vice versa) was reached in October 1967 when the band (billed as Tomorrow *with* Keith West) set out on a ten-date UK package tour, and then headed to Ireland for four shows.

'October '67 was a bloody busy period for us,' says Keith. 'We were part of a package tour with Traffic, Vanilla Fudge and amongst others The Flowerpot Men – seriously! Tony Blackburn was the original host, but he got so much stick on the coach – mostly because of his terrible jokes – that he got upset and dropped out.

'I had just done *Teenage Opera,* so we were promoted as Tomorrow *with* Keith West and we'd close the first half… we were not doing *Excerpt from a Teenage Opera,* though, which caused a massive problem because people expected to hear me do that, which was impossible.

'Vanilla Fudge didn't last long. They left the show after one day, the Finsbury Park date, because they were way too loud. The whole thing wasn't working at all, so we were asked to put a few more numbers in our set which wasn't a problem.

'The whole thing was bloody hard work though. We only did a 40-minute spot, so it was a lot of travelling and then hanging around – day after day – and we'd be writing songs and mucking about in general. I remember Twink played a terrible joke on Steve Winwood of Traffic; we had this chair that was all in bits, and it was like a jigsaw puzzle; you put it together, and as soon as anybody sat on it the whole thing collapsed.

'Twink invited Steve, on the first day of the tour, into our dressing rooms, 'All right Steve, come in, have a smoke,' he said. 'Have a seat' and Steve collapsed on this chair.

'He's such a lovely guy. I mean, he's the wrong person to do it to, really, and he didn't take it too well. But it was all right after that; it was all fine after apologies were sent round, and it did lighten up the tour a bit.

'Steve [Howe] got on well with Dave Mason [the guitar player from Traffic], I remember. Dave's a well-respected musician as well; a very talented guy. He wrote *Hole in My Shoe* and *Feeling Alright* amongst others. We all had a lot of respect for Steve Winwood too; he is a great singer. I saw him at The Marquee when he was about 17 or 18, amazing voice, I mean incredible, and just a great musician all round. He has everything.'

While the teenyboppers who were turning up in England were disappointed not to hear Keith perform his smash hit single, things got worse when the band headed across to Ireland. As Steve Howe recalls, 'When we went to Ireland, it was more confusing as they expected a show around the kind of music that was on *Teenage Opera*. Our reputation as a psychedelic band had not gone that far, and they didn't know who Keith West was, other than the singer of *Teenage Opera*. Tomorrow, as far as they were concerned, was just his backing band.'

With the promoter in Ireland refusing to pay the band unless they performed Keith's big single, they sought advice from Tony Howard. He agreed that things were getting confusing and that they should just play the song in Ireland. Steve Howe remembers once more, 'I felt easier about that than

Twink and Junior, especially as I was part of the *Teenage Opera* story. Sometimes that just helps you empathise with where you find yourself. I had to come up with an arrangement that the band could play and I didn't think too much about it. I just took the chords, summarised the orchestral arrangement, and kept it simple.'

Keith, too, remembers the gigs in Ireland.

'The tour in Ireland was crazy. We went all the way out there, and *Teenage Opera* had just charted, which was a big problem, as they expected us to play that.

'We had to play it as a three-piece. We had to get through it, and it must have sounded god-awful. There was so much screaming going on, you couldn't hear much anyway, but we did it, and we got away with it.

'I said to the other guys in the band that we didn't have to do the shows and we could just walk away if they wanted. But they had a 'fuck it, we'll do it' attitude, so we rehearsed it, and did it, and got away with it… thankfully.'

While the chart and radio success for *Teenage Opera* was still increasing, Tomorrow were gamely trying to move their career forward with the release of their second single: *Revolution*. This was a fact that had not gone unnoticed in the media, and as Nick Jones of the *Melody Maker* reported on September 9th, 'Keith's solo success has thrown the recording plans for his group into turmoil.'

Written following their famous night at the UFO, and the march on the offices of the *News of the World,* the single is another example of innovative production from Mark Wirtz and his episodic approach. It also possesses a strong chorus and a simple, repeated message.

The single, however, was victim to many changes in its scheduling as EMI kept delaying its release so that they, and the record-buying public, could focus on investing in one Keith

West product at a time. As seems to be the norm around all things related to *Teenage Opera,* there was no linear story to ensure the media and the public were kept informed. A report in the *Melody Maker* of the 26th of August reads: 'West's group Tomorrow have now decided to postpone the release of their new single *Revolution*. Producer Mark Wirtz told the MM. '*Revolution* was supposed to be released on September 1 but quite honestly I am not happy with the recording, so we're doing it again. It'll be issued on the 8th or the 15th.''

Twink, too, recalls that *Revolution* was not being given the focus it should have by the group's management or record company as a pivotal release. 'I remember going to a meeting at Bryan Morrison's office one day with Keith, and it was just before *Revolution* was coming out. Keith was called into his office first, and I'm sort of sitting there like a dummy in reception. Then I go in, and Morrison says, 'Well, you've got your single coming out soon, it's going to do really well, we're going to have a big party at the GPO tower.' You know revolving tower, *Revolution,* get it? Which never happened.

'The single was due out in September '67 and kept getting delayed because of *Teenage Opera,* and that should never have happened; they should never have delayed anything.'

As it was, when *Revolution* was finally released on the 22nd of September, it attracted many positive reviews. *Disc and Music Echo* attested to its 'certain mad charm' while *Record Mirror* called it a 'solid beater that should make the fifty'. *Melody Maker,* a constant supporter of the band, were effusive in their praise: 'Tomorrow have made a complex, driving record full of power and feeling, and it should chase Keith's *Opera* success up the chart and into the sunlight for all to dig.'

However, Steve Winwood, reviewing the record as part of a celebrity column for the *Melody Maker,* highlighted what would be the overall view of DJs, and the general public at the time, when he said the song was, 'A bit jumbly – a lot of good ideas that aren't properly connected.' A review which probably earned him a ride on Twink's collapsing chair when the two parties toured together a couple of weeks later.

Keith comments that 'We all weren't very happy with that production; the band arranged that song and threw everything at it embracing the whole song, but I feel Mark let us down. The edits were poor, and although we were making suggestions at the time, nobody seemed to listen, unlike the *My White Bicycle* sessions.'

As history shows, *Revolution* failed to reach the charts, and by this time Keith was being pulled in so many directions that his communication around his plans became totally inconsistent. In one interview, his responsibility to the group is maintained; in another, or even the same, he talks of developing the *Opera* and the labyrinth of ideas which that involved.

At the same time, Bryan Morrison was certainly steering Keith towards a solo career as can be seen from some promotional pictures at the time which show Keith in all sorts of solo pursuits such as horse riding, shooting, and falconry. These pictures, in truth, reveal more about Bryan Morrison's interests and pastimes than Keith's, who was happier watching football or reading a book!

As Keith recalls, 'He loved it, Bryan, having a pop star. All those silly things with falcons and that. They were all his ideas. Horse riding? It was all lies.

'The embarrassing thing was doing *Juke Box Jury* when, on the way back on the plane, one of the panellists said, 'Ooh, I've seen some of your publicity shots. I didn't know you were into riding. Why don't you come over for the weekend? I've got horses in the stables.' I couldn't fucking ride to save my life, so I just said, 'Okay, I'll get back to you on that.''

If Keith's head was being turned, and turned again, by the multitude of offers and possibilities that were being pushed towards him, the loyalty, patience, and friendship of his bandmates was also being tested by forces outside their collective control.

Unbeknown to the band and Keith, Mark Wirtz's *laissez-faire* attitude to the exclusive nature of his publishing contracts was going to have serious ramifications for them all. Mark's problem was, according to him, 'EMI's legal department suddenly discovered that my production contract with the company included a clause, to which I had ignorantly agreed, automatically rendering the publishing rights for all of my compositions to EMI's publishing company for the term of the agreement.

'I was also signed to an exclusive songwriting contract with Robbins Music, and I suddenly found myself in breach of both contracts. A serious publishing dispute erupted, which temporarily halted all my recordings and put *Sam* into suspension, pending a settlement.

'Fortunately, my agreement to give up 50% of all of my royalties to EMI, thereby making up for their lost revenue to Robbins Music, settled the matter sooner than feared.'

Mark's memories of his publishing problems are somewhat glossier than they were in real life. His loose attitude to contractual agreements, and indeed the ownership of material, caused a rift in the Tomorrow camp as – before the band's album was even released – cover versions of their songs started to be played on radio and released as singles by other artists.

Keith provides more details, 'Before Mark was even done recording the songs [for the Tomorrow album], he was doing covers of these songs behind our back. He never told me about Kippington Lodge [who covered *Shy Boy* just before Nick Lowe joined them]. He never told me about Steve Flynn. He never told me anything. I asked him if he had released a record, as a cover version of *Hallucinations* had been released by an artist called Steve Flynn. Mark denied knowing anything about it even though I suspected it was an alias he was using.

'He changed the arrangement around, and I don't know why he wasn't more upfront about it. Maybe he thought I wasn't going to like it or something, but it's a nice little version of the song.

'He had a publishing deal with Ardmore & Beechwood and I think he would do things like this because he owed them so much money. If he put out a song, they'd just grab the royalties, pull back the money that he owed, so he wouldn't see a bean.

'He called himself Philwit, a derivative of 'Mark Philip Wirtz', which was his full name. He also later recorded under the name Philwit and Pegasus. He used it as an alias so he could get royalties. It was very naughty as he signed to Robbins music when he shouldn't have done, because he was already signed to Ardmore & Beechwood, *and* EMI.

'He also used my name and photograph on a German record that I didn't sing or appear on called *Engel Fallen Nicht Vom Himmel*. The B-side is Ken's and my song *Shy Boy*; the songwriting credit shows Hopkins/Burgess/Fleming – although we can only fathom an educated guess as to who Fleming is.'

Even today, when you check the original label on the *Excerpt from a Teenage Opera* single, it says words and music Philwit and Hopkins. Mark Wirtz was hiding his deception in plain sight.

But Keith's memory of being completely oblivious might also be unreliable here as, in an odd quirk of fate, his appearance as the celebrity reviewer for *Melody Maker's Blind Date* column on September 2nd 1967, coincided with the single release of *Mr. Rainbow* [the re-titled *Hallucinations*] by Steve Flynn.

Keith's review of the single reads: 'Oh it's a nice tune isn't it! I seem to remember writing this about a year ago. I think that's right. Actually, the number's from Tomorrow's album, but we took off this track and changed the lyrics about for the single version. We altered the arrangement and did some things with it. We never saw Steve, the singer, again. Hope he has a hit with it. Fab-gear Robbins music! I prefer the group version actually, but the lyrics might be a bit dodgy. It's more commercial than this one though.'

Keith subsequently remarks, 'Yes, that is confusing. I think I was probably asked to go along with it at the time, although I had nothing to do with the recording or arranging obviously, that is all Mark's work. But it's hilarious when I say, 'We never saw the singer again', when it was actually Mr. Wirtz.'

What Keith knew, and what Keith suspected, are somewhat immaterial as what cannot be doubted is the negative effect this leaking of their material had on the remaining band members.

With the band becoming divided into two camps, with Twink and Junior in one, and Steve and Keith in the other, and Keith becoming worn down by his schedule and the continued uncertainty around the future of *Teenage Opera*, he started to debate both privately, and in the media, what his future role with Tomorrow would be.

Keith's personality obviously plays a large part in his decision-making around this time. Keith, by nature, avoids conflict. He is a pacifier, someone who will look to create a solution which is acceptable to all sides. His protestations at the time, particularly in the media, should be viewed with this in mind.

As early as the end of September 1967, the rumours started to leak out. On September 30th, the *NME* ran a story that said: 'Keith West is considering leaving Tomorrow in order to pursue a solo career. He begins a tour with Tomorrow next Wednesday. It is likely he will leave the group as soon as the tour ends, provided a new lead singer can be found. He would continue to act as Tomorrow's record producer.'

On the 21st of October, the same paper carried a story saying: 'Keith West has now decided to remain as lead singer with Tomorrow for the time being, although he will at the same time also follow his solo activities.'

Just two weeks later, on the 4th of November, a story appeared in the *Melody Maker,* with a picture of a smiling Keith surrounded by the Brownie pack choir from *Sam,* which was again different: 'Keith West is to retire from live performances. With the exception of major concerts and TV dates, he intends to concentrate on writing and producing records for his group, Tomorrow, in collaboration with Mark Wirtz. Tomorrow are now looking for a singer to replace Keith on one-nighters.

'Keith will however feature on the group's next single as well as writing and co-producing it. Recorded this week it is *The Incredible Story* [sic] *of Timothy Chase.* A new album *Tomorrow Meets Keith West* will be released before Christmas.'

On the same date, *Disc & Music Echo* ran with a slightly different version of the same story: 'Keith West has left his group Tomorrow and is to retire from all live appearances for an indefinite period, with the exception of radio, TV and major concerts.'

As with all things to do with Keith, Tomorrow, and *Teenage Opera,* it was rumour, counter-rumour, confusion and what these days would be politely termed 'spin', as all the parties jostled for position.

Keith lays the blame squarely at the door of The Bryan Morrison Agency, 'That's where the management failed. They should've advised me not to do the single but to just carry on with what we were doing. They should have been strong enough to advise me if I didn't want to do it, then don't do it.

'Bryan should have backed me up, but he didn't. All he could smell was more money. He was flying off to New York, trying to do deals on the film rights [to *Teenage Opera*] and all this sort of stuff. Obviously, I was paying for it all indirectly.

'At the end of the day, I don't know what he was doing in New York. I mean there was no film rights I ever heard of. He did talk to Disney, apparently, at one point. But it was all getting ludicrous. I said to a film producer I met at the time, 'Am I going mad? Does anybody really want to make a film out of this?' And he said, 'I doubt it. The main character dies in the first song. Where do you go from there?'

'It should have been one hit single; it should have been left at that. I wish it had been. Just a one-off. I did think about changing my name and just going off on a completely different tangent. But it is what it is, and I'm not complaining. I'm not bitter or anything like that.

'People who liked the band accepted it better than I thought, and there's nothing like a hit to raise your profile. I actually hated it for a while, although I can listen to it now.'

Mark Wirtz points the finger at a different culprit. 'In truth, what killed Keith's career, as well as mine in the UK, was EMI's persistent refusal to give the timely go-ahead for the development and complete recording of *Teenage Opera*.

'Had EMI given the green light when it first became a hit, I would indeed have been able to put my full time and concerted effort into the creation of the entire work as originally intended instead of wasting time and money on making all kinds of routine records which collectively cost a lot more and, though enjoyable, yielded very little.

'*Teenage Opera*, in its entirety, would have been ready for release by October 1967, and instead of pushing for a crap-shoot chance of a follow-up hit with the randomly-recorded

Sam release, EMI could have chosen the most suitable follow-up single from an entire collection of tracks.

'Keith, in the meantime, could have freely continued his pursuits with Tomorrow. His presence for *Teenage Opera* work would only have been required for the relatively brief periods of time it would have taken to co-write lyrics with me, and to record his relevant vocal passages.

'Quintessentially, what killed *Teenage Opera* was EMI's blind and stubborn procrastination and political tomfoolery, which ultimately shot us all to shit. Nevertheless, even in its incomplete form and ultimate failure, *Teenage Opera* entered the history books as a bright torch and shining star, having set a precedent and broken down barriers to pave the way for others to succeed where I had failed. Like The Who with *Tommy*, The Moody Blues with *Days Of Future Past*, and, above all, Tim Rice with *Jesus Christ Superstar* [who credited *Teenage Opera* as giving him and Andrew Lloyd Webber the idea to release singles from yet-to-be-completed musicals in order to prove their viability and help with their financing].

'Though flattered [by others referring to him as an innovator], I learned the hard way that being a pioneer carries a costly price, a lesson which prompted me to coin the phrase, 'Never be the first at anything – someone else is bound to take it through the finishing line.''

To escape from it all – and to give him some time to think – Keith, now with some money from the success of *Teenage Opera*, booked a two-week holiday for himself and Steve Howe in Jamaica. Steve Howe remembers that as being 'an outrageous thing to do' and the two of them set out on Tuesday the 5th of December 1967 armed with acoustic guitars and the hope that some winter sun and some local culture (mainly of the smoking kind) would relax them both, inspire some creative freedom, and allow the dust to settle on what had become a heavy scene at home.

Keith remembers being particularly run down at this point and, having had a vitamin shot from a doctor which did nothing, sought the advice of his accountant, Neville Shulman, who recommended a break in Jamaica. A huge fan of the James Bond novel *Dr. No,* Keith did not need much persuading and after fainting at the airport (if any further proof was needed of his wrung out physical condition), he felt the weight of the situation lift off him once on the plane.

What Twink and Junior thought – having been left behind in the cold and dark of London in December – while their bandmates jetted off for two weeks' of tropical luxury can only be imagined, but Keith did not feel too guilty.

'The band had benefitted from my success also,' he says. 'Junior had bought himself a sports car, and I recall walking in on him inadvertently at our hotel in Ireland when he was in bed with a beautiful girl, and they were sharing a bottle of champagne.

'He was enjoying the fruits of my increased profile. I was writing the songs and was conscious of the fact that while improvised live performances, and theatrical interludes in our stage show, were all well and good, record companies simply did not care at all.

'This is an incredibly important point which has been missed in all of the previous coverage about the band. If we were to move beyond being a mere support act, then we had to write and produce hit records. It's as simple as that. The record companies wanted songs which would sell records and get airplay which would bring in money. It's called the music *business* and Steve and I were always conscious of this in a way that Junior and Twink didn't seem to care much about.

'It's the story you hear a thousand times in bands from musicians who don't write songs. It may not be right, but the revenue in the music business was, and still is, always focused towards record sales, royalties, publishing, and copyright ownership. I took my responsibility of putting bread on the table for me and for them seriously. I was the one stuck in my room writing away while they were out partying. That's the Faustian pact you all make.'

14. When you missed your moment

Tanned and relaxed from their Jamaican holiday, Keith and Steve flew back into the UK, which was in full Christmas Party Season swing, on the 19th of December 1967. There wasn't much time for a leisurely re-entry as, on Friday the 22nd, they were to join up with their fellow Tomorrow bandmates and play *Christmas On Earth Continued,* a pre-Xmas all-nighter being held at the Kensington Olympia, in London.

The event brought together, from a musical point of view, one of the most incredible line-ups ever assembled with headliners The Jimi Hendrix Experience to be joined by Eric Burdon and The Animals, The Who,[4] The Move, Pink Floyd, Soft Machine, the Graham Bond Organisation plus… Keith West 'and' Tomorrow.

The relegation of Tomorrow to Keith's backing band, on posters which were plastered all across London (and which are still available to purchase now, given the profile of the event and its place in musical history) must have felt like a smack in the face for the group, especially for Junior and Twink who hadn't just experienced two weeks of 'R&R' courtesy of their putative leader.

It didn't affect their playing and performance on the night though, and any bad feelings were pushed aside, which is a testament to the professionalism of each member. Tomorrow's performance (as mentioned in Chapter 11) that evening was recorded and is available on various bootleg albums. While only of average standard, in terms of sound reproduction, the recording is an energetic and musically innovative example of

[4] The Who did not appear and were replaced by an un-billed Traffic.

their power as a live band including the, as yet unrecorded, version of *Caught in a Web.*

While January 1968 would see Keith once more travelling across Europe on *Teenage Opera* promotion duties, the band would also record *Caught in a Web* at Abbey Road, and at the very end of the month – for a second time – venture into the BBC's Maida Vale studios to record songs for what would be the first-ever John Peel session. The former *Radio London* DJ had literally been forced to jump ship when the government closed down all the pirate radio stations, and he was now part of a revamped BBC offering.

1968 was a 'cold, austere year', according to Steve Howe and when *Tomorrow,* the album by Tomorrow 'featuring' Keith West, was finally released on Friday the 9th of February 1968, it was into a vastly different world than that in which it had been conceived.

Labour Prime Minister Harold Wilson's government was experiencing enormous economic difficulties, which would ultimately lead to a spontaneous awarding of a bank holiday in March to prevent a run on the pound. Coal mines were being closed, and the government was reduced to endorsing such unrealistic initiatives as the *I'm Backing Britain* campaign, which encouraged people to work extra time without pay to help boost the country's competitiveness. It has come to be regarded as an iconic example of a failed attempt to transform British economic prospects.

Despite its now out-of-step counter-culture vibe, the album still picked up many positive reviews upon its release and the band were still viewed as having a bright future by the music journalists with whom they had forged relationships. The media rightly saw the four band members as bright, talented lads who hadn't got above themselves and were still approachable and helpful – unlike a good many of the musicians who they now dealt with.

Among the reviews, the *Record Mirror* from Feb 10th 1968 reads: 'A very imaginative group are Tomorrow. And this LP spotlights a wide variety of songs most of which are contrasting – and they have a varied selection of styles too. They also use reverse tapes, insidious harmonies and good percussion work. Obviously, a lot of work has gone into this – it deserves to sell.'

While the *NME* review, from February 10th 1968, read: 'Do not adjust your record players, this is the way this progressive group plays! Featuring Keith West as lead vocalist, the boys make interesting jangle sounds for this varied set, which includes The Beatles' *Strawberry Fields Forever* plus ten tunes by Hopkins (Keith) on his own, or with co-composers. There are some distorted but fascinating sounds on *Revolution* and *Hallucinations,* which bear out the sleeve notes' contention that this is the sound of Tomorrow. And I like the way Keith, Steve, Twink and Junior are each mentioned four times, each getting top billing once!'

The NME review is one of the only positive mentions of Roger Fennings's sleeve notes (who Keith remembers as being an artist friend of Mark Wirtz) which have been widely derided and pointed to as a reason for the album's commercial failure (although how much sleeve notes can affect the sales of an album is up for debate). There's no doubting that, as sleeve notes go, they are somewhat odd:

Roger Fennings' notes read:

Today's today,

Today's OK

But then there's Tomorrow (Keith, Steve, Twink, Junior)

and that's something else

Here now, today tonight

In the wide-eyed listening dark
hear and feel
feel and dig
now, today, the sound of Tomorrow (Junior, Keith, Steve, Twink)
Here are four as one, with but the sound of the future
(Tomorrow) (Twink, Junior, Keith, Steve)
to offer
Yesterday (the past) is known was seen, was heard, was loved
Is dead
But the sun of today is yet still warm
and excites
and creates
and conceives
new lives, new things, new days
and one of these is Tomorrow (Steve, Twink, Junior, Keith)

Driving, changing, moving, building, sometimes gentle,
sometimes fierce, always creating, never still.
This is Tomorrow.

Hippy-dippy sleeve notes aside, the *Melody Maker* review of February 24th 1968 points to the record's major weakness, it's belated release, while at the same time praising it highly. The full review reads: 'Somehow *My White Bicycle*, the opening track, completely sums up the long, dead days of the hippy summer of 67. It brings back a whiff of burning incense, the jingling of bells and the sounds of the UFO, the Saville Theatre, Primrose Hill, Chalk Farm and various scenes around

Marylebone, Earl's Court and Paddington. The madness may have faded but the music lingers on, and these Keith West compositions have a charm of their own. Songs like *Shy Boy* should have been hits. Well-produced and performed and above average material.'

Flashback magazine in 2012 highlighted the 'elegiac' tone of the *Melody Maker* review, and a damp fog of sadness permeates the band members' language when they recall the record [which despite its chart failure at the time is now considered a classic of its time and has sold solidly for more than 50 years].

Steve Howe said of it, 'We couldn't really get there in the studio. We couldn't transcend the white coat atmosphere.

'I wish we'd been encouraged to be ourselves more in the studio, but we didn't quite know how to play without an audience responding to us. Mark tried very hard to get on our page, but his work beyond Tomorrow was very poppy, almost cheesy, and he wasn't really a band producer, more of an orchestrator and arranger. I think if he'd simply said, 'Just jam guys; we'll edit it later' – it might have benefitted us.'

Twink also recalls the deflation at a time when the group should have been at its most dynamic, 'We were starting to feel really, really let down, and then of course the album; myself and Junior weren't involved in any of the mixing.

'We weren't involved in the album sleeve design, and we had ideas for the album sleeve, and the first time we played the album we said, 'That's terrible.' Because it could have been better.

'The mix could have been better with our input. I think I'd have given the tracks a little bit more of a psychedelic touch to them. And, of course, the sleeve was horrible. The sleeve notes were horrible. So, when the album came out, we just said, 'Well, that's it.''

Keith adds to Twink's point, saying, 'None of us were actually involved in the mixing, we didn't have a say in any of the recordings, as there was just a limited time to perform, especially my vocal parts. I always seemed to be in a rush! At one point, I do remember helping Geoff with a mix as Mark was out of town, but it was an isolated incident.'

'Keith and Mark had a falling out around about the same time as well,' remembers Twink. 'I moved in with Mark Wirtz. It was just before I joined The Pretty Things, so that would have been about March, April 1968. There was no communication with Keith at all at that time.

'Anyway, Junior and myself, we started to plan another band, and we decided to call the band, The Aquarian Age. We wrote a great song, which Mark Wirtz produced, called *10,000 Words in a Cardboard Box* which was about Keith [who famously squirrelled lyrics and song ideas away in various receptacles]. Junior came up with the title and the core sequence, and I finished off the lyrics.'

According to Steve Howe, when looking back on this period, at which point he and Keith were living in a house together in Muswell Hill, 'The group dissipated rather than suddenly and spectacularly falling apart. Junior and Twink released their record [May 1968], but the opportunities didn't come for them, nor did they come for Keith really because – although *Sam* was a lavish production – EMI turned off the tap and I dawdled on and got some sessions.'

Keith, as we know is his nature, was still trying to placate all parties across this entire period, and trying to come up with solutions to their mutual predicament. But not all his good intentions were so well-received; he failed to gauge the depth of feelings which Twink and Junior had.

As Twink recalls, 'We went up to a meeting at Keith and Steve's house, and Keith had obviously done the deal with EMI because he'd started to produce his own records by that time.

He suggested to us that he was leaving the band and we could carry on as a three-piece with him continuing to write our songs and produce us. Junior said, 'That's not going to work for me' and they got into a bit of a heated argument.

'I remember that night we told Steve about the song that we were recording with Mark, but he never actually played on the single. We had some great songs, really good songs. We did some demos with Mark Wirtz, of other songs, but they have all been lost. I don't know where they are.

'We had a lot of theatrical ideas for the live show too. Also, Junior did most of the early writing for a stage play, which was called *Good Wizzard Meets Naughty Wizzard,* which he wrote because we did an ad-lib thing [with the same title] on the B-side of *10,000 Words in a Cardboard Box*.

'He started to write this stage play, as a follow-on idea, and it was great. We started rehearsing with friends of ours. I was a good wizard. Obviously, Junior was a naughty wizard. We had gremlins involved in the play. Mr. Badger. It was fantastic. And we incorporated what existed at the time of the *Teenage Opera* songs into the play excluding *Excerpt from a Teenage Opera*. It was taking shape; we had great friends taking the different parts. It was fun.

'But then, one day, myself and Junior went up to the Bryan Morrison Agency, our booking agent at the time, to tell Tony Howard and Steve O'Rourke where we were at and what we were doing with a view to them getting us some bookings.

'Anyway, Dick Taylor – of The Pretty Things – was there. He was looking all flustered and he told me that their drummer, Skip, had left the band and they were facing some problems as they needed to fulfil several bookings in Rome, and would I be prepared to stand in? It was no problem, so I went to Rome that week after a couple of days rehearsing and it went well.

'I only planned, because of my commitment to The Aquarian Age, to stay with The Pretty Things for a month, but I ended up staying for a year and a half because they had a lot of work on. They had a film to do, they were recording *S.F. Sorrow* and I got involved and played on that. Junior was twiddling his thumbs; he joined The Jeff Beck Group for a short while, but then he had a big argument with Mickie Most and left.

'Junior just gave up on me because I got so involved with The Pretty Things and I can understand that. I don't regret anything in my life, but if I did have a regret, that would be the one regret, not carrying on with Junior and The Aquarian Age. In fact, I have just finished writing a song called *Sammy Sunshine*, that's what Sheila Cohen from *Granny Takes A Trip* used to call Junior, 'Sammy Sunshine', so I wanted to dedicate it to him.'

Just prior to the release of the album, with the group in turmoil, Tomorrow and Keith also decided to leave the Bryan Morrison Agency. In his book *Have a Cigar,* Bryan Morrison recalls the meeting between him and Keith taking place at a restaurant in Soho Square known as the Romeo & Juliette Café and that Keith fired him because *Excerpt from a Teenage Opera* did not make #1 in the UK charts.

As with many of the colourful agency head's stories, the truth does not paint him in such a kindly light. Keith reveals the less emotional reasons behind his departure from the agency, 'Bryan Morrison only appeared, and announced himself as my manager, when my record charted. I didn't get on with him at all, and I was stuck with him for months. We just didn't hit it off.

'There were financial problems as well. My accountant at the time said, 'You've got to get rid of this guy, he's a nightmare.' I paid him off, basically. God knows what it cost, I've got no idea, but it cost me big time. I paid him off because

Robert Stigwood called me up and said he wanted to take over the management.

'But, he didn't want the group. He didn't want the band at all; he did not want anything to do with the band. I still don't understand it. He saw it as a solo act and wanted to produce it, and they [the Robert Stigwood Organisation] would have been offering me songs to cover and stuff like that, but I didn't want to do that.

'I might have been a fool, and other artists might have jumped at it. To do covers, have hits, but I just didn't want to do it. I didn't really want to be a solo artist; I wanted to be in a band. It was a really difficult thing to be faced with.

'He [Robert Stigwood] offered me £12,500 to sign with him [more than £200,000 in today's money] and Neville Shulman, who was one of London's top accountants with many clients including Twiggy, told me I should take it as it was a lot of money. You could buy a house for that in those days.

'I turned it down. I just wasn't interested. He had the Bee Gees and Cream and all types of other stuff going on. There wouldn't be room for me there, I didn't think. I used to go up to his house for parties and stuff and hang around, and I can remember being around there once, and we were larking around and Eric Clapton was up there, so was Maurice Gibb – a mate of mine at the time – and Lulu was there too.

'Suddenly we hear a 'Toot, toot, toot', and we all looked out of the window and Barry Gibb and his wife, who was a nightmare – she used to boss him around something terrible – turned up in a Rolls-Royce. It was a horrible sort of candy red colour, and I can remember Eric saying, 'For fuck's sake.' He used to call Barry Vera Lynn. 'Here comes Vera.' He took the piss out of him constantly.'

While not exactly in the manner of Bryan Morrison's retelling, there's no denying that Keith did unceremoniously fire Bryan Morrison, and even Bryan's most ardent supporters admit that the management job he did with Tomorrow and Keith was pathetic.

Gita Renik, who worked for the Bryan Morrison Agency at the time, and who remains a big defender of his reputation admits, 'Tomorrow for me were like The Spice Girls of the 60s, and I could have done a better job of promoting them than Bryan did.

'They were naturally set up to be perfectly packaged. Junior was Baby Spice, he was like a young James Coburn and always looked funny and cute with his little sandals. Twink was Scary Spice with his cravat and his enormous hair. He was full of fun and when he walked into a room, it was like 'King Kong' had arrived. Steve Howe would be 'Sporty', he had an angular strong face and was electrifying to watch, and Keith would have been Posh Spice, as he always looked brilliant, was smart, good-looking, nicely spoken and polite.'

Ultimate (and ever-lasting) revenge would be had on Bryan Morrison, however, through lyrics to the song *The Incredible Journey of Timothy Chase* which Keith had written for the *Tomorrow* album. The central character in the song is labelled 'a fool' whose ideas are worthless 'The things you plant they just don't seem to grow/ The ground you tread it just screams out 'Oh no'. As cynical kiss-offs go, it's one of the best examples. The lyrics read:

Think your clever image outer

Makes you any better inner, fool

They never really see right through you

That's because they just don't know you

And you just laugh and say 'thank you'

I think I'll take a voyage real soon

Wipe that smile off your make up
With another piece of paper
You don't need to own a thing
Why don't you just pull a string
Everyone's doing tricks but you don't know
When tomorrow comes you'll see a different show

Can't you see we're there in the front row

I believe dawn is light
Wrap it up tight
I mean the contradiction guiding light
Kiss the flame, that changed your name

Been a laughing meter lately
Mask off you're just imitating now
Creeping, crawling, going very slow
The things you plant they just don't seem to grow
The ground you tread it just screams out "Oh no"

The simple just becomes absurd
I don't know a single word to describe
Looking from a thoroughly different view
You could almost fit there too
But the man's not in who has the clues

It's just us and we're here too

Looking back slowly now

Don't know why

You didn't take the truth as just a lie

What you fear, we're still here

Despite the Peel Session, the new recording at Abbey Road and what would turn out to be the band's final gig on Saturday the 3rd of February 1968 at Middle Earth on Kings Street, Covent Garden (billed oddly as 'The' Tomorrow 'plus' Keith West and supported by Tintagel and The Spice), the band was sadly in its final throes. The album *Tomorrow* received next to nothing by way of marketing support from EMI (Keith remembers a meeting with Ken East, managing director of EMI, to discuss promotion during which the executive spent the whole time avidly watching cricket on a small black and white television in the corner of his office) and the only appearance by the band to promote the record was on *Discs A Go Go,* a regional TV show for Wales and The West.

The band at this point was firmly divided into two camps, as Keith recalls, 'They brought it upon themselves Twink and Junior. Both Steve and I were getting fed up with their antics, mucking about, charging about on stage in the middle of songs, just doing their own thing. I was like 'What the fuck's going on here? You know?'

'They would just start doing crazy stuff, and it wasn't working for me and Steve, it really wasn't. EMI, the management, even Robert Stigwood all spelled it out to me, that we were in danger of losing our record deal and we needed to focus on the songs in the live set more.

'We needed hits to carry on, or we'd just be a supporting act forever. Plus our act was feeling dated… extended miming with no meaning attached to it. Things were changing fast and the hippies had all but gone. Their advice was to lose the band and go solo!'

Speaking about where he saw responsibility for the group's break-up, Steve Howe says, 'I wouldn't put all of the blame on Keith and his success. There was a demise in interest also. Promoters were looking for new things and there were new things. At this point, Tomorrow were definitely on the back burner, but I didn't care as I thought Keith and I were going somewhere or would go somewhere after Tomorrow.'

A rarely heard voice, unfortunately, due to his death in 2016 and his disappearance from the music scene between 1968 and 2012 (when, with some brilliant detective work, *Flashback* magazine managed to extricate an interview from him), John 'Junior' Wood provides a clear-eyed appraisal of the band and the sad way their career ended (of which all the band members express regret).

Junior said, 'There was never an official last gig – we just reached a point where none of us had the enthusiasm to keep going. We drifted apart like marriages can.

'We could have gone a lot further, but we missed our opportunity. I think we could have been bigger, but we had the wrong management – it was a much harder life for touring musicians then than now, and we didn't have access to good advice in the way young bands have today.

'Once Keith had his hit, there was no way back. The whole *Teenage Opera* thing was a fiasco and turned us upside down.

'By the end, the enthusiasm had gone – and we certainly didn't want to keep playing *Excerpt from a Teenage Opera!* We were much better live than our records will ever be, and it's a shame the true character of the band, at its peak, never got out to more people.'

There was to be one final hurrah for the band when they appeared, minus Keith, as Tomorrow '67 at a one-off show at The Roundhouse as part of the *Christmas Spaced* event held in December 1970. Twink remembers, 'That was amazing. My heart still belonged to Tomorrow, even though I was doing other things, because we were a great band. We deserved better. That particular event, I organised with Nik Turner from Hawkwind.

'We had the underground press helping us, but I put the bill together. I said to Steve and Junior, would they like to do Tomorrow's '67 – a flashback kind of thing. Steve did all the lead vocals, and we put on a great show although Keith wasn't invited for obvious reasons.'

Through all the twists and turns, the highs of the UFO and the lows of the *Teenage Opera* confusion, how does musical history judge Tomorrow? It's a difficult question to answer due to the band's sparse output – but its influence as a live act that incorporated theatrical techniques and dance, its sonic innovation in the studio, and in the innovative structures and the strength of its songs must all be considered.

One school of thought, led on this occasion by Anthony Rufus Isaacs – their first manager – is that, 'In a different universe, Tomorrow would have been another Pink Floyd.' Others, such as Gita Renik, generally agree they had all the components needed to have been a greater commercial success than they were.

Others, Mark Wirtz among them, disagree, saying, 'Keith laments to this day that *T.O.* ruined his and Tomorrow's career. As much as I understand and empathise with Keith's reasoning, I don't agree.

'No matter how popular and creative Tomorrow were in their heyday, the band was ultimately bound to disintegrate. Their scope as a band was simply too narrow and limited to ultimately hold on to the talent of Steve Howe, who sooner or later would have been compelled to break away in order to find alternative vehicles which better suited his brilliance, and which offered him the freedom to express it.

'And, with all due respect to Keith and the other two band members, Twink and Junior, without Steve, there simply was no Tomorrow.'

Maddeningly, while discussing such variables is entertaining, opinions of this nature serve no purpose as they cannot be proved or disproved. What is certain, to the credit of all involved, is that half a century later, people across the world are still discovering the music of Tomorrow (and of Keith and Mark Wirtz) and getting turned-on to a hugely influential period of which they were all central participants.

15. Going solo

In March 1968, with his band not officially deceased but now – to all intents and purposes – a solo singer-songwriter, Keith found that his singular adventures would get off to an impressive start when he was nominated for an Ivor Novello award and invited to the ceremony on Tuesday the 26th of March at Grosvenor House on Park Lane.[5]

'I got a phone call from Tony Howard saying that I couldn't tell anyone, but that I had won an Ivor Novello Award. I was really quite surprised as I'd never really thought about winning any awards in the songwriting world.

'I turned up, collected the award, and the first person who came over and congratulated me was Tony Hatch, Petula Clark's main writer, the man responsible for such hits as *Downtown, Don't sleep in the Subway,* and many more. Later on, he also wrote the theme tunes for *Emmerdale Farm* and *Neighbours*. He's a famous and well-respected writer, who by a strange coincidence also has a property on the island of Menorca where I have spent a lot of time over the last 50-odd years. I used to bump into him at the island's tiny airport now and again, but never took up his invitation to visit, which I do regret now.

'I was nominated for the Best Novelty Song award, and The Beatles won one as well for *She's Leaving Home,* but they weren't there on the night as they were away touring or something.

[5] Named after the entertainer Ivor Novello, the eponymous awards are for songwriting and composing, and have been presented annually in London by The Ivors Academy since 1956.

'Tony was the first one to come over and congratulate me, telling me how much he loved it and all that sort of stuff. Because it was so different [*Excerpt from a Teenage Opera*], they made a special category for it. It was a bit last-minute, almost as if they had to acknowledge it – 'Oh, we've got to put that in' – and everybody was saying nice things about it. So we went and picked it up and gave a little speech.

'Of all the awards, it's the one I'm most proud of,' says Keith. 'It's like the Oscars for music and presented by the Songwriters Guild of Great Britain, so it's from other songwriters, and it's all big songs from that year. You get a certificate, a bronze statue. I gave it all to my mum at the time, but following her passing I now have it.'

With nothing concrete, but a loose plan to work with Steve, EMI decided to see if lightning could strike twice and gave the two some studio time to see what they could come up with. For many, fans and critics alike, what they would produce would match anything they had done previously in terms of pure pop music sensibility.

Keith takes up the story, 'EMI let us go into the studio and fool around for a couple of days, and I came up with *On a Saturday*, which I had written at our Muswell Hill flat. We did a couple of other tracks as well, one of which was *The Kid Was a Killer* which is based on a book by Caryl Chessman, who was executed for murder in the USA and is a true story.'

Although EMI signed Keith to a recording contract for *On a Saturday*, and released it as a 7" single, there are multiple reasons why – behind the scenes – they didn't put their full weight into promoting it, despite it being a truly great pop record which DJs continue to play to this day. Former *Radio 1* Breakfast DJ Mike Read spontaneously sang the song down the phone when asked about it in an interview, and Ken Bruce regularly spins it on his *Radio 2* programme.

'It's a lovely song,' acknowledges Keith, 'but things were tense between myself and Mark and also between EMI and Mark [who would soon leave EMI to pursue an independent career]. I'd refused to do any more *Teenage Opera* tracks after *Sam*. He played me a couple of ideas, but I told him they weren't really right for me and things got a bit tetchy. I didn't want to fall out with Mark, but nor did I want to be involved with his type of music anymore. I was moving in a different direction.

'With Steve's help, I'd bought a really nice little Martin acoustic guitar – model 00018 – and the main reason I chose this instrument was because the serial number was dated from 1944, the year I was born. Paul Simon played one of these guitars on *Mrs Robinson* and I loved the sound of it, it's still my favourite guitar today.

'Steve and I were hanging out, and he was showing me a few bits and bobs on the guitar. I have to say he was a great teacher, plus his guitar technique and knowledge was off the scale as far I was concerned. He had to keep it very simple which – thank the Lord – he did.

'Anyway, I found a couple of chords that I liked, A minor 7th, I think it was. I got hooked on that and a diminished chord as well, which I liked. I worked on the basic structure, intro, verse, chorus – classic stuff for writers – and for some reason, probably Steve's influence, I fancied using a double bass on the song and made a demo of it.

'I played the demo to Mark, and he thought it was nice and asked me what I wanted to do with it. I told him I wanted to bring in Aynsley Dunbar on drums, who I had already met with and struck an agreement with, and he was dead against the idea. He thought Aynsley was just a blues drummer, but I was adamant because he can play anything; he's fucking brilliant.'

Aynsley Dunbar was a well-respected drummer who, having been through The Jeff Beck Group, had formed his own band – The Aynsley Dunbar Retaliation – which issued four albums. He would go on to have a long and successful career drumming with the likes of Frank Zappa as well as Nils Lofgren, Journey, Jefferson Starship, and Whitesnake.

'And I wanted a double bass on it,' continues Keith. 'I didn't want a normal bass. Steve was going to do all the guitars, and I thought perhaps Mark could add a bit of piano or something? And that was what we did. He didn't suggest putting anything bigger on it, like strings, or to boost it up, or anything like that. It was a very basic recording, just one or two takes.

'He didn't really put his heart and soul into it; it was pretty basic. I think everybody expected the strings and a big arrangement, all that kind of stuff. Although to be fair to Mark, I wanted to get away from that, to a certain extent.'

Mark's production skills were not even required on the B-side, *The Kid Was a Killer,* which Keith produced himself. 'Yeah, that song wasn't Mark's thing at all. He thought it was influenced, to a degree, by Bob Dylan, a comparison which to be frank I was flattered by.

'Bob Dylan changed everything as far as song lyrics go and as a songwriter, if you weren't influenced by Dylan, you should hang your head in shame.

'I co-produced *On a Saturday,* really, to be honest. Mark wasn't around much. He played a bit of keyboard on it and mixed it. But, *The Kid was a Killer,* that was just me, Steve and Aynsley.

'Listening back to it, you can see the two sides of my character there on that record. One trying to produce another hit and get back in the charts, and then the B-side is completely dark and something a lot of people would have hated. It was a bit of an 'Up Yours' to EMI.'

Which perhaps explains their reluctance to promote it…

Despite receiving some decent airplay, *On a Saturday* was not a hit and Keith was losing a little heart, and his confidence, at this point.

'Obviously, I was a bit disappointed with *On a Saturday.* I thought it could have done a lot better. I thought I could build something up. I went back; I evaluated what I was going to do, and where I was going to go. I thought that I couldn't start another band; it's not going to happen. This *Teenage Opera* thing is always going to come back to haunt me. I really didn't know what to do.'

As far as others were concerned, there was a simple answer to the question of why *On a Saturday* did not catch fire as hoped. Twink says, 'Keith is a great songwriter, and he really does come up with some good ideas. But he lost his producer. The single *On a Saturday* was so totally under-produced. But it's a great song. I love it. I used to play it all the time when it first came out.'

Keith's fragile state of mind is reflected in an interview he gave to *Record Collector* journalist Andy Davis in 1995. The article says of the songs that: 'Although commercially unsuccessful, the single's B-side particularly is a highly regarded postscript to Tomorrow, fashioned from the same distorted rhythms and trebly guitar work which had become the group's trademark. But, with the demise of Tomorrow, Keith's confidence had taken a beating, 'I didn't know if these songs were commercial or even if they were any good. *On A Saturday* didn't have a big enough sound [Backing up Twink's theory even if Mark Wirtz was the producer in name]. Mark Wirtz wasn't interested in it, and we only spent the usual couple of hours in the studio.''

Keith admits to feeling a little 'lost' at the time.

'I went back home for a while, a month or so, I hadn't seen my parents for quite a while. I'd been going through all of this and I'd forgotten all about them, basically. I went back for a bit of advice, also from my brother-in-law Barry Gough, who was married to my sister Anne and was a successful businessman; he was a great guy and gave me a lot of advice in those days. I stayed with them for about a month before I moved back to London again.'

Reinvigorated by a trip back to his see his family, Keith called on some friendly faces – who had all cut their teeth on the music scene through the R&B boom – to help him re-discover his mojo. Forming, in November 1968, what might be considered rock and roll's first 'Supergroup', Keith once more pulled together Steve Howe and Aynsley Dunbar but added Ronnie Wood, who was becoming increasingly disenchanted with life in The Jeff Beck Group, and Nicky Hopkins, the pianist/ organist who was also in The Jeff Beck Group. Nicky would be one of only a handful of rock musicians to contribute to a Beatles song (*Revolution*), and his list of sessions is a veritable 'rock's greatest hits', from the Rolling Stones to The Kinks to The Who, and beyond.

Ronnie would obviously go on to achieve rock and roll immortality in The Faces and the Rolling Stones, but he and Keith were close friends at this point and hung around together often. Keith recalls one famous occasion when, 'We were in Ronnie's parents' council house, and he was stripping his Fender Precision bass to get the paint off it, which was quite trendy in those days [sadly it devalued the guitar by a huge amount]. And then the phone went, Ronnie was like 'It's Rod [Stewart]. He says he's coming down the pub and he's got one of his girlfriends in tow.' I was OK with that, and we went down the pub.

'His girlfriend happened to be an ex-girlfriend of mine, a typical leggy blonde, which he didn't like at all. It didn't go down too well, to put it mildly, and Rod left pretty quickly after

that. As soon as we were introduced, I said, 'Oh hi there, darling, how are you doing?' Rod said, 'Do you two know each other?'

'I didn't say she was my ex-girlfriend, but it was a bit awkward. Ronnie then said to me, 'He's going to be off in a huff now.' He was so jealous, such a jealous guy.'

As Keith says of Ronnie, 'You'd always want a guy like Ronnie Wood in your band. He was just a great guy to have around. He, like some other musicians I've had the pleasure of working with, has a knack of giving 100% to a new song, adding ideas on guitar, getting the feel just right, and generally spreading enthusiasm that spills out to the whole band.

'He's also a talented artist. I remember when we were hanging out together, he was always sketching, and he showed me some of his work one day; beautiful drawings of horses, which other artists have told me are notoriously difficult to draw. He also can play anything with strings on!'

The 'Supergroup' recorded two tracks, both of which remained unreleased until 1995. Firstly, *The Visit,* which begins with a crashing drum intro from Aynsley Dunbar and, according to *Record Collector,* '...links the sound of Tomorrow with a new, transatlantic sensibility, blending those twitchy guitar patterns with a sparse, mellow production and country-tinged harmonies.'

It doesn't take too much imagination on the part of the listener to hear the loose style which would soon see The Faces achieve enormous success (particularly in the USA) in *The Visit* and, as ever, Keith had his finger if not directly on, then certainly around, the pulse of where things were moving musically.

She is an altogether different beast, though, and betrays Keith's love of Anthony Newley. It's a number that wouldn't be out of place in a West End musical. It's an example of

elegantly arranged British pop, and Keith both wrote the arrangement for the string quartet and produced the song himself. But, sadly, EMI didn't see an outlet for the songs, and they languished in the vaults for nearly 30 years.

As for the 'Supergroup', as we know, Aynsley Dunbar and Ronnie Wood would soon be gainfully employed in other projects and as Keith summarises, 'Nobody was too excited about taking it forward. We just left it, basically, and I wandered off.'

Steve Howe too, in his pointedly pithy way, remembers, 'We did those fascinating sessions with Aynsley and Ronnie, and I drifted along with Keith to see if it would go... but it didn't go.

'*On a Saturday* was a lovely song and with the other guys coming in, I thought 'we have an opportunity here'. Keith was a writer, I was a guitarist, and we could have ploughed away but didn't get the breaks we needed soon enough.'

While more material like *The Visit* could have led to a longer life for the 'Supergroup', it's revealing that Keith's material was so wildly different at this stage – with genres changing completely from song to song. While *On a Saturday* was an (albeit brilliant) straight pop song, *The Kid Was a Killer* was alternative in both its subject matter and delivery. As for *The Visit*, as much as it can be seen as a forerunner for the material with which the likes of Buffalo Springfield and Crosby, Stills and Nash would achieve global mega-stardom, *She* must have been a confusing step back towards *Teenage Opera* for all involved.

As Keith's *annus horribilis* of 1968 came to an end, perhaps it was time for a break for all concerned? What could be better than that most English of 'cure-alls'... a refreshing trip to the seaside!

16. Write me a song for Elvis

'Write me a song for Elvis' was Freddy Bienstock's parting words to Keith as he set off for a holiday to visit his sister Anne in Spain at the end of 1968. Shrewdly, Keith was taking the opportunity to escape the cold of the English winter to spend some time with her and her husband, Barry, at their home on the island of Menorca.

Freddy Bienstock was the legendary owner of Carlin Music, and his Elvis comment was no throwaway gag. His impressive claim to fame was that, for the first 12 years of his career, Elvis wouldn't look at a song unless Freddy had seen it already. Bienstock was responsible for pairing the King with such material as *Jailhouse Rock* and *Heartbreak Hotel* – the very song that had originally turned Keith on to rock and roll.

Keith would run into Freddy often, as he regularly visited Malcolm Forrester, his publisher, who was now acting as General Manager for Carlin Music (which was, in turn, administering his company – Getaway Music – the publishing company for many of Keith's songs).

'That's why I wrote *The Power and the Glory,*' says Keith recalling the time. 'Because Freddy said he could get me a cover with Elvis – although he probably said it to everyone, to be honest.

'I thought that song was going to do really well, when I'd written it. I thought, hang on a minute, that's special.

'Contrary to popular belief, Ken [Burgess] didn't write any of it; he didn't have anything to do with writing it. I wrote it on holiday. But in those days, we gave everything off as being by Hopkins/Burgess.

'Yeah, I thought this [song] was going to be a hit. There was a big argument going on, because when people started sniffing around the song, I said to Malcolm that Ken hadn't written any of it and I didn't want to throw away 25% of my share. Ken got a bit iffy, but that's the sort of thing that can happen in the business. Maybe I was out of order; I don't know.

'Nothing happened anyway, but they were talking about all these people who were going to cover it... and Malcolm's going to do this and that with it. Elvis did a demo of it, apparently, which I would have loved to have heard obviously, but it never saw the light of day. It was a real opportunity though as Clive Westlake, who was at Carlin Music as well as a songwriter, used to get the odd Elvis cover such as *It's a Matter of Time* and *Twenty Days & Twenty Nights.*

'So, I wrote it for Elvis, whilst on holiday. There's a Graham Greene novel called *The Power and The Glory*. That's where I got the title from. I took a lot of books with me. I was big on Graham Greene at the time. I'm a bit of an all or nothing guy. If I like one book, I'll go and buy the whole set. *The Quiet American*, I read that and *The Honorary Consul* too. They're all great books. I thought, what a great title, *The Power and The Glory*. Wow, that's Elvis, you know? That's a big song, with big themes – as he's religious and all that kind of stuff.

'But looking at what it's earned, that song, in royalties... it's nothing. It's a terrible waste, really. I thought somebody would have promoted it more or got somebody bigger to do it.'

While the thought of an Elvis demo version of *The Power and The Glory* languishing somewhere deep in the vaults of Graceland is a tantalising prospect, the song did attract the attention of other artists. The Fortunes released a version of the song in 1972 but only in France, and the well-known English pop act Pickettywitch again covered the song in 1973, but it generated little by way of airplay or record sales.

The song would, however, act as a segue into another fascinating chapter in Keith's career, as he says, 'I wrote some lyrics down, wrote down some basic chords, and brought it back to London and played it to Malcolm Forrester who was bowled over by it; he thought it sounded like a big song and likened it to *Bridge Over Troubled Water.*

'Malcolm asked me how I felt about working with Andrew Oldham as he was not doing too much at that moment. He suggested myself and Ken go down to the West Country and do some more stuff, come back, and we'd work something out. And that's what we did.'

Malcolm Forrester would continually be a positive presence in Keith's career (as was seen earlier, when he introduced Keith to Roy Pitt), and was at this time something of a 'big fish' in the music publishing world. He came up through the ranks at Essex Music, where he was responsible for signing the first songs by the fledgling Rolling Stones, and headed Gunnel's Music which he acquired and re-named Getaway Music when the Georgie Fame song of the same name became an enormous hit.

At this time, Malcolm was ferociously busy. As well as being GM at Carlin Music, he was also heading up the publishing side of Immediate Records, the record company owned by Tony Calder and Andrew Loog Oldham which was famous for such acts as The Small Faces, Fleetwood Mac, and Rod Stewart, as well as being the UK publisher for The Beach Boys (allegedly, Malcolm once paid a courtesy visit to Brian Wilson who did not emerge from his sandpit for the entire meeting).

Tony Calder and Andrew Loog Oldham's rock and roll pedigree is also the stuff of legend as Calder worked with Brian Epstein as a press agent for The Beatles, and Loog Oldham produced some of the first Rolling Stones records and handled their day to day management. Keith was certainly still keeping some well-connected music industry company.

With the offer of Malcolm's Bentley S1 as transport, Keith – along with his writing partner Ken Burgess – departed for the tiny village of Marshwood in West Dorset to write some more songs. Keith takes up the story, 'We went down to the West

Country and wrote another bunch of songs. We wrote *West Country,* which is one of my favourite songs, and a bunch of other stuff and brought them back to Malcolm in London. We'd both got into the piano a bit as well, so it changed our writing perspective slightly, which was good. I sat down at the piano, and Ken at the guitar, and we just hashed out this stuff.

'We were literally in the middle of nowhere, in a place called Marshwood, which I wrote an instrumental about. There was one local pub in the village, and when these two long-haired guys walked in one afternoon – for a drink – all the locals just stopped and stared at us. Literally, the door opened and they all just stared at us.

'Luckily, one of the guys behind the bar was quite young, and he did a bit of journalism on the side. He asked me what we were doing down there, and I told him we were songwriters and who I was. He got very excited and organised a local TV crew to come down and film us down there. It was great publicity for everyone.

'Because of that, we started to entertain them with a few songs. They loved *West Country,* obviously. We got invited, too, on a few days out and they looked after us. They cooked for us, great big pub lunches I remember, during the three or so weeks we were down there.'

With their idyllic sojourn in Dorset over, and having returned to London, Keith and Ken played their new songs for Malcolm and Andrew Loog Oldham who, according to Keith, 'Loved it; I mean he actually loved it. He wanted to record three or four of the songs and signed us to Immediate [Records].

'He booked Olympic Studios in Barnes, which was his preferred studio, with Alan O'Duffy as the engineer. Andrew knew him as he'd worked with him there with the Stones, and he obviously knew my kind of stuff. And off we went.

'Oddly enough, when we were in the studio recording with him and Andrew, Thin Lizzy were downstairs recording and Andrew was mates with one of them. Oh God, they were tough! They were doing cocaine, drinking; it was all going on. They came up to wreck one of our sessions completely one afternoon. They came up, and we all got out of it... it was a different world.

'We did a song called *A Little Understanding*, which I had in mind for Joe Cocker. *The Power and The Glory* got bigger and bigger and bigger as the days went by. It started off as a simple sort of ballad and then spilled out, got built out.

'There was a choir... I came in one day, and Alan O'Duffy said, 'Fucking hell, you want to listen to what he's [Andrew] done to your song. He said he's gone a bit too far, I think.' He really did, but it seemed to work.'

Writing in *Record Collector* magazine in 1995 about these sessions, Andy Davis wrote, 'All that remains from the sessions are three acetate demos. The first *A Little Understanding* boasts an uncluttered, sophisticated sound, while retaining Keith's gift for melody. With its layered horns and overdubbed harmonies, *The Power and The Glory* is a production big enough to have whetted Phil Spector's appetite. *West Country* meanwhile is a meditative paean to the rural idyll, with CSN flavoured harmonies and even a hint of that trio's partner, Neil Young.'

There would even be an entente cordiale of sorts during the recordings in Barnes when Keith pulled Twink in to play drums on *The Power and The Glory*.

'Andrew liked working with crazy people,' Keith reveals. 'He didn't like working with professional musicians very much. He quite liked people who were a little nuts. I think he felt a little bit threatened by them [professional musicians].

'I always thought that he wanted to be the main attraction. He's a frustrated pop singer, really, to be honest. When he went out to dinner or something, he'd always be the one that showed off and got in trouble, or he'd just do crazy things.

'There's a story where his hair caught alight. He was drunk one night at his house; his leg was in plaster because he'd kicked the door down to try to find his wife, who was having an affair with the plumber. It was like something out of a magazine. He was drunk, he lent back, and there was a load of candles on the shelf behind him. He had very thin, very fine hair, and must have had lacquer on it because when he lent back close to the naked flame – woof, it went up.

'On another night, Malcolm arrived in a brand new car, and as we came out and were saying our goodbyes, Andrew came out and stood on the bonnet, stood on the roof, walked across the roof. I thought Malcolm was going to kill him, but I told him not to do anything – to just let things calm down – and then send him the bill.

'Malcolm snarled at me, 'He hasn't got any fucking money.''

With three new songs in the can, the plan was for Andrew to take the new material to America and see if he could get some major artist interest. 'After the recording finished, Andrew planned a trip to America,' says Keith. 'He was going out there to visit Bob and Dan Crewe who were quite a famous duo in the industry [Bob co-wrote *Lady Marmalade*], and we were hoping to get a couple of covers from them. And the interest ... it all sort of just fizzled out into pretty much nothing again.'

Chief among the reasons for this 'fizzling out' was the financial problems which Immediate Records was having. In the stage play *All or Nothing – The Mod Musical,* based on the story of The Small Faces, there is a scene where Steve Marriott is having a meeting with Andrew Loog Oldham to discuss money the band is owed. During the scene, bailiffs remove the office furniture one piece at a time until there is a bare stage. Keith recalls fiction, on this occasion, not being too far from real life. 'I remember being round at his house in Richmond when the bailiffs came for the fittings and took his cars away.'

Keith was left feeling disillusioned once more about his prospects. 'At that time, I decided that I didn't want to front anything anymore; I didn't want to sing the act. I wanted to write the songs, to produce them, but get somebody else to record them, basically... that was the way I was going. I wanted to be a writer, a composer, and maybe do a bit of production. I wanted to keep out of the limelight.

'I could see it wasn't working for one reason or the other, maybe partly it was my fault. Perhaps I was not giving it enough commitment; perhaps I didn't have enough desire to do it. I'll take the blame for that, definitely, no question about it.

'I was very happy at home, with my girlfriend. I was having a really good time of it there. I probably got a little bit lazy. I didn't have the desire of Rod Stewart; the desire that these guys have got to succeed. I didn't have it in me. I've always been very happy. I've always been a very happy, contented sort of guy – stress-free – so my career, it's kind of suited me in a way.'

With Keith's connections at Carlin music (amongst others) and the fact that *Teenage Opera* had been a huge hit, he had a calling card that would last his entire life; opportunities as a songwriter and a producer would regularly come his way. One of the first would come from a familiar source... a familiarly framed request from Freddy Bienstock.

''Keith, write me a song for the Eurovision Song Contest,' I can remember him calling after me. He was very much like that. It wasn't really my thing. I think Don Reedman, who at the time was a manager at Carlin and tasked with finding songs for artists – and who later had a huge career in the music business – was sort of sniffing around this idea, and was doing stuff like that.

'He said, 'Come on, you can make a bundle. This is fucking easy. The songs I've heard that they're putting forward are dreadful. Go on, write one.'

'I said to him that it wasn't really my thing, but he told me to just bash something off. So, Ken and I literally sat around, and came up with *Many Rivers,* a Jewish folk song-sounding thing, and it was a good song. It was catchy.'

The song which Keith and Ken wrote, *Many Rivers,* would be recorded by Irene Sheer and released as a single in the UK and Germany in 1971. Irene Sheer is an interesting artist in her own right, as she was born and educated in Romford, Essex, but concentrated her pop career in Germany where she has had numerous hits and even represented the country in the Eurovision Song Contest (finishing sixth in 1978). She continues to release records and make TV appearances up to this day.

Keith remembers the recording session, 'Irene turned up to the studio, and it all went very smoothly. She was a very attractive lady and a real professional; I was so impressed by her. As the session progressed, I was helping her to get the feel of the vocal right, and after she nailed it, we embraced. As I looked in her eyes, a voice in my head suddenly said, 'Whoa, No. No, no, no. Don't even think about it.' I think she had the hots for me and she's quite upfront, as well, certainly an emancipated woman. But, that song didn't get voted for by the powers that be, for the Eurovision Song Contest entry.'

Keith also remembers another opportunity which came his way, one which reveals a great deal about his artistic nature as opposed to any purely professional approach to work and music in general.

'Lou Christie wanted Ken and me to produce him,' recalls Keith. 'His angle was that he had a falsetto voice and he had recorded about five or six really big hits; *Lightnin' Strikes* was one. I told Freddy that it wasn't really my thing, and that I couldn't do a good job on it. He tried to convince me, saying it was a good job with good money. But if I'm going to do something, I've got to put my heart into it. If not, I can't do it.

'So I then suggested that perhaps Ken might want the job? But no, he didn't want to do it either, so that was it. We just passed on it. Lou and his managers walked out. They had just been turned down by two third-rate producers, two guys who hadn't had a production hit between them. It must have been a bit embarrassing.'

More to Keith's liking was the chance to work with a fellow songwriter who he admired, producing an album for Clive Westlake. Clive already had an impressive songwriting CV when he came to work with Keith. He is most associated with songs written for Dusty Springfield, including *Losing You* and *All I See Is You* — both of which peaked at #9 on the UK Singles Chart, in 1964 and 1966 respectively. Plus, *I Close My Eyes and Count to Ten,* which reached #4 in the UK in 1968. Across a long and successful career, he also wrote songs recorded by for Shirley Bassey, Vera Lynn, Elvis Presley, Petula Clark, Cilla Black, Tom Jones, Roger Whittaker, Crystal Gayle, and others.

Keith remembers the period, 'Clive was buzzing around the office at Carlin, and we were up there quite a lot. I had a flat around the corner, just off the Edgware Road, so it was walkable, and I'd be in there sniffing around. I got on with Clive really well, and the singer/songwriter thing was popular in those days. Writers were actually starting to step forward, people like Carole King, they were all making their own solo albums. Somebody suggested to Clive that he make a solo album and his reply was typical. 'Oh, I don't know about that, boyo,' in his thick Welsh accent.

'He wasn't too sure about his vocal ability, so I reassured him that he was a great songwriter and that he could trust me as a producer and we'd give it a go, and so that's what we did.

'We used to go down the pub, have a couple of pints of Guinness, more than a couple of pints sometimes, and we'd do all the backing tracks for him. All he had to do was get in there and sing. I had to hold his hand quite a lot, but we got through it.

'I didn't write any songs for him or anything; it was all laid out. I haven't heard it for years. We did another album, a similar thing with a guy called Roger Morris who was heavily into The Band. If you listen to the album, (a copy of which, on the Regal Zonophone record label, is now highly prized… and priced), it's very like them. He was a lovely guy. I think he went on to join The Psychedelic Furs for a while, and he played on a k.d. lang album and worked with Tom Jones later, too.'

'Roger sent in a demo tape one day. I used to sit and go through them all. I think Carlin probably put out an advert or something saying, 'Looking for writers' or similar. They were always looking for new songwriters.

'He had a song called *Trail of Tears*, which was a nice title and all about the Native-American experience. *Bury My Heart at Wounded Knee* was a big book at the time, which was all about the Indians, and what the American settlers did to the Indians. It was a big seller, and there was a lot of people looking back at that period, like The Band with *The Night They Drove Old Dixie Down*, you know.

'That's what he was heavily into; unashamedly really. He didn't care that what he wrote was derivative. He had an extremely high voice too, and for a lot of people, it wasn't that palatable. He had a high range, and you couldn't get him to go any lower. That was his key; it was right up there.

'We got in Bruce Rowland out of The Grease Band for some of the drums, and had really good players... Glenn Ross Campbell on pedal steel. We had all those guys, all of our mates. Lisle Harper from Stealers Wheel on bass, Rod Coombes on drums, too. All that bunch.

'I played a bit on it, a bit of guitar. But none of these songs or these albums took off on their own right, really. I wouldn't think they made any money. But they're collectors' items now, because of the rarity value.'

As ever with Keith, nothing would be thrown away, and he would work closely with many of these musicians again in the none-too-distant future – on what some consider to be his best recordings.

[illegible] in Bruce Rowland out of The Grease Band for some of the drums and had really good tracks. [illegible] on pedal steel. We had all those cows, all of our animals [illegible] from speakers vibrating [illegible] [illegible] that. All that bump [illegible]

[illegible] of putting [illegible] these early [illegible] they made any money, but they're collectors' items now, because of [illegible] value.

As ever [illegible] would be different [illegible] would work closely with many of these [illegible] in the distant future [illegible] what some consider to be his best.

17. Bodast

Following the sessions with Ronnie Wood and Aynsley Dunbar, and with Keith away either visiting family or on songwriting breaks, Steve Howe was getting involved in different projects and with various musicians. One such project, which would have a recurring impact on Keith's professional life, came when he joined the group, Canto.

As Steve says, 'I was looking for something else to do, and got involved in a group being put together by Deep Purple's management which Keith eventually ended up producing. That album shows where we were at, as a partnership. If I did something, Keith might come into the project; or if he did something, I could.'

Canto was comprised of Steve Howe on guitar, Dave Curtiss on bass, and Bobbie Clarke on drums. With the addition of Clive Skinner on vocals, it quickly morphed into Bodast. (The name is derived from the first two letters of the Christian names of Bobby, Dave, and Steve. No one recalls why Clive didn't get a credit!)

Keith sheds some light on Dave Curtiss and Bobby Clark's history, too, 'Those two used to play with Vince Taylor and the Playboys in France; they were an Elvis knock-off band.

'Vince Taylor, now there's a story. Steve Howe ended up living in a house with these guys in Lots Road, Chelsea, opposite Battersea Power Station, and he [Vince] was an acid freak. He just used to wander around that house; literally, he would just stroll into one of the rooms out of the blue while we were going over songs or chatting. David Bowie apparently based Ziggy Stardust on him. He was a black leather, rock 'n roller, but he was yet another acid casualty, sadly, albeit harmless. He died pretty young.'

Initially, the new group seemed to have an exciting future. 'With Bodast, we thought we had a big opportunity in America because the sound of the band was suitable for the USA post-psychedelia,' says Steve Howe, 'and it was great that Keith could come onboard as producer to wrestle with the recordings. He booked great engineers for us to work with at Trident studios.'

History shows that the group recorded an album for Tetragrammaton Records – a label which had experienced success in the United States with Deep Purple – but who went out of business just before the scheduled release date of the Bodast album in 1969, placing it in limbo.

As Steve Howe recalls, 'That was it for Keith and me; the parting of the ways. If the Bodast album had come out and had charted, or if we had become a touring band, it would have been a reward for all the hard work we had put in. But there was no reward; the material was buried.

'After that, opportunities came, but nothing ever came to much and it got depressing. Then [in January 1970], I joined Yes.

'Essentially,' Steve adds jauntily, 'I knew when to leave a sinking ship.'

Of the other Bodast members, bassist Dave Curtiss went on to form a folk duo with Clive Skinner (now working under the name Clive Maldoon) called Curtiss Maldoon. They recorded two albums, and the first – *Curtiss Maldoon* – was released in October 1971 (with Steve Howe playing on two songs). The second – *Maldoon* – was released in November 1973 (Dave Curtiss asked for his name to be taken off the album's name, as he was not happy with it!).

Although largely unnoticed at the time, a song on the duo's first album called *Sepheryn* was to have a remarkable re-birth more than 30 years later… but we'll come to that.

Other songs from Bodast also had second lives with a portion of *Nether Street* being renamed *Würm* and re-used as part of the song *Starship Trooper* from *The Yes Album* in 1971.

Of the project, Keith recalls, 'Again, the record company went bust, and although it was nothing to do with me, from a business point of view, I was the producer. I remember we recorded it at Trident Studios in Soho with Ken Scott who was David Bowie's engineer. It was a good album, although it was done very quickly as the budget was low. After the record label went bust, I bought the tapes before they were thrown into a skip.'

The tapes for the Bodast album would physically sit with Malcolm Forrester and Getaway Music. However, they weren't technically part of the company's catalogue, and were only re-discovered in 1976 by an eager, young beaver just starting to learn his trade in the music publishing industry. His name was Martin Costello. He listened to the tapes and questioned his boss, Malcolm, as to their provenance, but never seemed to get a straight answer.

Costello recognised the names of Steve Howe and Keith West and, as it was his job to make copies of the songs that his publishing company was attempting to push to artists, he knew the Getaway Music catalogue inside out. He also knew there were many Keith West songs in the catalogue, and that he was labelled as 'producer' on this curio.

A few years later, having hustled his way up the greasy music industry pole, and now making a name for himself in music publishing, Martin Costello would be introduced to Keith West backstage at a gig by The Cars at The Lyceum in London. The two struck up a friendship and started working on a way to 'get a deal' for the Bodast album.

This project would ultimately have many repercussions. Firstly, it would lead to Costello being fired by Malcolm Forrester; secondly, it would signal the start of a close friendship between Costello and Keith which continues to this day – they are the best of friends. Finally, it would lead to Costello, through his connections to fledgeling independent label Cherry Red Records, helping Keith to secure a release for the Bodast album more than a decade after its completion.

The Bodast Tapes – Featuring Steve Howe was eventually released by Cherry Red in 1981 with a tongue-in-cheek cover shot of Keith digging up the tapes in the middle of a wood. The record sold a highly respectable 15,000 copies and, as mentioned, the reverberations from this project would continue to be felt for many years to come.

18. Family life calls

With his musical life slowing a little, and without the late-night commitments of gigs and the periods away from home when touring, Keith was starting to settle down having re-started his relationship with Pat Stebbings in 1971.

Family has always been important to Keith, but it's something that doesn't fit easily with a career in the music business, and Keith increasingly missed that element in his life. In stories of individual success, the burning desire to achieve and be recognised can, most often, be traced back to an unhappy childhood or some sense of abandonment or emotional isolation.

Keith's story – and perhaps why he recognises that he didn't have the pathological need to drive forward once he had earnt a certain level of success, money, and fame – is one of a happy childhood and warm, loving relationships. Something he would soon bring to his own family.

Keith Alan Trevor Hopkins, his birth certificate reveals, was born on the 6th of December 1944 at 11, Hunters Square, Dagenham. His father, Sidney Hopkins lists his occupation as 'Lorry Driver', and his mother Annie Hopkins records her maiden name as 'White'.

'Sidney was my father,' recalls Keith. 'He worked for a manufacturing company, May & Baker, that supplied pharmaceuticals and many other speciality products for hospitals.

'He would drive stuff over to Ireland every two weeks and be away for a couple of days, and that was his main job. Obviously, it was Keith Hopkins and not Keith West at that time. In those days, if you or somebody at the record company didn't like the sound of your surname, or it didn't sound rock and roll enough, then you'd change it.

'In my case, somebody came up with some ideas, and we started to work them around and then somebody suggested 'out west' or something like 'east west'. I thought that was OK and that I'd settle for that. It was that easy. It's better than Alvin Stardust or something that's ridiculous.'

Keith's mum, Annie, was a seamstress who worked for Hector Powe, a tailor for gentlemen, and he had two older sisters: Anne, the eldest, and Mavis (both now sadly deceased). Being the youngest of the family, Keith felt totally protected by these women, but by Anne, especially.

'My older sister always looked after me. We were very close,' reflects Keith. 'We lived in Hunters Square which was a two-up, two-down council house in Dagenham. At the back of our garden was the playground for our school, Richard Albion Primary School.

'I don't recall much about that school, but I was encouraged to play sports, and I was okay at high jump, running, that kind of thing. I was quite sporty believe it or not, and I was crazy about football. When I was ten, they thought I had contracted a form of TB, which turned out to be Pleurisy. It wasn't too serious, but I was banged up in hospital for quite a while, and my sister Mavis was as well.

'Pleurisy causes a shadow on the lung, and I can remember taking this horrible medicine every day. I was in bed for a long time because it was difficult walking. I would have difficulty breathing; I can remember that. I missed out on school for about ten months, and then I'd been in bed for so long that my feet were all soft. I had a bit of making up to do when I got back to school, but when I was in hospital, one of the guys had a crystal radio.'

'That's where my music thing started from. He had a crystal radio. It was a terrible sound obviously, but you could get *Radio Luxembourg* on it, and they played pop music, and rock and roll, and stuff like that. It was a different kind of stuff than you got on the normal BBC. That excited me quite a bit. I can remember laying under the sheets listening to them on this crackly old radio.

'There were thrillers on there, Dick Barton and stuff like that; things that we used to be into. It was an escape, actually, from the nightmare that was going on in that hospital. It was boring as hell, obviously.

'Hearing rock and roll was like something from another world. It was the defining moment when Elvis's *Heartbreak Hotel* came on the radio.

'It's been said many times before, but it still rings true… *that* was the defining moment. Everything changed after that.

'I was a big fan of Ricky Nelson, too. He had a lot of hits. Not equal to Elvis, but it was pretty close, and I loved his voice. I saw films like *Blackboard Jungle* – with its title song *Rock Around the Clock* – that was on at the local cinema. We went and saw that, and it was true; I mean all the Teddy Boys ripped the seats out and were dancing in the aisles. I'd never seen anything like it.

'The times I heard an electric guitar prior to that, which excited me a lot, was on the Les Paul and Mary Ford records. That was the first kind of music that really turned me on when I was younger.

'Les Paul was a musical pioneer; he also invented multi-track recording. He was buying and customising all kinds of recording equipment and doing all this music in his house. I believe he set up a bunch of microphones in his kitchen, he would then multi-track the guitar parts over a simple backing track and then his wife, Mary, would sing harmony with herself. They're amazing records still, when you think that the technology in those days was nothing compared to today.

'To get me up out of bed in the morning – this is true – my parents would put on a Les Paul and Mary Ford record, *Bye Bye*

Blues or *The World is Waiting for the Sunshine,* and I was straight up and out of bed as soon as those records came on. I was very excited by it all.

'I did meet Les Paul in the 90s. Steve Howe was playing in New York, and he asked me to get up and sing *White Bicycle* with him, which I did. We then went to Fat Tuesdays, which is a club where Les Paul played, and Steve got up and played a short set with Les's trio as he knew him well and because Les had arthritis in his hands.

'Les came over to the table and asked us to do a few numbers as he was tired. Steve got up and did some tunes which you can find on YouTube. It was fantastic.

'Then Les came over, and I told him I was a fan and he was lovely. Apparently, he used to video his shows and check them all out. A real pro! He signed something for me, which was a Les Paul pickguard I bought earlier that day. Happy Days!

'In our house, my parents played a lot of music. They regularly bought records. We had a piano in the house, too, that my dad used to play the odd Hank Williams tune on. That's where my interest in country music came from, I guess. He also liked to play a bit of jazz. Ella Fitzgerald and stuff like that.

'My dad used to like Erroll Garner a lot, too, and would buy pop records as well. A bit of Russ Conway, a bit of Winifred Atwell, who was very popular at that time. He'd play them on a gramophone with a radiogram built in. It had a big old speaker on it, and you got all kinds of bass out of it. So, that was good.'

Bar the extended stay in hospital, Keith's early experiences of school and life had been carefree and happy. Secondary school was to be a much greater challenge.

'I went to Eastbrook Secondary Modern,' remembers Keith, 'which was less than a mile away from our house, so still walkable. My sister Mavis was there, but Anne had gone to the grammar school, so we were now split up.

'A bunch of us decided we were going to fail the 11+ and we didn't want to go to grammar school, but sadly my best friend – Ken Burgess – did take it more seriously and he got into grammar school. He was an only child, and I think his parents probably pushed him a bit harder. I missed him at school, but a bunch of us agreed we weren't going to stay on at school as we wanted to leave at 15 and get out in the world.

'Eastbrook was a single-sex school, and it was a bit rough; there were a lot of Teddy Boys around and you had to be careful. There were a few rituals. You might get thrown over a wall. You might get press-ganged. If you really got out of line, they'd pick on you and probably stick your head down the toilet and flush it. Stuff like that. We had one female teacher, once. I think she only lasted two weeks.'

Keith's best friend at the time, Ken Burgess, would go on to have a colourful life as well as an on/off relationship with the music business. Now married to Navah Baruchin, a well-known singer, and living in Israel, he has converted to Judaism but was sadly not well enough to contribute to this book.

Keith remembers him as, 'Middle class in my eyes, because his parents owned their own house. He was just around the corner from us, but his house was a semi-detached with three bedrooms.

'Through him, I came to join Tony Colton and The Teenbeats which, looking back, is something of a high-profile start, isn't it, for a couple of 13-year olds? All three of us went on to amazing things and were right in the centre of the music business, which is weird from a little school band from Dagenham.'

Keith's formal education lasted for little more than a decade but his childhood, which came to an abrupt end at the age of

15 when he joined the working world, was a straightforward and happy one. It was this kind of environment which he wished to create for his children who, having re-united with Pat in 1971 following her split from Steve Howe, were now on the horizon.

Keith has a close family. His oldest daughter Shelley (who amongst other things is a qualified masseuse and budding film director) was born in 1973 followed by twin-daughters, Carrie and Jodie, in early January 1977. 'My father's brother had a twin sister, my sister Anne had twin boys, so there are genetics involved here,' says Keith. Jodie lived in New York with her family but has now returned to the UK. Carrie is a marketing consultant and action girl.

Balancing domesticity and a career in the music business has proved impossible for the vast majority of people who've attempted it. Keith seems to have been more successful than most, and has maintained a normal home life for his family, while at the same time still pursuing a myriad of musical adventures.

An anecdote, relayed by one of Keith's music business associates, nicely summarises his career from the 1970s onwards. 'At a music industry awards evening, a table of men, approaching middle age – who have worked with Keith or know of him – are hitting the drinks hard and taking regular bathroom breaks to 'powder their noses'.

'The talk amongst them is of where they will go on to later, and of their latest girlfriends, and of their divorces or their ungrateful children and step-children.

'Someone delivers a general question to the entire table, 'So what's Keith West up to now then?' 'One of the music industry men quickly retorts, 'Probably sipping a cold Chablis and watering his hanging baskets,' at which the group of men break into guffaws of laughter. However, the laughter quickly subsides as the men reflect on the gentle nature of Keith's life and the mess of theirs.

'As the men look around at each other, one of them pipes up, 'He's probably got it right then, hasn't he?''

19. One last tilt at stardom

The early 1970s saw Keith moving between musical projects, searching for the one which would replace his time with Tomorrow, from both a commercial and artistic point of view. His name would be briefly associated with David Bowie, the hottest artist of the time, when on the 16th of June 1972, Bowie released his classic album *The Rise and Fall of Ziggy Stardust and the Spiders from Mars*. Pictured on the front cover of the album is a shot of Bowie, in full Ziggy outfit, stood underneath a sign which simply reads 'K. West'.

Keith West watchers have often debated this rather curious appearance of his name on the front cover of this legendary record. Keith was certainly known to Bowie from his days in Davy Jones and The Lower Third, and they certainly met at The Marquee when both had residencies. They even possessed a girlfriend in common, Dana Gillespie, (who had featured on the *Ziggy Stardust* album) and Keith had been a frequent visitor to the Lots Road house where Vince Taylor (who Bowie based the Ziggy character on) was resident... along with Steve Howe, his wife and son, Gita Renik, and bass player Bruce Thomas.

While further investigation reveals that 'K. West' was, in fact, the name of a furrier whose shop happened to be on Heddon Street, where the cover photo was shot, it seems impossible that Bowie wouldn't have appreciated the ironic mystery which the name on the sign created. It might even have been a little sardonic swipe at Keith, depending on how he [Bowie] felt about his girlfriend's association with a former peer.

Keith had reservations, but there were those in the music business that still saw him having a future as a recording artist in his own right. Such thinking saw him signed by Decca in 1973 for a couple of 7" singles on the Deram label *Riding for a*

Fall B/w *Days About to Rain* and *Havin' Someone* B/w *Know There's No Livin' Without You* which came out in 1974.

Keith sheds more light on this period of his career, 'I was working at Command Studios in Piccadilly Circus, doing some production work. I was working for Carlin Music, and I was interested in going into the back room and writing songs and doing production. I didn't want to be a face out there for a while; to do anything particularly.

'Everybody kept saying, 'Oh, you're a wasted talent, you should be doing this, you should be doing that.' Eventually, Decca signed me for a couple of records... under protest from me. One was called *Riding for a Fall*, which was like a country-rock sort of thing. *Having Someone* was the other, and there was a lot of interest in it as a song to be covered by a few people. Again, it didn't really live up to its potential.'

Keith even did some media work at the time, and while two-thirds of the interview – published in *Music Week* in November 1973 – focused on the potential for a *Teenage Opera* follow-up, you cannot fault Keith for lacking ambition as he eyed a return to live performances. The article excerpt quotes him as saying, 'There are some nice venues available now. The Festival Hall is a really nice gig. I'd like to start somewhere like that.'

Despite the failure of the two Deram singles to dent the charts or establish Keith as a solo artist in his own right (beyond *Teenage Opera*), they had at least given his self-confidence a boost. This, plus another coincidence, would see him back in the studio to record his first, and only, solo album.

The catalytic coincidence tale is told by Malcolm Forrester, then GM of Carlin Music (which administered the Getaway Music catalogue that owned the publishing rights to *My White Bicycle*). As Malcolm recalls, 'In a way, it was just a quirk of fate. Panache Music [a Carlin sub-brand] looked after Nazareth, and Dan McCafferty – the singer from the band – came into my office and asked if I knew who the publisher of

My White Bicycle was, because they wanted to record a version of the song. Obviously, it was easy to answer that question and simplicity itself to organise for Nazareth to issue a cover version.'

Nazareth's version of *My White Bicycle* was released on the 14th of June 1975 and reached #14 in the UK Singles Chart staying in the top 40 for eight weeks, of which four weeks were in the Top 20. The success of Nazareth's version of the song also gave Keith's reputation as a hitmaker something of a boost, and the budget was quickly found to capitalise on this, and to record an album.

Released in September 1974 on the German label Kuckuck, *Wherever My Love Goes* is, arguably, Keith's most consistent work from a songwriting and production viewpoint. As he recalls, 'The production on that record was done by Ken Burgess and me. It's joined-up from a production point of view. All the songs sound like they're meant to be together, and there's a thread running through it where you think, this kind of works'.

'But we were experimenting down there really, and trying stuff out, without too much thought about it being commercial or not. They gave us a free hand, Carlin, I have got to say.'

The album's opening track is actually the original version of *The Power and The Glory*, as produced by Andrew Loog Oldham in 1969 at Olympic Studios in Barnes, following the trip to Dorset. This shows, again, that nothing of merit in Keith's career is ever totally discarded. While the Andrew Loog Oldham track is acknowledged as being a 'huge production', it is equally matched on the album by a re-recorded version of *West Country* which comes complete with an incredible pedal steel outro solo from Glenn Campbell.

Keith remembers the recording sessions, 'We made it at Command Studios right by Piccadilly Circus. It was an odd studio; it didn't last very long. I think the only big record to come out of there was *Virginia Plain* by Roxy Music, and they left immediately afterwards because it was a strange place to mix. Every time you did a mix down there, it sounded completely different when you took it out. There was something wrong in there, and it didn't last.'

Checking the credits of the album, you can see Keith is working with familiar musicians from his earlier production work for artists like Clive Westlake and Roger Morris. Rod Coombes is on drums, and Lisle Harper on bass (both of Stealers Wheel – *Stuck in the Middle With You* fame). Johnny Almond is on sax, and Tommy Eyre is on keyboards (Tommy played on the mega-hits *With a Little Help from My Friends* by Joe Cocker and *Baker Street* by Gerry Rafferty, and went on to be the music director for Wham). Tommy also provided the superb intro to *Power And The Glory* and the lovely keys on *Sad Song*.

John Weider featured on violin and banjo. He was formerly the bass player in Family, and Eric Burdon's Animals for whom he co-wrote *San Franciscan Nights*. Glenn Ross Campbell is on pedal steel, and Ann Odell and Roy Young on keyboards, too. Keith and Ken Burgess are credited with electric guitar and acoustic guitar, respectively, as well as vocals.

While the album is certainly a strong one and features superior recordings of earlier Keith West compositions (such as *The Visit* and *West Country*), it would be released in Germany only on the Kuckuck label. A decision which, at the time, bemused and infuriated Keith. 'I asked Malcolm Forrester what happened and why he hadn't managed to get a UK record deal on it, because Martin Wyatt, who was at Anchor Records at the time, he was interested in it. He really liked two or three of the songs, one of them was *West Country*.

'Malcolm was having a bit of a problem and couldn't close the deal. He left it too late, and by that time, something else has always come in the door. It happens a lot. If something generates some interest [from a record label], you have got to close that deal quick. Because they'll get bored with it after a short while.

'But that album, I kept asking him if he had got a deal on it and he would always reply, 'No, no, I'm working on it, I'm working on it.' But he wasn't. He was taking Valium at the time; it was big and trendy in those days. Everybody was chilled out on Valium, and nothing – I mean *nothing* – got done. So, it got buried, until some German company picked it up.'

Despite its frustrating history, Keith still looks back on the record fondly. As he says, 'Songs like *Liet Motif,* and others like that, they are full of really, really musical ideas. It's stuffed full of tunes, basically. *Sad Song's* nice, but Ken wrote that, and I only helped him out on it. It was his song and when he asked my opinion, I reassured him that it was nearly finished and that there was no point in me getting involved in it.'

'He said, 'It needs a hook in it or something.'

'I said, 'I'd just do it *as it is,* if I was you.'

'So, Tommy got up and started playing the piano, I played guitar on it and a bit of bass, and that was it. And it's a nice simple tune. I had started playing him Neil Young records, and Ken loved *I've Been Waiting for You*. He loved that song and *Sad Song*'s influenced by it, but I warned him to be careful not to go too close to it.''

Ironically enough, the album performed relatively well – from a sales point of view – in Germany. This was probably due to the fact that *Excerpt from a Teenage Opera* had been a big hit there, and that the TV show *Beat Club* continued to use the song as its theme tune. Nonetheless, it was not enough to secure a UK or US release, and the album is something of a neglected gem in Keith's work.

Far from being deterred by the lack of success of *Wherever My Love Goes,* Keith's creative juices had been stimulated, and he had also made new music industry contacts who he wanted to mine while still fresh. Plus, he had made a connection with John Weider during the Command Studios sessions, and wanted to see what else he and the stringed instrument maestro could conjure up between them.

Keith recalls the time, 'I'd moved down to Walton-on-Thames and had been working with John Weider who, as well as being in The Animals, also played with people like Johnny Kidd and the Pirates and all sorts of bands. He was a very talented guy. Anything with strings on, he could play. Violin, bass, mandolin, guitar. He was an all-rounder, a lovely guy and a good songwriter.

'We teamed up because he was doing sessions for me at the time, and we got on like a house on fire. We both liked Neil Young a lot; we liked that kind of country-rock stuff, so we started writing some songs together. We started jamming around.

'I was getting a bit better on the guitar by then, and we started bashing out some tunes. John said, 'I'll tell you what, I reckon we can get a deal on this. In America, this is what they're all buying.' So I said, 'OK, let's get a few guys in and let's get a rehearsal going.' We advertised, and John knew Chico Greenwood, so he pretty much got the gig on drums straightaway; and Bruce Thomas, who was subsequently in The Attractions with Elvis Costello, he came in.

'Actually, Bruce wasn't the first choice,' remembers Keith, laughing at the memory. 'We put an advert in the *Melody Maker* as we didn't have a bass player. Various people turned up and auditioned, but they weren't right, or they didn't look right, or we didn't like them as performers. We held the auditions somewhere around the Kings Road, which we booked and paid for ourselves.

'One bass player we turned down was Cliff Williams, the bass player for AC/DC. We turned him down because he was far too good-looking, and you don't want a bass player to get the attention, do you? He's a lovely guy, but he wasn't right for us.'

'I remember this God walking in, with massively long hair. He was really well-dressed and carrying a brand new mega bass and a brand new amp. His girlfriend was really hot as well; she looked like something out of a modelling agency, which she probably was.

'He walked in and said, 'All right guys?', then he played.

'He was great, but I said to the guys, 'Forget it, he's not joining the band. I'm not standing next to him on stage.' Then I made up some other reasons, 'He won't last. He's a gold digger. He wants to make too much money. Forget about it.'

'This was before AC/DC, so I did him a huge favour. It was probably the biggest favour of his life not getting that audition and joining Moonrider!'

In their search for a bassist, Keith continues, 'I knew Bruce Thomas from Lots Road and the Bodast era, so I gave him a ring to see what he was doing. I loved his bass playing. He's probably one of my favourite bass players. Look at the stuff he's done with Elvis Costello – it's fucking dynamite – and he was good with us as well.

Bruce Thomas is scathing about his time in Moonrider, saying in his autobiography *Rough Notes... and grainy images*, 'There's a band I don't ever talk about – it's one I happily leave out of my resume.' He did, however, agree to an interview for this book and while most of his hilariously acidic memories are told with the benefit of 50 years of hindsight (and are potentially libellous), he does recall behaving unprofessionally in his time with the band.

Bruce was, he maintains, at odds with the musical direction of the band. Having seen the J. Geils Band at The Lyceum, he was more interested in hooking up with Wilko Johnson to play the overdriven R&B-style music which would soon lead to punk and the new wave revolution.

'John's girlfriend suggested we change our name to Clam Chowder to appeal even more directly to the American soft rock market,' says Bruce. 'That sums everything up for me; Moonrider – Born to be Mild.'

'We used to rehearse at The Marquee,' remembers Keith, 'and I invited Martin Wyatt and Ian Ralfini to come down and check us out. Ian Ralfini was my original publisher at Robbins Music and was now running Anchor Records; Martin Wyatt was his A&R guy. Martin was credited with having signed Van Morrison before *Astral Weeks* and was originally interested in *Wherever My Love Goes*.

'Martin loved *Our Day's Gonna Come*; he thought that was going to be a massive hit. He liked a couple of other tunes as well, but that was the one that sold it to him.

'Anchor Records was financed by MGM, and they had Steely Dan among their acts, who we were fans of at the time. They had also had a big hit with Ace and *How Long,* which was written by Paul Carrack. They came down and saw us and wanted to sign us, but said the band would need to get a management company before they would sign anything off.

'They said, 'OK, look, we're really interested but have you got management yet?' And we said, 'Noooo.' They replied, 'Well, that's OK, as soon as you get it... we'll sign you. You need to get a management deal in place pretty quick if we're going to do it.'

'I didn't want to make the same mistake as with *Wherever My Love Goes,* and said to John, 'Look, let's do this fast because they're going to get bored with it. It will be the same old story. Let's get some management in quick.'

'A friend of mine recommended these guys from America called CTA, which stood for Creative Talent Associates; they had Three Dog Night, who were big in America, and a couple of other bands, but they wanted to develop into the UK. I phoned them up and told them we had a deal with Anchor but didn't have management, so we were doing things in reverse. They were interested and invited us to meet them for lunch. We went up to their offices in Kew, a very nice office, and it was all lovely and we ironed out a deal.

'We got Neville Shulman in to do the financial side, and did a nice simple deal. We then took it back to Ian and Martin and agreed to sign with them. We needed management as they gave us a big advance, Anchor poured in quite a bit of money. We got about 30 grand as an advance (around £250,000 in today's money), which was quite a lot in those days. After we'd split it all up, and paid everyone, it must have come out to 10 or 12 grand each for John and me.

'It was a nice easy deal to put together, but then this guy called Bill Utley, from CTA in America, decided he was going to come over and take over our management, which was a big mistake and we didn't like him. He was a real tough New Yorker; he turned up and we thought, 'Oh, fuck' because we liked Tony MacArthur, the English guy we had been dealing with. The American guy could smell money, obviously, after we got a deal he bought us all this gear; we had these fucking acoustic amps, and the most expensive PA, huge great big stacks, great big drum kits, guitars, the works, and off we went on tour.

'It was all going smoothly. We went on tour and appeared on the BBC's famous *The Old Grey Whistle Test* music show in July 1975 performing four tracks live. I'd love to get a copy of that. I bumped into Bob Harris, the show's host, a few years ago, and he said that even the BBC don't know where the tape is.'

'We supported John Mayall and the Bluesbreakers at the Royal Albert Hall. We did all the big venues, as well as doing club gigs and college gigs. We even did a couple of gigs with Chaka Khan.

'It was going well, and then Anchor went bankrupt. They pulled the plug. Our chosen producer, Gary Katz, Steely Dan's producer, fell by the wayside. He had shown some interest in Moonrider, so we were getting really excited about that. But, because of all the financial shenanigans, he wasn't going to come over from America to do that job.

'We did a couple of tracks with Ace's producer, John Anthony, but he was out of his tree most of the time. We went round to his place, and he was very positive and said that he had listened to the songs and thought they were great. He even buttered me up saying I looked great and was going to be a star, all that sort of stuff. We all thought, 'Oh dear, fucking hell, here we go.'

'He asked us if we knew who Joe Walsh was and then he played us *Rocky Mountain Way* really loud, on these huge speakers; it was ear-bleedingly loud. He then told us that's what he wanted our album to sound like. We were confused and said to him that our songs were not like that; not as upfront as that. They really weren't.

'We did a couple of tracks with John, but it didn't work out.

'In the end, at Ian Ralfini's request, I ended up producing the album myself. We had to do it pretty quickly, mostly at Olympic Studios in Barnes. We did one of John's ballads, *As Long As It Takes*, which was a Beatles-style ballad, a big song, but again it didn't really take off.

'Then a guy called Pete Gage came in and produced one song, *I Found Love*, which I hated. But I recorded it anyway; it's one of John's songs and very, very poppy. We had a conversation saying that the album needed a hit. If we could get a single away, we could use it as a launchpad to push the album as the songs were good enough. Given that, I decided to just go along with it, and spoke to John and said that he should sing it as it was his song. But, in the end, everyone wanted me to do it. So, it was OK; it's an OK thing. It's all 10cc harmonies on it, all loaded up.

'There's a nice story about that, actually. We'd finished recording that song, and we were on tour; I think we were up in the Midlands, Birmingham, somewhere like that. I got a call from Ian Ralfini saying that I needed to come back to London because Pete Gage wanted me back in the studio to do some more harmonies and put something else on the track. I was pretty pissed off, but Ian was insistent that I return to the studio and sent a car for me.

'Anyway, a limo turned up, and I didn't want to have to go on my own, so I talked John into going with me. We both got in the car and ended up in Olympic Studios. We left Bruce Thomas and Chico in the bar at our hotel around midday. No word of a lie, we drove to London, did the overdubs, drove back. God knows how long that would have taken. Birmingham's 120 miles and when we got back, they were still in the bar... we were supposed to be on stage by 8pm, and they were absolutely hammered.

'We had two singles out, and an album. The singles were *I Found Love* and another attempt to record and release *Havin' Someone*. Anchor put the album out and then the whole thing tumbled down. Ian Ralfini went off to manage Norah Jones while the record managed to generate some sales and got some airplay; it did earn some money.

'It's funny because we went to a party at Anchor Records, and there was about ten other bands there, and I was saying, 'What's happening with your deal? What's happening with your record?'

'And the other artists were saying, 'Nothing's happening. There's a rumour they're going to go bust.' I couldn't believe it, but in the end, the money got pulled out pretty quick, which wasn't really a surprise. If you just think about our deal, they were pouring out money; giving out money all over the place with no returns.

'Sadly, I had gotten sick and tired of it all by now. Things always seemed to go wrong that were outside of our control. I walked away from Anchor completely, but John Weider stayed on and did another album under his own name. It bombed because they were struggling, and he did it as a contractual thing, I think.

'It was a piece of spectacular bad luck. Moonrider was a good band; it was just starting. We had a bunch of songs; we'd written the first songs, and put them together, and we were going to go from strength to strength. Annie Nightingale was big on us and was pushing the record on the radio, and 'Whispering' Bob Harris, he loved it too. It was all cool.

'Then the whole thing changed, punk came in, and it was all suddenly very old hat.'

Not that Keith, as it turned out, was to be a complete stranger to the punk scene as things developed.

20. Punk and a masterstroke for Masterswitch

Approaching his mid-30s, and now a father of three young girls, Keith was not the most natural of punks when the pop culture phenomenon approached its height in 1977. However, by chance, living in close proximity to Keith in Walton-on-Thames was a peer of his, from the R&B and mod days of the 60s. Someone who would drag him into the heart of the movement as it turned commercial and played out in central London.

Jimmy Edwards had been lead singer in The Neat Change, a popular mod band who scored a minor cult hit with the psychedelic single *I Lied to Auntie May* at around the same time that Keith was dominating the European charts with *Teenage Opera*. The two were essentially singer-songwriters and therefore hit it off.

As Keith recalls, 'A good friend of mine, Jimmy Edwards, was a fellow singer/songwriter and had a couple of record deals. He never really sold records in any great number, but there was always a bit of an interest in him from record companies as he was talented and very good-looking.

'He'd written a bunch of songs that were semi-punk, if you like, they were quite aggressive. He got together with a bunch of musicians who weren't really punks either, and I managed them. Along with Neville Shulman, my accountant, we secured a potentially massive deal for them with CBS.

'They didn't have any money, the guys in the band, especially Jimmy. His girlfriend, Natalie, and her friend were 'sort of' managing them and weren't making a very good job of it.

'He played me a load of the songs, and I thought they sounded really good; they were not really punk, but they had a lot of energy. I thought that they could ride the wave that punk had created, like The Police and other bands were doing.

'He was a standard songwriter, Jimmy, just like me. He can write standard, melodic songs and Natalie came to the conclusion that as I knew a lot of people, then I should try and get a deal for them.

'Initially, I was hesitant and said that I wasn't really a manager. But Jimmy was keen; he told me, 'It will just be a bit of fun, it won't last.' So I agreed and ended up taking things over and got them a couple of showcase gigs, one at the Marquee. For that show, I invited Maurice Oberstein from CBS down. I also invited Don Arden from Jet Records, who sent his son David down. Plus, a couple of other record labels.

'I remember David Arden was hiding in the club because there was all this spitting taking place, and it was mayhem on the stage. He was in a corner, and as I walked past he shouted, 'Keith!'

'I looked around; it was Dave, and he was terrified and said that he was only there because his dad wanted to sign a punk band. I told him that it was great he was interested but that there were many other record labels interested in signing the band also.

'Then CBS turned up. Maurice Oberstein, with his dogs. He just looked at them for about 10 minutes, had a drink with me, said that we had a deal, and that I should make sure to call him the next day. CBS were just buying anything that sounded like punk.'

With a highly lucrative offer from CBS on the cards, Keith was a little perturbed when he received an invitation to visit the infamous Don Arden and discuss Masterswitch being signed up by Jet Records.

For moral support, he asked John Jessup – a friend who he had recently met in hospital where his wife was expecting a baby at the same time as Pat, Keith's partner – to accompany him.[6]

John relays the story. 'Keith and I were close neighbours, and I helped out for about a year with Masterswitch.

'One day, Keith said he had been invited to Don Arden's house to look over a contract for Masterswitch. I didn't know who he was, but Keith said he was a bit dodgy with a bit of a reputation. I just naively thought that everything would be alright!'

'We went along to this huge house in Wimbledon, a real mansion, and we were let in by these guys straight out of central casting; they were your classic villains with flat noses and bulging jackets. We were shown into Don's office, which was a room of about 500 square feet with one heavy mahogany desk at the far end, and a bloke in dark glasses sitting at it.

'We made our way over and then we heard the door close behind us, and one of these guys is standing at the door. I looked at Keith and thought 'Shit! Are we going to get out of here alive?'

'I found out, subsequently, that to all intents and purposes Don Arden was a gangster and the way he ran Jet Records was by coercing people into signing for him and then ripping them off. We sat nervously in front of him, and we managed to get out of there without signing anything. We made some excuse about another deal being on the table.

'We were saying, 'We want to sign for Jet Records, it's a great company, but we just need to have a look at this other deal to be fair to the band.' He wasn't happy at all. He wasn't

[6] Keith's twin daughters arrived on the same day as John's daughter, and the two buddied up and stayed friends.

happy about letting us out, but I was elated to get out of there! We never went back…'

Keith remembers it well, too. 'Don threw a contract across his big old desk and said that we should sign it because it was a great deal. He even said he would give us an office in the house to work from.'

'I thought 'fuck that'; he would be all over me. I wouldn't stand a chance, and if the band did take off, I could end up as part of a support under a motorway bridge. Anyway, John and I made it out of there safely past the two stooges, who could have been armed for all we knew.

'I put Neville Shulman up as the fall guy, telling Don that he had to approve any deals. That's showbiz, folks!'

John Jessup was also with Keith on another potentially dangerous occasion, when the two of them found themselves in a tight situation with John Miller, the ex-SAS soldier who ran The Vortex (a punk/new wave club situated at the top of Wardour Street). As well as having a well-deserved reputation as a violent hardman, John Miller is also infamous for later masterminding a plot to kidnap Ronnie Biggs and bring him back to the UK (to then sell the story to the red top media). He is remembered by all who have met him as something of a character.

John Jessup recalls, 'Masterswitch were playing The Vortex, which was a big feather in our cap. I remember it was the night Elvis died [August 16th 1977] because an announcement was made and all the punks cheered – that was the kind of people you were dealing with.

'They were playing a punk showcase alongside Sham 69 and The Art Attacks, the Royal College of Art punk band. We were in the green room at the back with all these bands and lots of people wandering about when John Miller came over and said that he wanted us to sign a contract because they were going to be recording the show for a *Live at The Vortex* album.'

'Keith made some non-committal noises and said that we would have a look at the contract, but it could have potentially screwed the other deals we had on the table, and he managed not to sign it. For the rest of the night, we were being followed about by these ex-soldier, bouncer mates of John. They took a particular dislike to me and roughed me up and shoved me outside the door; all the while, I was protesting 'I'm part of the management!'

'Anyway, I was thrown outside into Wardour Street, and I couldn't see Keith, so I didn't know what was happening to him, and I couldn't get back in. Then, outside the club, I saw Jimmy Pursey, of Sham 69, having a cigarette and I said to him, 'Hang on a minute, Jimmy, your band's on stage, now!' He said, 'Yeah, they've thrown me out.' The same bouncer had thrown him out because they wouldn't sign the deal either. That's how crazy it was.'

One element that separated Masterswitch from their peers, aside from Jimmy's cocky demeanour and song-writing ability and history, was their musicianship. As Keith summarises, 'The songs were great, and the band were a lot better than the rest of the punk bands as they were musicians.' This did cause them some trouble when, occasionally, the band's punk authenticity was questioned.'

Keith remembers one example of this, 'I had trouble getting them some dates because CBS had an agency downstairs in their building, and the guy in charge didn't like them. He didn't think they were 'real' punks.

'All the other bands at CBS were getting bookings through that agency, so I went down to see him. I was mates with him as well, and asked him what his problem was because I needed to get the band some dates. His response was, 'They're not really punk. Let's be honest, they're Pop.'

'He had a point because they were accomplished musicians, which wasn't really what the punk ethos was all about. I asked him to do it for me, as a favour, and we started getting dates in, and we did really well. They played with Sham 69 and people like that; they were mates with Sham too.'

Jimmy Edwards recalls how the band got together. 'The first line-up wasn't the same as the one the public saw. It was Martin Lee on drums, and Ray Simone was the original guitarist and leader of the group until I joined. Steve Wilkin came in later as another guitar player. The bassist was Mark Steed.

'We were a punk band because I'd started writing punk songs before punk began. I was ready for punk. We played a couple of pubs and then the Roxy; so right from the off, we were in the thick of it.

'We did a lot of rehearsing because we wanted to be good, which wasn't really the ethic in those days. It was more 'I can't play so let's get up and form a band'. Which was great, but I was a bit older than most of them and could already play and had already put records out.

'I was lucky in that the punk scene embraced me. Mark P from *Sniffin' Glue* [an influential fanzine] liked what I did. Savage Pencil, the cartoonist and singer with The Art Attacks, liked us. We were like the Genesis of punk, our drummer was a really good drummer, and the guitarist was a great guitarist.

'I had to fight the group to play the music I wanted to play. I still didn't get it how I wanted it. I wanted it even more punky, more thrashy, not so arranged. I had to tell them what to wear, to get their hair cut. They ended up near what I wanted, but not perfect.'

While not a natural manager, Keith still negotiated Masterswitch a reputed $1 million record deal which Jimmy Edwards recalls, 'We signed to CBS for a phenomenal amount of money. But we had to deliver six albums to get all the lucre, and we never even made the first one.'

Until a compilation album rounded up all their demo material in 2010, the only Masterswitch material to see the light of day at the time was the 7" single *Action Replay* B/w *Mass Media Meditation*. However, if you are only going to record one single to be judged by, then *Action Replay* is an incredibly good offering. It has, over the years, become recognised as a punk anthem.

As Keith recalls, 'I was mates with Vic Maile, who engineered The Who *Live at Leeds,* and Masterswitch were looking for a producer. He'd just done *2-4-6-8 Motorway* for Tom Robinson which is a great record and nice and simple. He's only got a simple studio, and he works quickly; I knew he'd be great for the band.

'Vic wanted to do it live-ish, but the band went in and they were all disappointed; they thought that it was going to be some massive studio, especially the guitar player. He was a real moaner, Steve Wilkin, but he was a pretty good guitar player. 'It's fucking cardboard,' I remember him saying, because there were egg boxes on the walls of the studio. I told them not to worry, as Vic would make them sound like The Who.

'They were a difficult bunch, and they didn't like me much either, although I always got on with Jimmy, and he was the band, basically. He was writing all the stuff.

'The drummer thought he was going to be in Kiss or something, one of the biggest drum kits you've ever seen, which obviously you can't take on stage at a punk club.'

Jimmy Edwards' version of events corroborates Keith's experience. He says, 'As soon as we got signed, I noticed changes in the group. They all became like superstars, instantly. We hadn't even had a fuckin' record out.

'They wanted Ampeg amps; they wanted thirty thousand drums. It was only me and the bassist Mark Steed who adhered to the punk ethic of not wanting all that equipment. Our contract said we could get CBS to buy us gear, but – of course – we'd have to pay for the equipment down the line, once our records were selling. The rest of the group went into the office demanding these amps, these drums, these this, these that! I didn't know about this at the time.

'We were being managed at the time by Keith; he was a friend of mine. He phoned me up and said, 'Your fucking group have run into CBS and demanded this, that, and the other.' I thought here we go; they think they're rock stars and our single isn't out yet. *Action Replay* had been recorded, and everyone was pleased with it, but it hadn't even been pressed yet. The group got the equipment they wanted too, but CBS complained to Keith about their attitude and the expense and asked him what the fuck he thought this group was doing.

'In response, I sacked the band apart from the bass player Mark Steed. That was it; I was finished with them. No more Masterswitch.

'Then, Keith said CBS wanted me to put a new Masterswitch together. In the meantime, *Action Replay* was released. It didn't do much; it didn't get promoted. Everything was all over the place. Keith wasn't really a manager; it was a favour for me because we were mates. He's a musician. He was fed up and quit, although we worked together musically after that.'

When *Action Replay* came out on the 21st of April 1978, John Peel supported it, and Annie Nightingale played it on her radio show too, but there was next to no promotion from CBS due to doubts over the band's future. The song is now considered to be something of a punk/new wave classic but at the time – aside from attracting some critical acclaim and some airplay from a few influential DJs – it did nothing.

With Masterswitch breaking up, Keith and Jimmy remained on friendly and collaborative terms. As Keith continues, 'After The Jam split up in 1982, I worked with Jimmy and Rick Buckler. We had a band called WEB – West, Edwards, Buckler – at least it was a better name than Bodast. We wrote a bunch of songs.

'Rick's a smart guy, and very easy to work with. He pretty much transformed all the drum parts and was really good at programming. Jimmy and I wrote the songs. I wrote the music, Jimmy co-wrote the lyrics with me; he was very easy to work with and always had interesting ideas. We wrote a bunch of good songs; they'd probably sound very dated now. They were done on my little Tascam Portastudio 4-track studio at home, and some of them have been released.

'That band never got out of the studio really. We went to see David Howells at PWL [Pete Waterman Limited], who was an old chum of mine. Jimmy took the songs up which David thought were great, but he couldn't see what he could do with them. It was all Kylie and Jason at the time. He said he'd like to sign us but that even a publishing deal would be a waste of our time. So, we messed around with a few ideas, and then decided not to take it any further.'

Keith's relationship with Jimmy Edwards and Rick Buckler would continue into the mid-1980s. Jimmy and Rick linked up again with Ray Simone, who was in Masterswitch, and formed Time UK. The band released three singles and were unfortunate not to achieve greater success.

Typifying the sort of luck and ridiculous behaviour that occurs in the music business, their first single *The Cabaret* sold 60,000 copies but was excluded from the charts, and from BBC Radio 1 airplay, due to accusations of chart rigging by their record company; accusations that subsequently turned out to be false.

Their third single, *Playground of Privilege,* issued in 1985 has Keith's song *Puppets Don't Bleed* on the B-side, and when the band evolved into Sharp (with the addition of Bruce Foxton also from The Jam on bass), they recorded Keith's *Sunday Mood* which has only more recently become available on the Time UK compilation album *One More Time*. A track from that time, *Peter Pan*, written by Jimmy about Keith, remains unreleased.

21. Grocer Jack refuses to die

Even with punk and new wave ruling the charts, talk of making a *Teenage Opera* in one form or another continued to surface frequently. As Keith recalls, 'Many people have expressed interest in producing a *Teenage Opera* and, over the years, there's a lot of people who have started to develop productions.

'One of them who approached me was Ray Davies of The Kinks. I had a meeting with one of his management guys and also present was Bruce Foxton, the bass player from The Jam. I was a bit confused at this meeting, I really was. I just said, 'Look, you can do whatever you like with it. If you want me to write a couple of songs or co-write some, I'm up for that. You've got my blessing to do what you like with it. Come back with a draft, and I'll look at it.''

While nothing came of this particular project, a more concrete development came through the formation of a new company called, pointedly, Grocer Jack Promotions. With it came a new business associate, David Prowse-Jones, who was introduced to Keith through the ever-magnanimous Malcolm Forrester.

As Keith says about his new employer, 'He was a real hard case and a handy guy to have around if there was any trouble. He was an ex-policeman, and he looked a bit like Tom Jones; all the ladies loved him.

'He put quite a bit of money behind the *Teenage Opera* project; we made an animated short film and played it to some producers. We hired a theatre and a projectionist, and I'd even written a couple of new songs for it along with David who played piano. When it came down to it, I think he was asking for too much money; he was trying to turn it into a movie. When he first came to me, it was a theatre production. That drifted away, much to my relief to be honest with you.'

While the focus of Grocer Jack Promotions was on trying to realise the multitude of ideas around *Teenage Opera*, David Prowse-Jones also had his fingers in many other pies. 'They had a successful advertising agency as well, with the Guinness account,' recalls Keith. 'They teamed up with Jim Bowen from Bullseye and Guinness and took it out as a package on the road, which was a marriage made in heaven in marketing terms. They were making a fortune out of it and pumping the money into this, that, and the other.'

One area that received some investment was a record label, Video Records, and a music publishing company, Video Music. They were established as Prowse-Jones was a songwriter and was also keen to exploit any rock and roll kudos and connections that Keith still had. Keith reflects on the period, 'I had a lovely big office at the company's base in Windsor, opposite the castle, and I was sitting in this office doing pretty much nothing, along with a secretary with no other tasks to perform other than brewing Italian coffee, and pretending to be busy on the phone if anyone from upstairs deemed to visit.

'I was still trying to work out what I was doing there in the first place. I had some publishing deals on the go but needed a hand with the practical, administrative aspects.'

It was at this point that fate, and Bodast, would once again raise their heads in Keith's career.

The tale is best told from Martin Costello's perspective: 'I started in '76 with Malcolm Forrester and Getaway Music, and it was my job to do all the tape copying. I would be told to 'Get this song out to that bloke' or to 'Get that song out to these guys'. And, of course, when you do all the tape copying, you get to know the catalogue really well.

'Amongst various tapes was a thing called Bodast/Steve Howe. I can remember asking Malcolm what it was, and he told me it was a Steve Howe album, produced by Keith West. I mentioned to Malcolm that I thought I could get a record deal for the album because I'd become friendly with Iain McNay at Cherry Red Records.

'I spoke to McNay about the Bodast album, and he wanted to put it out, which was great, so I went to dig it out, and Malcolm seemed pleased.

'Anyway, at the last minute, Malcolm got cold feet. He started to question who really owned the tapes, and he said that Brian Lane [manager of Yes] would come down on him like a ton of bricks.

'I spoke to Iain and explained that Malcolm now didn't want to go ahead and told him why. Iain's attitude was bullish, and he started to question if Malcolm even owned the masters.

'So Iain, showing true indie label spirit, said, 'I don't care. I'll do it anyway. I'll still do a deal with somebody; we'll sign a bit of paper and we'll see what happens.' So, I teed up Keith with Iain McNay, plus it transpired that *Keith actually owned the master tapes*. They worked a deal out. I advised Keith what he should be asking for, points-wise and money-wise, and that's it.

'The publishing was put in Sunset Music, which is Keith's company. I was seriously just advising. He had a little company called Sunset Music; I wasn't an owner, shareholder, director or anything. It was nothing to do with me.

'In the meantime, I was embarrassed because Iain had just signed a new band called the Dead Kennedys and offered us their publishing for five grand, which I thought was a brilliant deal for us.

'But, Malcolm said, he couldn't possibly sign a band called the Dead Kennedys and scuppered the deal. I was a bit put out and felt better about advising Keith on his deal because I kind of figured my days there were numbered. I also sent out the album, on Keith's behalf, to a few of my affiliate mates in America thinking they might want to license it, and if they did they should contact Sunset Music. Anyway, Keith and Iain do their deal and I go away on holiday.

'Unfortunately, while I was away, a letter came to the offices from one of these USA affiliate partners wanting to license the Bodast record. Someone saw the letter and told Malcolm that, basically, I'd got a joint venture going with Keith West and I'm fucking around and doing deals behind his back and blah, blah, blah. The upshot is, Tony Calder [formerly of Immediate Records and now advising Cherry Red and doing all their overseas deals] and Forrester phone McNay to see what's going on.

'I then get a phone call from McNay telling me he had received a call from Tony Calder and Malcolm. He told them it was nothing to do with me. It was Keith West. That I was just helping him out, but he warned me that when I got back to work, the shit's going to hit the fan.

'I went back to work, and the shit hit the fan. Malcolm fired me. It must've been middle to end of '81 when he fired me. I remember I said to Malcolm, 'You know about this record. I had fuck-all to do with this record. You know that, I know that. But, obviously, there's a lot of people in here that don't want me around.'

'What I didn't realise was that half the staff hated my guts. I was then just 21 or 22-years-old, and I was doing all the deals and going to meetings and dealing with Rainbow, and dealing with all the big bands and managers and the other people in the office had got the hump.

'Years later, Malcolm said to me, 'Martin, they fucking hated you. I had them all at me. They all hated you.'

'Anyway, I got kicked out of there and I rang around all my mates telling them I had been kicked out of Panache Music; asking have they got anything for me? There were a lot of 'We'll call you backs', and as many 'I can't hear you properly you're cracking up'... followed by the dial tone. It was a harsh lesson learnt early on in the music business. The only person that called me back was Keith West.

'He's the only guy that called me back, and he felt really bad about it. He couldn't believe that Malcolm had sacked me.

'So, anyway, I spent three months painting the ceiling at Tesco's on Sutton High Street. Chocolate brown it was; my brother got me the job down there as I had no money. In the meantime, Keith was being managed by a bunch of advertising guys who he had met through Malcolm Forrester. David Prowse-Jones and George Hales.

'David Prowse-Jones was a budding songwriter, a terrible songwriter, but Malcolm took a shine to the fact that he had an advertising background. I had no interest. I was trying to sign bands like The Clash to publishing deals, so some bloke who's in his forties who wears a suit doesn't interest me. I kept out of it. Anyway, he put Keith together with this guy, David Prowse-Jones, to try and finish off the opera.

'He thought – with Prowse-Jones's advertising contacts – it could all be great. Anyway, the upshot was, David Prowse-Jones ended up managing Keith West. So, in-between my departure from Panache and my painting the ceiling at Tesco, these guys had set up their own agency called Grocer Jack Promotions.

'They gave Keith the job of setting up a record company and a publishing company, and after a couple of months of painting ceilings, I got a call from Keith saying there could be a job for me. He knew they had a bit of money as they'd given him a car, so he thought there might be a bit of work for me to get myself back in.

'He saved my life, Keith West. He really did. He was the only one who rang me back. He was the only one who did anything. All the guys I thought I knew, like his songwriting partner, Ken Burgess, I rang them all up, and the only response I got was that they'd 'call me back'. Keith was the only one who rang me back.'

Video Music and Video Records – so named as to jump on the back of the nascent video technology boom – seemed to be going places when Martin Costello arrived to join Keith at the tail end of 1981.

'We signed Miles Davis,' says Keith proudly. 'We had the whole Miles Davis catalogue, including my all-time favourite jazz record *Kind of Blue*. And we tried to sign *Poison Arrow* by ABC which Martin spotted and liked.

'We were going out, drinking lots of wine at lunchtime, schmoozing and looking at other deals. We went to MIDEM – the music publishers' annual event held in Cannes every February – and we did well there. Everybody knew us, and we ended up organising a deal with Shalamar who went on to have hits like *A Night to Remember, I Can Make you Feel Good,* etc. and also The Whispers, another soul band that had a load of hits. We had a deal with them to sign their publishing; it was $20,000 for the whole lot and we came back and put it to the board – but they rejected it.

'I was the frontman for this kind of stuff, and they rejected the deal. I remember Martin, when these records started to chart, he would ring them [David Prowse-Jones, etc.] and tell them how much money they had passed up or he would even buy the records, along with copies of *Billboard* magazine showing the chart positions, and put it on their desks to wind them up.'

Martin Costello, too, recalls the frustration of not being able to build Video Music. 'When I first got there, it was really busy as they were issuing a novelty Christmas song from a popular kids TV show, and they also re-issued *Excerpt from a Teenage Opera* [complete with new wave record sleeve]. I thought it was great, and I thought they had money, and again, Keith thought they had money. They had X-Reg cars, staff, and an office in Windsor, Coutts bank accounts, and all this stuff.

'We set up a deal with SOLAR [Sound Of Los Angeles Recordings] to publish Shalamar and The Whispers which would have been hugely profitable deals. But they had burnt through their cash. When we presented the deal, they said they had cashflow problems, and that they couldn't do the deal at that time. As time went on, I began to realise that this excellent deal was not going to happen.

'By now, we're sort of into March, April time, and I started to ask questions about where the money for this deal was. Anyway, it turned out they had no money, so everything fell apart. But their egos wouldn't allow us to walk out.

'I was literally saying, 'You're all chancers. You've got no fucking idea. We had all these deals lined up, and you screwed them up.' But, for some reason, their egos wouldn't allow them to throw me out.

'They wanted to appease the situation and would say that they wanted to work things out. So, as Keith and I were still getting paid, I thought we should hang in there. But Keith was getting pissed off at this point, and I had to work hard to get him to stay and take the money. 'Fuck 'em' was my attitude.

'We had a very bizarre meeting where they took Keith and me to meet their bank manager. It must have been the Coutts guy because I had already said to them that they should be investing in music catalogues which can be treated as assets. This is going back 40 years and, of course, now everyone realises that good catalogues are assets and I was trying to convince them to put some money up and buy some catalogues based on the bands in the catalogues.

'It's sensible business, but in those days people didn't trust music. So, I'm sitting with these two guys, Prowse-Jones and George Hales, and Keith and me. Anyway, the upshot was that the bank manager agreed to loan the business money to buy the catalogues, but he wanted to set a charge on a house. He's suddenly looking at Keith because I think the others already had charges on their houses. I had a bedsit in Sutton at this point, so no-one's interested in me.

'I'm looking at Keith at this point trying to get the message across, 'No, don't do this,' and the bank manager's looking at Keith with the same facial expression as me, 'Don't do this.' They basically wanted Keith to put his house on the line to raise some money to keep the company going, which is what another guy who worked there – who ran their film side – had done. He'd put his house on the line.

'Anyway, Keith didn't, and so it got very nasty. They were accusing him of not supporting the company and it got quite bad for Keith, but I kept telling him that we should hang in there as they were paying us. He hung in as long as he could. We both did… then we both fucked off, and I ended up setting up Bayswater Music as a joint company with Iain McNay.'

Despite losing his new best friend, Keith – as always – would not have to wait long until another opportunity came along. This time he would, once again, work with John Jessup who was now with Leo Burnett, the giant advertising agency based in London.

'I remember I asked Keith to produce a rocked-up version of *Really Saying Something* [later covered by Bananarama] for a Vidal Sassoon campaign which we shot some test films for, but never used,' says John Jessup, 'and we continued to collaborate on other bits and pieces.'

Keith really enjoyed the work he did in the advertising industry and recalls his time working with John fondly, 'The agency had the Texaco account and the Kellogg's account, stuff like that, so when they were pulling together a campaign, they would put a storyboard together – to show to the client – and they would ask me to put some music to it [the storyboard] to help sell the vision.

'If they won the pitch, I'd go into the studio and do it on a 24-track. I recorded at home too; I had a studio at home, so I worked there. I did a lot of stuff like that, and some of the contracts came through, some didn't.

'I had a nice little home studio in my house near Weybridge. At that time, I was running the latest software, doing it all on the latest sequencer, a Steinberg, and using a big Allen and Heath desk. Plus I had a plethora of outboard gear all running through my Sequential Circuits Prophet T8 – which I bought from Spandau Ballet when they broke up.

'I learned a lot about engineering, pretty quickly. Compressors and reverb, this kind of stuff. How to mic guitars up. I got reasonably good at that, I think. I did the whole thing on my own.

'I could programme the drums, play keyboards, bass, guitar, do the whole thing on my own. A one-man band, basically.

'Music is great for storyboarding; a little soundtrack to a storyboard is perfect. It's all you need. You don't need a full-blown production at that stage because you might not get it past the clients. You probably only use 30 seconds, something like that.

'I did one for Alan Sugar and Amstrad computers. The ad was only 28 seconds long, and it was only about eight seconds of music at the end of the day.

'That was good fun for me. It was easy, really easy. Plus, a friend of mine had a studio, a guy called Chris West. He was a good engineer and we used to work really fast in there. We'd get it all done in just a few hours. I'd have all the programming done on a disk, so I'd shove it into his system; it would all be programmed, everything I'd sequenced in. He was a good musician as well, so if I needed anything really hot on guitar or keyboard, he would do that.

'I enjoyed that and did it for quite a few years. It was really good money because the budgets in those days were enormous. I remember mad lunches, for hours, in Soho with the creative team and the client. L'Escargot was their favourite restaurant. It cost an absolute fortune; even just the wine bill was enormous. We also got the Boulogne Tourist Board account. We used to go over to Boulogne, and wine and dine their clients with the staff, and it was good to be in a team environment as well.

'It was great fun as they were a great bunch. They were all frustrated film directors, essentially, who wanted to make their own little movies – but getting it past the client is the difficult thing. You can't be too self-indulgent, they want to see the product.'

John Jessup, it transpires, would also join the ranks of those who attempted to develop *Excerpt from a Teenage Opera* into some type of coherent production. When he first met Keith, he recalls, 'We got chatting about the *Grocer Jack* thing which was part of my growing up as a teenager, and we wrote a story that could possibly have been made into a show or film or whatever. It was the whole opera; the rest of the story we just sort of re-imagined and we started to get some interest.

'We made an 'animatic'; a film of illustrations that was over an hour-long complete with narration, and then some other people got involved [David Prowse-Jones], and I backed out because I didn't really get on with the other people. It was a shame because I thought we'd written an interesting take on who this guy was, and it all became quite fantastical which – at the time – was the style.'

Frustratingly, a copy of this animatic has proved impossible to track down, although John Jessup thinks it may be in a storage facility he has. Mike Read, the former Radio 1 DJ, who also attempted to develop a *Teenage Opera* script, believes he could also have a copy in storage. Keith believes he may have sacrilegiously thrown his out, in a cull of material in the late 1980s.

Try as he might, *Teenage Opera* is something which Keith has been unable to shake off during the more than 50 years since it was created. In 1996, the project once again reared its head when the record label RPM produced what they called *A Teenage Opera: The Original Soundtrack Recording* which was an album produced in conjunction with Mark Wirtz.

The album is an odd one though, including as it does, Tomorrow tracks such as *Shy Boy* and *Colonel Brown* but omitting *Sam* and *A Thimble full of Puzzles…* songs that were originally written specifically to be included in the opera.

'I've not really listened to it closely,' explains Keith, 'but it's all orchestral music, and there's like 12 pieces of it, or something. It's all bits of stuff that he'd written and tried to cobble together and shove it on there, but it didn't work. The show that they put together, it didn't work either. They weren't songs. They were just sketches.'

The show which Keith is referencing is the National Youth Theatre production of *Teenage Opera* which was staged to celebrate the song's 50th anniversary in 2017. 'I told them to include some different material,' says Keith, 'and the response was, 'Well, Mark's been over [he resided in the USA at the time], and he wants to do this; he wants to do that.' So, basically, he'd taken it over. I thought, if he wants to take it over, I'm quite happy to let him do it. I'm not really interested in it.

'I did go and support the show, but it only ran in a theatre in Brentwood for four nights. It was fun, and I had a nice chat and a catch up with Mark and his wife, Amanda.'

It would be the last time that the two central protagonists in the *Teenage Opera* saga would meet as, in August 2020, Mark Wirtz sadly passed away in the USA.

22. An original indie kid

While Keith was busy with his advertising projects in the mid-1980s, his partner in crime from the Video Music days, Martin Costello, was steadily building his music publishing business with Iain McNay of Cherry Red Records. Bayswater music, formed after Costello left the ailing publishing and record company, would eventually merge with Cherry Red Music and form Complete Music in October 1984.

Complete Music would be a great success, establishing a strong partnership with Creation Records, and publishing such big names as The Stranglers, Primal Scream, Nirvana, and The Manic Street Preachers. It would also become the de-facto indie publishing house with such bands as The Primitives, The Go-Betweens, Aztec Camera, Everything But The Girl, Felt, Loop, and dozens more under its banner.

While Complete Music was a separate entity to the record label, Cherry Red Records, they shared offices and Iain McNay had a commercial interest in both. As much as music publishing is a part of the music business, it is firmly located at the 'business' end of that spectrum. Running a record label is much more rock and roll (as the man in the street would see it) as the label swings from high to deep, with gay abandon, on the back of finding the next big thing. The two ends of the spectrum don't necessarily sit together happily. Adding to the problems caused by this clash of cultures was the fact that Iain McNay was prone to taking extended sabbaticals.

Martin Costello recalls the period. 'Iain went off again, but this time he was away for four years! He started off él Records, a subsidiary of Cherry Red, prior to his departure, and he brought Mike Alway back in. Mike had worked for Cherry Red previously, and been partly responsible for the putting together and signing of Everything But The Girl – who sold a lot of records.

'Iain buggered off. We'd moved both the records and publishing business to Fulham High Street, but the records side was haemorrhaging money. James Kyler, who's sadly dead now, was running the label and Mike Alway was responsible for A&R.

'I just knew that the bills weren't being paid. The record company management kept sending stuff to Iain McNay saying that everything was going brilliantly, and I just knew there were hundreds of thousands of pounds of unpaid bills.

'So, I got the accountant to contact Iain and make sure he saw the real numbers. Anyway, the upshot was I got a call – I was in Hong Kong on business at the time – from Iain saying that he'd seen the real numbers and it was bad, and could I sort it out or he would shut down the record label.

'Anyway, Iain offered me some cash, and I came back and had to sort out all these artists and record projects. Some people wouldn't work with me. They just went sulk, sulk, sulk, to which my reaction was, 'Fine. You're off the label.'

'But others, for example Louis Philippe – whose real name was Philippe O'Claire – was one of the acts that was selling records, so we made an album under my stewardship which was *Yuri Gagarin*. A great record. I still had lots of the old stuff hanging about and got Keith in to finish it all off.

'I didn't want to handle all these maniacs, so I just got Keith in to sort a lot of stuff out, and that resulted in people leaving. But Keith was being brought in not just to produce, but to try and arrange stuff as well, and talk to the artists because I didn't have time for it. I got Keith in because I needed some back-up, frankly. I put him on a retainer, just to deal with these people.'

As Martin Costello recalls, 'The publishing company ended up being bigger than the record label by a mile. That's what everyone said. It was the tail wagging the dog in the end, because around the offices, we had gold discs everywhere. They weren't Cherry Red's. They were all Complete's.'

Working as 'in-house' producer, manager, artist babysitter, songwriter, and arranger for Cherry Red Records would be a highly productive period for Keith, with a couple of genuine highlights. As Keith recalls, 'Mike Alway had all sorts of trendy and weird acts. I produced a couple of records for him. One was by a group called the Would-Be-Goods, which was two girls. One was a model, one was her sister, but they couldn't sing to save their lives, but I managed to get an album out of them. I don't know how I did it. The engineer said I deserved a gold watch. He couldn't take it, at times, and left me alone on the desk while I rewound the tape machine back and forth – there was no Pro Tools in those days!

'Jessica Griffin was the name of the girl writing the songs and they're clever songs; little, posh girl ballads. I did it on a budget with Monochrome Set, another band on the label… they did all the back end. They were kind of an in-house band and did all the backing tracks.

'Then Jessica and her sister Miranda came in and sang out of tune most of the time. I just kept working them. In the end, I was enjoying putting them through it because they were such a pair of stuck up posers, they really were. Making them go over and over it again, so they'd get it right.

'What kept me going was that Jessica's voice had a certain fragile quality about it, and I wanted to make her sound good; the quirky songs had decent lyrics in them too. We never got on, obviously, but after it was all done Jessica did actually say to me that she didn't know how I did it, how I made them sound that good. There was appreciation at the end of it all, but it was painful.'

As well as professional integrity Keith's tenacity can be traced back to another source. As Keith recalls, 'Two or three months prior to recording the Would-be-Goods, I woke up covered in bruises. My GP asked me if I had been in a fight, which I hadn't obviously.

'I was sent for a check-up, and the doctor ran some tests. She informed me that they would be in touch in a couple of weeks. I arrived home, and later that afternoon, the phone rang; it was the hospital, and they requested that I return immediately. The consensus was that I might have leukaemia!

'The doctor took some blood tests, and bone marrow samples, and – luckily for me – leukaemia was ruled out. The problem was with my platelets, so I was basically a haemophiliac. That meant no sports – racketball with Martin Costello – and sharp knives were a no-no.

'The reason I'm explaining this is that I was put on a course of heavy dosage steroids, to kick start my adrenal glands which really pumped me up. I felt like Superman for a short period, right in the middle of these sessions. I think that helped me through the production and kept my mind off a very stressful period for me.'[7]

Listened to in 2020, *The Camera Loves Me,* the album by the Would-Be-Goods, and especially the single of the same name, is a great example of the literate, spartan style of music which was dominating the indie scene at the time. It was well received by the music press and sold reasonably well.

Another highlight would be working with the brilliantly named Bad Dream Fancy Dress. As Catrin Rees (Cat) from the band recalls, 'We did our album *Choirboys Gas* with Mike Alway, and then he and Cherry Red parted company. I believe we were made to choose between Alway or Cherry Red, and I wanted to go with Alway, but Cally [band member Cally Davis] was insistent on going with Cherry Red.

[7] A big thank you to our wonderful NHS as the treatment worked.

'We went with Cherry Red who obviously thought – as ska was all the rage – that they would get Keith to knock out a few ska tunes, *Flair* and *You Wind Me Up,* for us. We recorded these at his impressive studio at his house, but we only ever met him the once.'

Keith remembers, 'They were great fun to work with, the exact opposite of the Griffins. It was a joy, and they gave great vocal performances in the studio on the track, *Flair*. Full of bounce and laughter all through the day; lovely girls really down to earth.'

The 7" single *Flair*, released on Cherry Red in 1989 (B/w *You Wind Me Up*) is an interesting record in Keith's career, marking as it does the first time he would combine his passion for football with song, on record. As he explains, '*Flair* was all about Stanley Bowles and George Best. It was a tribute song to the players that had a lot of flair at the time. My mate, John Jessup, and I wrote the lyrics on that one.'

Combining an understanding of football and an ability to write and record decent songs quickly (and to a budget) would prove to be a sideline income for Keith and John Jessup for the next few years. Titles included: *The Don's are comin', We're backing Strachan, The Boys in Green, The Glamour boys, Follow the Eagles,* and many, many more.

As Martin Costello says, 'Jim Phelan, who was the artwork guy at Cherry Red, he did a Villa track. It was a parody. It was 'Dwight Yorke, Dwight Yorke', to the tune of *New York, New York* and Iain McNay couldn't understand why EMI came down on him like a ton of bricks.

'The EMI, head of copyright, she said, 'No way. 'Dwight Yorke, Dwight Yorke?', 'New York, New York?' You're not having it.'

''Ooh, aah, Cantona, ooh aah Cantona' was on it too, and John Fogarty – who published *Oops Up Side Your Head* –

stopped that record coming out as well. There was loads of football records coming out of Cherry Red at the time because we were all crazy about football and there was a guaranteed return from the fanbase. You'd do a Brighton record and immediately sell 1,000 to the fan club, for example. There must have been ten football albums.'

At around the same time, another notable visitor to Keith's home studio was indie 'legend' Lawrence Hayward, more commonly known as Lawrence from Felt. Despite a #1 indie single (*Primitive Painters*), they never made it big, but they signed to Creation Records and released *Forever Breathes The Lonely Word,* (published by Complete Music) which is lauded as one of the decade's best indie-pop albums.

As Keith recalls, 'I met Lawrence at the annual MPA [Music Publishers Association] Christmas party, at the Park Lane Hilton, and we got on really well. He admitted that he thought the event was going to be awful – full of executives and not the kind of people that 'artists' like to associate with.

'He asked me to help him put together a couple of songs, so I picked him up at Weybridge station, and we recorded in my home studio. Everybody warned me that he was very shy and moody, but I didn't find that at all. He seemed relaxed with me, and was just happy drinking tea and eating buttered toast.

'I do remember he had a very soft voice, and it was difficult to get a decent level on the track, but I worked it out so he was happy. I dropped him off back at the train station, and the next time I spoke to him about the tracks, I introduced the topic of publishing, as we had developed the music together and I had even written the bulk of the music for one track.

'Surprisingly, he told me that he alone writes the songs, and there was to be no credit where I was concerned. It wasn't worth arguing over… any income would have been minimal. So, I took him off my Christmas card list!'

As the 80s drew to a close, and the early 'noughties' came into view, there would be another fun collaboration with his great friend Martin Costello. It would bring Keith an indie top 10 hit and airplay on Radio 1.

As Martin Costello recalls, 'Taboo's *Number Six* was released on Anagram Records, which is an offshoot of Cherry Red, and sold the most of any record they ever released. But Taboo was basically Keith and me messing about.

'Anagram was originally a punk label that had been going since about '82. Anyway, I was running the record label, and a lot of people were putting records out. I thought, 'Fuck it, I'm going to put a record out.' So, I had the idea of doing *The Prisoner* [from the iconic 1960s TV Show] with Keith producing and providing vocals.

'I said to Keith that we should just nick the theme. Take the theme, and whack some samples on it. In those days, people were sampling all over the place without giving any credit to the original track or paying anything. No one knew any better. As a publisher, I figured the shit would hit the fan at some point. You can't just sample anything you please. But everyone was doing it. So, we put Patrick McGoohan's voice on it, and we put it out, and we got loads of airplay!

'Keith and Chris West put it all together, and it was Simon Mayo's record of the week. We had people like Radio 1 DJ Mike Read going, 'And you won't believe who is actually behind this record.''

Keith even recalls the song being be banned in some countries. The hook on the record was a voice repeating the number SIX SIX SIX which was mistakenly interpreted as SEX SEX SEX!

In terms of Radio 1, Keith remembers, 'I phoned Simon Mayo up, he was the enormously popular host of the breakfast show which attracted millions of listeners at the time, and spoke to him. Martin encouraged me to ring him when he made us the record of the week, but I thought he wouldn't answer my phone call. Anyway, I called up and the researcher who answered just said, 'Keith West's on the phone, I'll put him through,' and there I was – live on the BBC's breakfast show – with an audience of five million people. Crazy!

'It was top 10 in the indie charts; back when the indie charts actually meant something!' continues Martin Costello. 'It was nearly a top 40 hit, and it actually sold between 12 and 15,000 copies in the UK. We gave away badges as well; remember the acid house smiley badge? We did those, but we had him behind iron bars as The Prisoner. Keith and I took a co-write on it, obviously.

'There was meant to be two Taboo songs. Keith was a big Tintin fan, and we made *Tintin To the Rescue*. He did the track with loads of vocoder on the vocals. It had a squeaky, mad voice and loads of spiky piano and it sounded great.

'I was rather annoyed when, a few years later, *Do you believe?* by Cher used exactly the same vocoder effects and was massive. We couldn't get clearance from the estate to use it, because we had a load of samples from Tintin on it. It was a great record. Keith put in a lot of time and effort, and it was really good, but it didn't come out.

'We thought we'd do it correctly that time. Go and see the people who owned the rights – the Hergé estate – and they were very clear in the fact that if we released the record, they were going to sue us. It was a bit of a wakeup call. We made test pressings, but it's a shame because it was really good and it would have done well.'

23. Guitar guru

As well as the advertising work that kept Keith gainfully employed following his departure from Video Music, he was also pursuing what today would be called 'a portfolio career', with several different strands operating concurrently. However, as might be imagined in the music business, these strands were wildly different.

As Keith recalls from the time, 'John Jessup had formed his own company with a guy called Neil Barker, so I worked with them for a while on several of their accounts. They were called Barker, Jessup and Partners, as I remember. But, budgets weren't what they were, and I had time for other things. Happily, I fell into selling vintage guitars.

'It happened by chance, really. I had a bunch of guitars, and I realized that they'd gone up in value by quite a bit – things like Epiphone Casinos and some Fenders and Gibsons I'd picked up along the way.

'I started to sell a few off to buy some other musical equipment –keyboards and stuff like that – for my home studio. Anyway, out of the blue, I started to get offered things from various people; I made some valuable friends in the business, and before I knew it, I was a full-blown vintage guitar dealer.'

Going into further detail, Keith says, 'The vintage guitar thing took over for a bit. I visited Boston two or three times a year, where I had a partner, a guy called Danny Boucher, and there was a shop in Boston called *Mr Music* and another famous chain called the *Guitar Center*.

'In America, shops work differently. If the stock hasn't sold within a certain period of time, they just get rid of it. That's where people like Danny and me used to come in. We would phone up the shops' managers and ask them how things were going, and normally they would say they were under pressure to move on loads of goods. So, we would go and have a look.

'I'd fly out there, meet up with Danny, and we'd make a list of what we wanted on the shop floor. Maybe 50 or 60 pieces, and then we'd cut a deal with them.

'All the guitars had cases; it all looked very professional. They were all vintage instruments, and I didn't think we could find anything at that price anywhere in Europe. Plus, they were models I knew I could sell in England. Also, we chose Japanese guitar brands licensed by Fender because that kind of market was growing in London, owing to the fact that they were high quality and better value.

'We chose a lot of 60s guitars too, including the weird and wonderful Teisco models, Rickenbackers, Hofners and some Burns models – all kinds of stuff that was fashionable in Denmark Street. The *Music Ground* shop was pretty much the leader in this market, and led a lot of the trends which gave me an idea of what to buy.

'We'd ship them mostly into Denmark Street, also some local stores, maybe six or seven smaller ones that we knew as well; they would buy eight to ten pieces at a time. We sold a few to pop stars, too.

'Sony, if they were making presentations, they would ask me what I had. Noel Gallagher is a well-known Beatles fan, and I found him a Gibson J 160 – a John Lennon acoustic which used to belong to the 10cc singer Eric Stewart. I sourced a case and ordered a badge which was engraved and read 'Presented to Noel Gallagher from Sony Music' and took it up to their offices.

'It was all going really well, and then the internet started to become more influential, and the business began eroding slightly. There was less and less interest because everybody started to know exactly what these things were worth, and where you could get them. You couldn't make the margins you needed to cover the trips to the States and the shipping.

'We were probably working at about 30% profit margin in those days; on the vintage ones you'd make a little bit more, but that was your bottom line. It just wasn't worth doing it otherwise.

'It was great fun though I have to say. I love guitars; I always have, ever since seeing Buddy Holly's Stratocaster. I enjoy cleaning them up, putting them in cases, shipping them off; it's not work by any stretch of the imagination.

'I learned a lot about guitars and the way that whole industry works; plus the dealers and the fakes and all the rest of the business that goes on, not unlike the antiques world. I used to set guitars up too, with Danny – basic servicing, intonation, polish the frets up. Many times, problems can come from the nut on a guitar; most people think you should change the tuners, but the nuts usually have quite a bit more to do with it than people think.

'I formed a business for all of this vintage guitar work; it was called Q-track. Then I met Barry Gibson, a professional musician and – unbeknownst to me at that time – a guitar builder.'

Meeting Barry was to lead to a largely unknown but relatively lucrative, and certainly great fun, chapter in Keith's career. Barry was playing in a rockabilly band called Rock Island Line that had a part in the David Essex movie *That'll Be The Day*, and as such he had become firmly entrenched in the rock and roll heritage scene, playing with various members of The Shadows and other luminaries. Through these connections, Barry had met Mike Read, then riding a huge wave of popularity as a Radio 1 DJ as well as fronting his own TV programmes such as *Saturday Superstore* and *Pop Quiz* (not to mention frequent *Top of the Pops* appearances), and was asked to help Mike form a band to appear at the forthcoming season of Radio 1 roadshows.

In their 1980s heyday, a typical roadshow summer season started in July and ran for eight weeks, broadcasting live on Radio 1 from seaside locations from 11am to 12.30pm each weekday. The first hour, from 10am, was a warm-up ahead of the 11am start of the live broadcast. The roadshows became a key part of the summer schedules for Radio 1, and attracted much support.

As Barry recalls, 'Mike asked me to play guitar and Paul Foss – who also played in the Rock Island Line band – was on drums, but we needed a bass player. I knew Keith had played bass so suggested he come on board in that capacity. However, as important as Keith's musical chops were, bizarrely, it was his ability to play tennis – in which I gave him a quick crash course knowing he'd be fine as I had played racketball with him – which counted.'

Mike Read continues the story, 'As well as doing all the games, I persuaded the producers that a live band – playing a mix of 50s and 60s covers and songs from the day – would be great to warm the crowd up, and so we formed The Rockolas with Keith on bass.

'The production crew would book us into hotels with tennis courts or with courts nearby. Every day, at the roadshow, we'd get to play a half-hour set to around 20,000 people. It was great fun. We'd be wearing our tennis shorts and would play songs like *White Wedding* by Billy Idol, *Woolly Bully* by Sam the Sham, and *Move It* by Cliff and The Shadows. I even remember we played *Born to Run* by Springsteen a few times!

'We'd then play tennis in the afternoon, and in the evening on a few occasions, we'd do a gig as a 50s and 60s covers band and call ourselves The Quivers. It was this that got us into playing with Cliff Richard at his 50th birthday party. I was talking to him, and he said he was going to make his birthday party 1950s-themed, and that he should probably get a band together. I volunteered us for the job, which made sense as we knew some of the material and were a unit already, and we played his party at his home in Weybridge in Surrey in October 1990.

'I remember Keith and Barry said to me, 'Do you think Cliff will want to get up and do a number?' I replied that the problem wouldn't be getting Cliff on the stage, but getting him off!''

Keith remembers his time with The Rockolas fondly also, 'It was a fun thing. We were basically all there to play tennis as much as play music, and Cliff's birthday was great fun too. We were at his house, which has a guitar-shaped swimming pool, and they brought in some white wine for us.

'We looked at the bottles, it was Vin de Pays, you know, two months old or something. The guy came back in; we said, 'Sorry, we don't mean to be rude. But we can't drink that. We really don't like this type of wine,' and we asked for something half-decent. Then Cliff came in; he was so embarrassed. He came rushing in saying, 'I'm really sorry, what have they given you? Oh no, no, this is all wrong.' Off he went and brought in some really good wines.

'When we were rehearsing around there, earlier in the day, Cliff was such a pro. I mean he was making cups of tea, bringing out biscuits for everyone. He was very relaxed and had a couple of days stubble on, but later he went up and changed for the evening. When he came down, he was absolutely immaculate. He had subtle makeup and the whole stage kit on, like he was going to do a TV show or something. It was quite a transformation but not entirely surprising.

'I remember Elton John didn't turn up, but there were a couple of The Shadows there, and some old school rock and rollers. It was a nice evening. It was lovely, and we got to play about half a dozen numbers with Cliff, which was great.'

Following their fun time in The Rockolas, but with Mike Read leaving the BBC and the roadshows being replaced by other Radio 1 events, Barry and Keith would still see each other regularly. As Keith says, 'I went round to his flat one day; he wanted some help to set up this Tascam tape recorder he had, as he was starting to explore home recordings.

'He had a guitar lying in the corner. It looked like a Burns guitar, a white Hank Marvin one which I remembered from my youth. I asked him where he had got the guitar from, and when he said he had made it himself, I was amazed. He'd trained as a carpenter and a cabinet maker, and he'd made the whole thing – the neck, the body – sprayed it, bought the hardware, and put it all together beautifully.

'I encouraged him to take it further, and he said to me one day – when having a drink in a local bar – that he'd like to buy the Burns Guitars' brand name. I thought he could probably pick that up pretty cheaply and advised him to go to Companies House and check it out. He went, and they told him that he needed to find the original owner before registering any trademarks. Plus, Barry didn't want to upset any of the die-hard Burns aficionados.

'Barry thought this was a dead end as he didn't know how he could find Jim Burns. So, I advised him to hire a private detective who I thought could find him in no time at all, if he had a social security number or something. Barry didn't believe me and thought I was joking but eventually took my advice. Anyway, the upshot was that he tracked him down, signed the deal off, and suddenly he became the proud owner of Burns London Ltd.

'Barry asked me to help him out as a consultant, and we went to trade shows together for years. Korea, China, Japan, everywhere, America, all over.

'I found a guitar once at one of the trade shows – a Brian May model on the Gretsch stand. I wondered what the guitar was doing on the stand as it had Burns Tri-Sonic pickups on the body. When I asked about the guitar, they told me that they were dumping the model as it wasn't selling well. I asked to borrow the guitar and took it over to show Barry, and suggested that Burns could make a Brian May guitar.

'He wasn't sure at first, but after talking to other dealers and friends, we convinced him that this could be a sweet deal for Burns and take us in a different direction – away from the Shadows connection. Burns agreed a deal with Brian and borrowed one of his Red Specials to duplicate. The guitar sold very well, and Burns even won *Guitarist Magazine's* 2001 'Best Electric Guitar of the Year' award for it.

'Then we did a couple of other things like that, to try and move the status of the company on a bit. In those days, it was mostly Hank Marvin fans who bought Burns guitars, but the company's actually got a great and varied history; Marc Bolan had a couple of Burns, and most of the top guys – Jeff Beck, Jimmy Page – all started off with Burns guitars.

'At trade fairs, I would use the old charm with the customers. I never tried to sell; I would just be on the stand, and if someone's interested I would talk them through it. We were doing meetings in the meeting rooms there too; meetings with distributors – trying to get them to order more.

'The trade shows themselves were hardcore; up early, finish late, crammed with thousands of people. You had to keep a beady eye open for thieves on the stand. The noise is horrendous all day. It's not for the faint-hearted; the only way to get through it is to meet up with some friends, and hit the bar in the evening.'

Keith adds, 'One of my fondest memories of a trade show was in Los Angeles. Barry and I set the stand up, and on our left there was a stand called Everly Strings. The following morning we found out that this company was run by Phil Everly's son [of The Everly Brothers] who was a lovely guy. I was chatting away to him, and he told me his dad was coming in that afternoon to help out. I couldn't believe it. The Everly Brothers were a huge influence on me, and just about every musician I knew said the same thing.

'Trying to stay cool, I completely forgot to ask Phil for a photo or an autograph! He did, however, give me a sample pack of strings which were, by the way, great!

'We were mainly looking for worldwide distributors; that was our main objective at the trade shows. In Japan, America, Britain, we had distribution, but in Korea and China, you've got to protect yourself with copyright and trademarks. Plus, there's a lot of sharks out there, so I kept an eye on that side of it, and let Barry do his technical stuff. He was the guitar builder after all.

'Some people mistakenly thought that Barry and I were partners in the company as I'd have a suit on and he'd be more relaxed in chinos and a shirt. At the time, he didn't mind going along with that. I didn't have any interest financially in the company, and when I was helping Barry negotiate deals, we played 'good cop, bad cop'. I would be the bad cop, always complaining about the quality, the pricing, etc., until we were happy. Some cultures have a different take on how to negotiate, so you have to be quite diplomatic and respect their way of reaching a fair agreement. I think we were pretty good at that side of it.

'I would never push customers, but they'd seem to come round. I never actually tried to sell; my technique was not to sell anything and let them talk themselves into the deal. It used to work; I did that for a long time.'

A long time indeed – Barry and Keith worked together on trade events and on factory visits for Burns Guitars from 1990 until 2012 when – due to the double whammy of the global economic crisis and the increasing influence of the internet – the company stopped attending trade fairs. In June 2020, just after Barry was interviewed for this book, Burns Guitars was sold to a group of investors.

Barry and Keith still get together to jam and Barry has played lead guitar, recently, as part of The Keith West Band.

24. Working with a legend

When their working paths diverged, following the collapse of the Bodast project in 1969, Steve Howe and Keith couldn't have led more different lives within the music industry. Steve, as you can glean if you read his autobiography, had a career which was carried out at an intense pace, and which achieved critical and commercial success with Yes and other bands. He was constantly touring and recording, and eventually inducted into the Rock and Roll Hall of Fame in 2017. Keith's career has been far less hectic, punctuated by regular high-profile activities, of course, but never with the white-hot intensity of being recognised as one of the world's great guitarists, and a member of one of the most successful (but also dysfunctional) bands of all time.

Given their wildly different lifestyles, and also the difficult family politics that inevitably stay in place having both been married to the same woman, it may come as a surprise to learn that they have remained firm friends and musical collaborators. As Steve said recently, 'Keith and I always maintained the idea that, every now and then, we would get together and do something.'

Keith expands on a number of their projects across the years, 'Some of the bands that he's formed, they all fell out for one reason or another. But he's always told me that one of his favourite groups was Tomorrow. He's always said that to me; that some of the best times he ever had was in Tomorrow. I think he liked being on his own on the guitar, whereas, he didn't always enjoy all those keyboards and stuff from later bands like Yes, Asia, and GTR.

'It's just my opinion, but I think he likes the freedom of playing guitar with just bass and drums, where he can be let loose and take his guitar to places where many would hit a dead end, so to speak.

'When we used to hang out at his parents' house, we both used to play records from bands like The Big Three with guitarist Brian Griffiths, who was way ahead of his time. We also listened to The Pirates, the track *My Babe* especially, with Mick Green's choppy, tight licks. Gene Vincent's guitarist, Cliff Gallup, was another pioneer.

'Steve, like me, was always interested in what the guitar players were coming up with on the records. Back then, a single would maybe be 2-3 minutes long and there was always a solo. James Burton was another favourite. Scotty Moore, Steve Cropper, to name just a few.

'Jazz was his thing, as well. He was only 18, if that, when I met him. I was a bit older, 19, 20. We were playing, amongst others, Wes Montgomery records round his house, and stuff like that. I'd never previously heard them.

'I wasn't really into jazz at the time, although I always liked classical music. In some of Steve's guitar playing, you can hear the influences.

'*Claramount Lake* by Tomorrow has a Steve Howe special on there; he doesn't bend the strings a lot, but his solo has hints of jazz and country contained in it. It's one of my favourites.

'He's had a hell of a career, but he's been ripped off quite a few times over the years, like many other bands. That can be a big problem when you're flying high with huge record sales, headlining tours, etc.

'When he was in the original Yes line-up, they were spending ridiculous amounts of money in the studio. I went down to a Yes session once, and they were in there all day putting their feet up, spending hours on what snare drum they were going to choose. I went in there and said, politely, 'How can you work like this?' When I'm in the studio, I'm in there to work. I want to get going. I want to get on the mic.

'I like to record my vocals in one or two takes. If it gets past that, I start to get frustrated. Engineers often want you to do a vocal take for sound production reasons, whereas I would rather they just recorded straight away as there might be bits of it that can be used. When I'm fired up, I want to do it quick. I heard David Bowie was like that. Marc Bolan also. Just get in there and nail it.

'Let's face it, if you do take after vocal take, you start to doubt whether it's ever going to end. At that moment, all the excitement and feel can drain away, and you're left with a soulless performance.

'Steve sent me a tape of *Lay Lady Lay*, a song which he wanted to include on a Bob Dylan covers album in 1999. He asked me if I would like to do a track on it, and that he would send a tape over so that I could record my vocal in a studio close to where I live.

'The engineer put it on and I think the manager, more used to the way Steve was working, was expecting us to be there for about six hours. Not me, a couple of takes and harmonies and it was done. The engineer was really surprised, too, that we worked so quickly as we had it finished in around half an hour. He said, 'Might as well go down the pub then.' So that's what we did.

'Steve got it back and thought it was exactly what he wanted. He was also surprised it had been done so quickly and asked me how. For me, it was straightforward; we had the master tape there, I knew the song. I even did a couple of harmonies which I said he could use if he wished.'

However, there was to be a fly in the ointment on this particular quick-fire experience, as Keith explains, 'Then, in typical Spinal Tap fashion, the phone rings and it's Steve sounding a bit sheepish, asking me to do it again. I was confused as he thought the first version was great, but then he admitted that he had fucked up and the tape he had sent was at the wrong speed. As a result, my vocal was in the wrong key. I thought he was joking, but he offered to pay me to re-do the vocal, but I declined and did another short session. The second time around, it was all OK.

'I love singing that song, and it all came out well. I really liked Steve's take on it, and I was pleased with the whole mix, and to be included on the album.'

The track would end up on the Steve Howe solo record *Portraits of Bob Dylan,* released in Europe on Eagle Records in 1999. Other vocal contributors would be Jon Anderson and P.P. Arnold. Keith describes the album, 'It's a well-thought-out record and Steve's regard for Bob Dylan's songs is obvious in his careful selections, plus It's got some very nice licks on it. There's pedal steel and a collection of Steve's various acoustic guitars all over the tracks.'

Some other Keith West songs that would eventually appear on the 2017 *Steve Howe – Anthology 2: Groups and Collaborations* record, had more complex histories. As Keith explains, 'I sent some songs over to Steve, four I think, and he expressed an interest in doing something with them.

'His business lawyer, at the time, suggested we should contact Robert Palmer's office, as he heard they were looking to sign new artists off the back of Robert's recent success. So a tape was sent, and we had a positive response back as they were very excited about my song *Cross that Bridge*. Another was called *Hypnotique,* which they liked as a potential song for Robert.

'They signed me on the basis of those two or three songs, and I got Steve involved as a possible producer, which got to the meeting stage. Steve had shown a lot of interest in these songs which, as well as *Cross that Bridge,* included *Heaven, Strange Little Girl* and *Curved Ball*. I think they were impressed with Steve, and it was looking very much like we were about to work together again.

'Dave Harper was Robert's manager and also managed UB40. There were two other guys working there who were managing me; one of them used to manage Elkie Brooks. Again, it didn't work out too well. They put me in the studio, I did a load more demos and Robert was still riding high at this point mainly because of *Addicted to Love*. I made the big mistake of telling a lot of people that I was going to get a song with Robert Palmer and when it didn't materialise, I looked a bit silly. I regret it. I'd never do that again. I'd keep it quiet until it came out and it was a hit!

'I did get quite excited as he was huge at the time, and they were good songs. Plus, he was a great singer. They [the management agency] literally disappeared overnight. I got stuck with an unpaid studio bill, and not one person in that office in Flood Street even bothered to inform everyone that the ship had sunk.

'They did a whole number on me on how I was going to have hits with my songs and I went through the whole image, styling rubbish which was popular at the time. I had an all-day photo session with a stylist, who was my nephew's girlfriend [Paula Keenan]. She had just finished working with Steve Winwood, who went through the same experience and must have hated it, I think.

'There were make-up artists fussing around, a huge clothes rail with the latest fashions, and all the while they were playing my tape over and over; it was driving me up the wall! I went to a party, and there was about four or five other people that they'd signed there, and they were all asking me did I know what was going on. I knew something was in the air then. They were a one-trick pony agency; they had Robert Palmer, but nothing else was working.

'Luckily, my negotiator at the time, David Gentle, who's another famous music industry figure – a great guy to have on your side – he really put those guys through some hoops. He represented Stiff Records and Nick Lowe, all that kind of stuff. He did the contracts, which excluded the publishing, luckily. There was a clause that got me out of that deal, and the songs reverted back to me and were then part of Steve Howe's anthology album, apart from *Hypnotique* which is on the B-side of the Taboo record; I threw it on there.'

Steve Howe talks fondly about the duo's work on the *Anthology 2* record which was released by Rhino Entertainment Company, a division of Warner Bros, in 2017. 'Those songs,' he says, 'are a nice tidy up of tracks that Keith and I started. I took them on and added Virgil, my late son, on live drums.

'They were going to be part of a separate album, but Rhino agreed to make it part of the *Groups and Collaborations* record. Keith gave me a lot of freedom with the tracks, but the way I finished them was important, and there was a lot of recording time spent on them. They were put into Pro Tools and tidied up and made to sound nice and clear.'

Keith adds, 'All the tracks were originally recorded at my house on a little Tascam four-track recorder with a drum machine, live bass, a few keyboards and guitars. Luckily, the vocal takes came out pretty well; otherwise, I don't think Steve could have used them. He did a great job getting them to that quality, and I trusted him completely.'

Finally, Steve wraps things up, 'Keith and I kept dabbling with songs and there's at least one there that we haven't looked at again – which is a shame – but it does show you that you can re-visit songs and make them sound good.

'All of these songs have musical ideas which are part of my story, as well as Keith's, and they demonstrate that we have stayed in touch over the years. The songs have come with us, and we have found a way to enjoy them.'

25. A Ray of Light

As the 1990s drew towards their close, and with a new millennium on the horizon, Bodast would, unexpectedly, once again enter Keith's life. On this occasion, the group would be the starting point for a complex tale which demonstrates how strange the music business really is and how – if you are lucky enough to get it right – the riches that can follow can be staggering.

Recall, from Chapter 17, how the failure of Tetragrammaton Records and the dissolution of Bodast led Clive Skinner (nee Maldoon) and Dave Curtiss to form Curtiss Maldoon. They released a couple of albums in the early 1970s, the first of which contained the song *Sepheryn*, before leaving the music business and disappearing into relative obscurity, with Skinner sadly passing away in 1978.

Let's flash forward to 1996 when English singer and songwriter Christine Leach, Skinner's niece, had recorded her version of the track. Leach said she had always loved the duo's work and *Sepheryn* was her favourite song. Vital to the story is the fact that Leach worked with William Orbit, the hugely successful producer and musician, and recorded a demo of *Sepheryn* over a melody on which he was working. Leach re-wrote the chorus and also removed certain elements of the original composition.

Around the same time, Orbit was invited to send some songs for Madonna to consider. He sent a 13-track tape to Madonna with *Sepheryn* among the tracks included, with Orbit under the impression that Christine Leach had written the song.

As this story wades deep into the murky waters of the music publishing industry, we'll hand over to Martin Costello at this point, now representing Keith's publishing interests (Complete Music having acquired Getaway Music from Malcolm

Forrester). 'I was sitting in my office in Fulham High Street with the radio on. It was a sunny afternoon in early May, and Steve Wright plays the new Madonna single *Ray of Light*.

'After playing the song, the DJ says, 'Madonna's people are trying to track down the songwriters who actually wrote the original song. It's a song called *Sepheryn* by Curtiss Maldoon. Does anybody know out there where they are?' Literally, this was on the radio, I promise you!

'I heard it and thought, I know that record. So, my first port of call was to John Craig, who ran Purple Records. Curtiss Maldoon were originally signed to Purple Records, and the publishing was with Purple Music. John Craig's an old friend of mine, who I've known since '76. I had a French company, Editions Complete Music – that Iain and I established – and we represented Purple Music in France.

'I rang up John Craig and asked him if he had heard the new Madonna single, but he hadn't. I told him that Madonna has done a version of a song called *Sepheryn*, that was in his catalogue, and that he was going to have a piece of a fucking great big hit!

'In the meantime, I'm feeling very pleased as I've got the French rights. I rang up Keith and told him that his old mate Dave Curtiss from Curtiss Maldoon had just had his song covered by Madonna, but no one knows where he is; no one knows what he's doing. I said to Keith that if I was him, if he knew how to get in touch with him, I'd get my arse round to see Dave Curtiss with a management contract.'

Which is what he did.

'That's what happened. He went round there, and he found him living alone in a small second-floor flat in Acton and driving a laundry van for a living. I said to Keith, 'Actually, you're doing him a favour because between you and me we'll put it together, and make sure he gets his money.' So, the upshot was that everyone got in contact with everybody else and pulled the deal together.'

It's at this point that the dizzying financial machinations of the music publishing business come into play (as brilliantly documented by Ray Davies in The Kinks song *The Moneygoround* in 1970).

Martin Costello explains, 'So Madonna says, 'I like that track, but I want to change it around a little bit,' and William Orbit is fine with that. So, the upshot was, Madonna wanted 30% off the top, and William Orbit received 10% as well, which left 60%.' Keith adds, 'The publishing deal that Clive and Dave signed would have given 50% of all royalties to Purple Music Worldwide, so I contacted Tony Edwards in Italy who owned Purple Music and worked with John Craig, and he agreed to lower his share to 30% which left Clive's family and Dave with a 15% share each in the song.'

Martin continues. 'Keith, who was then representing Dave Curtiss as his manager, did a five-year deal to take a 15% cut of Dave's earnings over that period. Dave wasn't a PRS member any longer, as they had no address on file, so Keith sorted that out as John Sweeney – who's a mate of mine – is head of membership. Without help like that, Dave would have missed out on a huge amount of money.

'It's difficult to answer the question precisely about how much money Dave would have got from *Ray of Light,* but I would estimate that, by now, it would be a few million pounds and in the first five years of that Keith would have earned £100,000, easy.'

Doing the maths, and using the £100k figure that Keith received as a round number (to save much head-scratching), we can calculate that in the first five years after its release, *Ray of Light* generated £4.4 million in publishing revenue alone. Dave Curtiss could have received in excess of £600,000 in the first five years for a song he co-wrote almost 30 years earlier… it's a crazy business.

Keith, unsurprisingly, is an enthusiastic teller of the tale also. 'I kept an old diary and found a phone number for Dave, I thought he'd never answer; it was about 20 years since I'd spoken to him, but he picked up the phone, and I said, 'Hi Dave, it's Keith West, you'd better sit down mate. Have you heard of Madonna because her new song *Ray of Light* – that's your song *Sepheryn.*' He told me to fuck off because he thought I was joking, but I just explained that, honestly, she had covered his song and that he could go down to a record store and buy it and listen to it.'

'The money was just lying in perpetuity somewhere; so that's where I come in,' continues Keith. 'I get hold of the publisher in Italy. He came over to England and we cut a deal, phone calls going off – left, right, and centre – all hours of the day, two o'clock in the morning, three o'clock in the morning, it was all kicking off.

'I got ill because it was so stressful. I was diagnosed with shingles which I've never had in my life. What the fuck, stress? I thought it was a load of mosquito bites. I said to the doctor that I had been through a very stressful period, and would that have something to do with it?' I tried to explain the nature of negotiating with Madonna's legal team, but she just said I needed to calm down.'

'All of a sudden, as Dave's manager, I get cheques coming in for hundreds of thousands of pounds, and Dave didn't even have a bank account! Suddenly he's on TV and Carol Vorderman's telling him that they've just found a quarter of a million pounds for him in royalties.

'Such typical TV hype. We had already sorted out the royalties weeks before, but Dave pretended to go along with it, bless him. I think he enjoyed all the fuss and I don't blame him as his life must have been pretty mundane before the hit.

'I would collect the money, take it over to him, give him his cheque, take off my commission, and that worked for five years; after five years, my contract was finished.

'But during that time the money kept coming in. For example, I was in Los Angeles on business and having a break in the afternoon in my hotel, and the Superbowl was on TV, and they were playing *Ray of Light*.

'About half an hour later, the phone went, and it was Dipak, Purple Music's accountant, and he told me that the Superbowl organisers were paying a million dollars to play that song for one day. Can you imagine that much on one song? It doesn't take much to work out that Dave and Clive's joint earnings that day were approximately $300k.

'The next thing was Microsoft. Their new software used the *Ray of Light* music to put over that it's quicker than a ray of light. They used the song, which was another great big chunk of money. This is where I could see a change in the business. Sync fees and some of the other stuff that was going on would be strong revenue streams.

'Luckily, *Teenage Opera* was still doing well, and my tracks were used on classic 60s hits compilation albums, some big ones. It was a good couple of years, financially. We purchased a flat in Minorca using some of the *Ray of Light* proceeds,' says Keith. 'It's a sort of retirement bolt-hole, and it's a cool little island; it's part of the Balearics. I've always loved it since I went there for a break in 1967 with my sister and her family. It was a very good move for us, as all our family also love the island. We spend a good part of the year there now.

'I was still helping out a few people for no money – friends, fellow musicians – just helping them out on a few songs. Jimmy Edwards, for example.

'Jimmy was such a lovely guy, and both Pat and I thought the world of him. He could be a nightmare, though, as he was pretty much a hypochondriac for most of his life. He had a death wish and thought he was plagued with heart problems when there was nothing wrong with his heart at all.

'He convinced me, one day, to take him up to London for an ECG he'd booked. After the test, his doctor took me to one side and showed me his file; in big letters it read, *There is NO sign of heart problems!* and he told me in no uncertain terms not to bring him in ever again.

'I was still helping him out with trying to get a deal. A lot of people in the industry, they go through all of this for nothing; they never ever have a hit. Dave Curtiss and Clive Skinner had been in the business for years and never had a smell of a hit when suddenly – out of the blue – Madonna comes along and bang. It was the best record she'd made for years. Luckily for them, it became a big dance hit; absolutely massive and still earning money to this day. Which is the position I am lucky enough to find myself in with songs I wrote a long time ago.

'The performance side of *Teenage Opera* has gone up by a dramatic amount, but the mechanical side of it – the record sales – has hit the floor; that's why everybody's out on the road.

'I get offered those sixties things, package tours. I mean, don't get me wrong, if I needed the money or something like that, I'd do it. A lot of these guys have to do it. They've got no other way of earning money, no source of income, and probably haven't paid their taxes over the years. They've probably got no pension, or got ripped off along the way. All kinds of things go on in this industry.

'I've been very lucky, I tell you, I really have. Pat and I have always been self-sufficient money-wise. But, if I had to do it, I would, and there's nothing wrong in it. It's a tough business to survive in, and there were some very fly-by-night characters around, but the Inland Revenue can be very unsympathetic – brutal – if you haven't paid your taxes.'

26. Today and Tomorrow

While this book has attempted to capture the major incidents in Keith's musical life, there are a few juicy tales, which either didn't fit into any specific chapter or were just footnotes along the way – but worthy of mention none the less.

The first relates to the time when Keith was present at the birth of a rock and roll behemoth… that of Led Zeppelin. As Keith says, 'Jimmy was the top session guitarist around EMI, where I was also working, so we would bump into each other now and then.

'I was in the Gioconda Cafe, in Charing Cross Road, where I'd first met and hired Steve Howe for The In Crowd, and Jimmy walked in.

'We had a coffee and a chat, and he asked me what I was doing currently, and then he told me that he was forming a band. At this point, he said he was trying to get Steve Marriott involved, but that didn't work out. He said to me, 'I've found these two guys, a great drummer [John Bonham], and his mate Robert Plant who has an amazing vocal range… what are you doing this afternoon?'

'I wasn't doing anything in particular, and he said that I was welcome to come down as the band were rehearsing at The Marquee club. I sat in there for about an hour listening to their songs which were loud and powerful and I was so impressed, although at that time I wouldn't count myself a fan of heavy rock.

'I could see they were already well organised as a band, the songs were great, and the musicianship was way up there. That was, as we now know, the virgin Led Zeppelin! Jimmy said as I was leaving, 'Write me a song like *My White Bicycle,* I'd I love that.' And that was the end of it. I didn't think anything of it at the time, and maybe I thought he was just being polite. They went on to do OK without my help, though, didn't they?!'

Another story Keith tells – with a rueful smile and a shake of the head – is when Andy Partridge, the new wave, XTC, pop legend responsible for such hits as *Making Plans for Nigel, Sgt. Rock* and *Senses Working Overtime* reached out after he expressed a desire to work with him. 'He sent me a cassette tape of demos over,' remembers Keith. 'I think I might've said something to somebody because I used to love XTC and I could never understand why they weren't a lot bigger as they produced such clever songs and arrangements.

'I know we met up somewhere [Martin Costello thinks it was at Andy's house in Swindon], but it was a little bit on the vague side. I don't know what he wanted to do, to be honest. It was just a cassette tape that I got; I don't know where that is either. It was a bit of a shame. I lost a box of stuff.'

A final, more recent meeting, in 2019, saw Keith bump into the modfather Paul Weller in a café close to where he was recording his most recent album. Paul seemed genuinely pleased to be meeting an original mod pioneer like Keith and knew all about Tomorrow and *Excerpt from a Teenage Opera*. Something of a Q&A session took place with Weller, and his guitar player Steve Craddock, delving into subjects with Keith which ranged from original 60s clothing to Lebanese hash! An invitation was extended for Keith to drop into their studio, but Keith deferred as – true to form – he doesn't like to impinge on studio time which he recognises as being a place of work.

'Paul's a really cool guy,' remarks Keith. 'Very friendly and down to earth, and still dresses sharp; even in Ripley High Street! I would love to visit the Black Barn Studio again, as I worked there many years ago and recorded my Decca sessions there with Robin Black, the original owner. Maybe next time… when it's quiet.'

One question that is often asked is: what does a former pop star, songwriter, and musician do 40 or 50 years after their major hits? Keith turned 75 at the end of 2019, but there is a surprising amount of income still being generated from his best-known songs. As he says, 'I'm still receiving royalties because the companies that I signed to, they've all gone to Sony now. Warner Brothers own the master rights, and Sony ATV own the publishing. Therefore, it's all done professionally.

'Some artists that have written stuff with small publishing companies that have gone bust, they never get their money. It's a disaster. I've got no complaints, looking back. I have had some terrible deals, but I'm still receiving income.

'It was all with EMI and Robbins Music, but EMI got sold. So that's good, for me. I know the guys at Warners, and they're fans of Tomorrow and our stuff. Actually, the MD of the company wrote me a lovely letter, because I said to him, 'Where are my royalties?' [There was a pause in payments during the sale of EMI, understandably.]

'He wrote me a lovely letter saying, 'Oh, you're going to get them. Don't worry. I'm going to put you in touch with somebody in the UK, and they'll be sorting it all out. By the way, we're big fans of your work with Steve in Tomorrow.' A nice touch in the digital, paperless world we find ourselves in today.'

My small footnote in Keith's history, and the circumstances that led to the writing of this book, began in 2012. I had moved to a small Surrey village and had dusted off my guitar, and wanted to pull together a band. A nicely-designed advert in the village magazine led to a certain Martin Costello getting in touch and offering his services on bass. Through Martin, I was introduced to Keith and over the next few years continued to be wowed by his – seemingly endless – stream of rock and roll anecdotes. Plus, 'inspired' by mine and Mr Costello's plans to gig our way around the highways and by-ways of Surrey in our new wave and post-punk covers band, The Subway Rats, he decided to come out of retirement.

Thus, with Keith onboard, The Detours were duly formed, a power trio with Keith singing and playing guitar, Martin Costello on bass, and Nigel Broad on the drums. They have played regularly ever since and the band's alternative covers of Chris Isaak's *Wicked Game* and Nick Cave's *Red Right Hand* really do have to be seen to be believed.

More recently, things have got a little more serious, and The Keith West Band have played a number of sold-out shows at the well-known music venue The Bull's Head, in Barnes in West London. Keith has even dusted off *My White Bicycle,* but he still refuses to play *Excerpt from a Teenage Opera* and, as he has continued to write songs and demo them in his home studio all the way through his career, there is still a rumour about a new 'Americana'-tinged album, possibly with old sparring partners Cherry Red Records.

As to the chances of Tomorrow reforming for one last hurrah, while there is huge affection for the band among the three surviving members, and a number of lucrative offers have been made, it seems unlikely. As Steve Howe says, 'It's a disappointment to me as I would love to play Tomorrow material again, but we haven't found the time or place to create that.'

All, of course, point to the obvious absence of Junior who Keith always credits with having been responsible for the genesis of everything, as the Four + 1 audition – all the way back in 1963 – came from *his* efforts. As Steve Howe continues, 'It builds my hopes to think we could do it, but I don't know how or when or if we can. I know how difficult going out with a band can be, and it's got to feel right, so I have not reformed too many bands. If we do it, I would like to do it right, but it might take some manoeuvring.'

We'll leave the final quote in this book to Steve, as it sums up the enormous good feeling which Keith has generated during his life. 'I love Keith,' says Steve, 'and we get on great. If we get together more who knows if a Tomorrow reformation might be a possibility.'

Unusual and extraordinary – the life of Keith West – original mod, R&B pioneer, counter-culture hipster, pop star, songwriter, father, AOR artiste, punk rock manager, indie producer, prolific songwriter, guitar guru, grandfather, rock and roll survivor, and laid back gentleman.

INDEX

CREDITS

'Excerpt From a Teenage Opera' Words and Music by Keith Hopkins (p.k.a Keith West) & Mark Wirtz © 1967, Reproduced by permission of Robbins Music Corp Ltd/ EMI Music Publishing Ltd, London W1T 3LP

'The Incredible Journey of Timothy Chase' Words and Music by Keith Hopkins (p.k.a Keith West) ©1968, Reproduced by permission of EMI Miller Catalogue Inc/ EMI Music Publishing Ltd, London W1T 3LP

PHOTO CREDITS

Arranged by insert page and image number. Keith West [Hopkins], or Unknown, unless otherwise listed. 7 [1,2], 8 [1,2] Antony Rufus Isaacs; 9 [1,2] Pictorial Press Ltd/Alamy Stock Photo; 10 [1,2] Barry Plummer; 14 [1] John Jessup; 16 [1] Nigel Broad.

OTHER MUSIC BOOKS FROM THE PUBLISHER

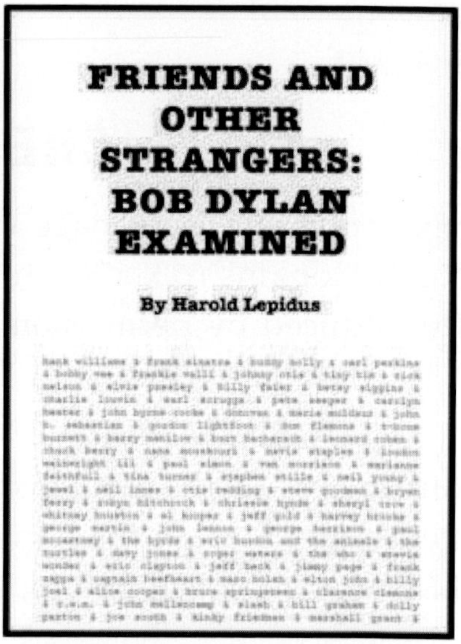

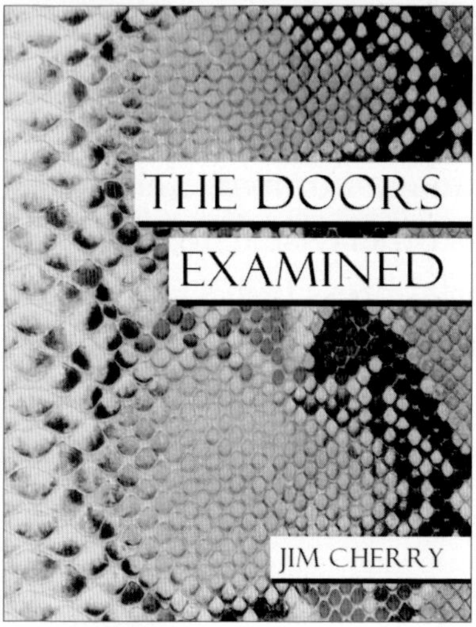

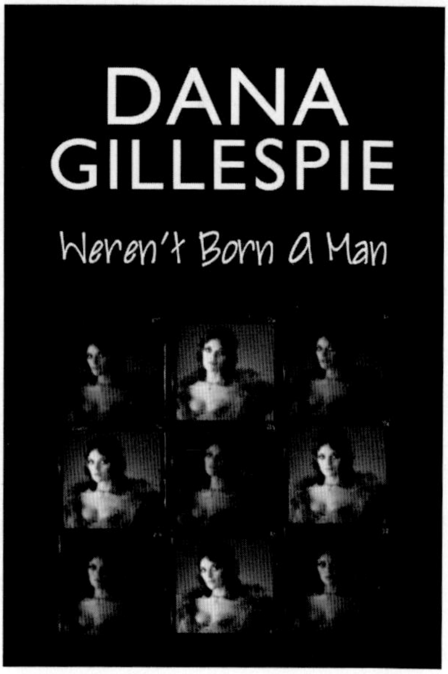